D0955580

Gold Bubble

Profiting from Gold's Impending Collapse

YONI JACOBS

WILEY

John Wiley & Sons, Inc.

Published by John Wiley & Sons, Inc., Hoboken, New Jersey.
Published simultaneously in Canada.

For general information on our other products and services or for technical support, please contact our Customer Care Department within the United States at (800) 762-2974, outside the United States at (317) 572-3993 or fax (317) 572-4002.

Wiley also publishes its books in a variety of electronic formats. Some content that appears in print may not be available in electronic books. For more information about Wiley products, visit our web site at www.wiley.com.

Library of Congress Cataloging-in-Publication Data:

Jacobs, Yoni, 1986–
  Gold bubble: profiting from gold's impending collapse/Yoni Jacobs.
    p. cm.
  Includes bibliographical references and index.
  ISBN 978-1-118-23935-3 (cloth); ISBN 978-1-118-28309-7 (ebk);
  ISBN 978-1-118-28413-1 (ebk); ISBN 978-1-118-28702-6 (ebk)
  1. Gold. 2. Gold—Prices—Forecasting. 3. Investments. 4. Commodity futures.
  I. Title.
  HG293.J25 2012
  332.63—dc23   2011050803

ISBN 978-1-118-23935-3

Printed in the United States of America

10 9 8 7 6 5 4 3 2 1

Contents

Preface

Someone with "perfect foresight" should have foreseen that the pro-
cess was not sustainable and that an implosion was inevitable.[1]
—Charles Kindleberger

G old is in a bubble that is set to burst.
I sit and write this without a clue as to whether we've reached the top in gold or whether we're getting ready for a parabolic rise. All I know is that gold is in a bubble, gold prices will come crashing down, and many people will lose a lot of money. I write this book after a year of intense analysis of gold, commodities, emerging markets, the dollar, and the stock market. After carefully, meticulously, and thoroughly analyzing gold prices since the 1880s, inflation trends, fundamental stories, chart patterns, investment behavior, news coverage, and a nearly endless amount of information from stock prices to economics to psychology—I boldly and justifiably claim that gold is in a bubble that is ultimately due to collapse and severely hurt the average investor.

I am not yet sure of exactly when the bubble will pop, though I have a few analysis-based guesses. What I do know, however, is that this book is an extremely time-sensitive matter; it must be made public as soon as possible. While this book offers an extremely in-depth analysis of gold and all of its driving factors, the lessons learned within and the clues pointing to a bubble will likely serve as a tremendous benefit for analysis of future bubbles across a wide range of asset classes.

At the height of the technology bubble and again at the height of the housing bubble, Yale Professor Robert Shiller released the first and second editions of his book *Irrational Exuberance*—a prediction of an impending collapse in the markets due to extreme investor enthusiasm and unsustainable speculative bubbles. Not only did Shiller make two of the greatest calls in market history, but his highly contrarian opinions were published despite the fact that the rest of the world believed the opposite: that technology and housing would continue to soar (though we now know they were all wrong). With gold prices up over 600 percent in 10 years, and with huge warning signs appearing that signal extreme investor enthusiasm, euphoric herd behavior, and an upcoming collapse to the Gold Bubble, I have written my own version of *Irrational Exuberance*. But this time, irrational exuberance has appeared because of massive fears and extreme pessimism over the future of markets and the U.S. dollar. This time, gold is the subject of irrational exuberance.

To make matters worse, unlike in the case of technology stocks and housing, gold's historical significance has created an aura and illusion that gold prices will never fall. Since gold has been used as currency and has been sought after by nearly every civilization for thousands of years, gold investors assume that investing in gold is "safe." But with gold now an object of mass speculation and subject to herd-like behavior, we are not far from the day when investors realize that gold is, in fact, an "unsafe haven."

How I Reached This Conclusion

After writing this book and putting all of the pieces together to form a coherent picture of gold's history and future, I cannot be any less than 95 percent certain that gold is setting up for a devastating fall. All the evidence I see, all the strategies I have learned in spotting bubbles, all the technicals, charts, stories, and commercials show me signs of a bubble. The entire world picture fits in almost perfectly with my view on gold. I finally see how economics, currencies, stock markets, reserve rates, inflation, forecasts, commodities, time, and the consumer all blend together to form a coherent big-picture view of the markets and the world.

To further support this claim, I have supported my analysis by applying some of the most prominent works written by industry leaders and highly regarded analysts. For studies of asset bubbles, speculative manias, financial crises, and their precipitating factors, I have applied Robert Shiller's bestselling *Irrational Exuberance* and Charles Kindleberger's *Manias, Panics, and Crashes*. For analysis of Elliott Waves and growth/decay cycles, I have applied Frost and Prechter's *Elliott Wave Principle*. For a better understanding of how different markets, sectors, indices, and asset classes interact, I have applied John Murphy's *Intermarket Analysis*. Finally, for behavioral studies and investor psychology, I have applied Martin Pring's *Investment Psychology Explained* and Carl Futia's *The Art of Contrarian Trading*. These books have not only provided a very thorough set of references, but have also strongly supported my analysis and claims of a bubble in gold.

In short, I have written a book because I have found a perfect example of a bubble—and one that I have followed for quite some time. I have provided plenty of charts and images that may better explain what I'm writing about—I'm a visual person myself. I have extended and further developed the gold bubble argument into a groundbreaking and ultimately accurate prediction at a time when the rest of the world is "irrationally exuberant" about the future of gold. Finally, because the opportunity presented itself, I have followed this bubble, analyzed it even to my occasional disbelief, and written a guide to the impending collapse of the gold bubble. I strongly think this book has the potential to become a foundational go-to guide for identifying bubbles and speculative manias.

What You'll Find in This Book

This book covers why gold has become so popular, what factors have allowed it to become so overvalued, what signs point to a speculative bubble, and how to profit from its collapse.

Chapter 1 launches our analysis of the gold bubble by asking the most basic question: Why gold? Knowing the importance of considering all sides and opinions, I have tried my best to present the standard arguments many have used for investing in gold. Understanding what arguments gold investors have used to support their claims helps put the gold theme in context, and gives us a better picture of the strong fundamental reasons and deep-rooted beliefs that gold investors have relied on to justify their decisions.

Chapter 2 presents the structural and precipitating factors that have allowed a gold bubble to form. It is one thing to know the reasons used for buying gold, but it is even more important to understand the specific events and contributing factors that have enabled a very risky asset bubble to form. Many stocks or investments have good reasons that may justify their purchase, but an asset bubble requires certain structural and emotional factors that enable a much larger speculative mania to take place. Identifying those enablers is the second step in determining the bubble's size, scope, and potential peak. In other words, if we can uncover when and how the bubble began, we have a much better chance of figuring out when and how the bubble might burst.

After determining the forces behind gold's surge in Chapters 1 and 2, we present an extremely thorough analysis of the many signs pointing to a gold bubble. Chapters 1 and 2 set the foundation for why a bubble in gold is possible, but Chapter 3 presents the many clues that signal that an actual bubble has formed. Breaking down the numerous signs of a bubble into four main categories, I have pointed to what I consider to be the most common characteristics found in nearly all asset bubbles—parabolic price increases, massive publicity, overspeculation, and extreme expectations. Applying them to gold, I then present very specific examples within each category of the bubble. After reading Chapter 3, readers should have tremendous doubts about the safety and future profitability of gold investing. Chapter 3 should convince readers that a gold bubble is almost obvious.

Once a gold bubble is essentially confirmed by the long list of warning signs and red flags discussed in Chapter 3, Chapter 4 discredits the claims made by many that gold is a "safe haven" during recessions. By discussing gold's performance during the Great Depression and past recessions, Chapter 4 presents the case that gold is an "unsafe haven" and is wrongly relied on as a safe investment during deflationary periods. Chapter 4 also shows how overvalued gold is by comparing it to other asset classes and their historical relationship. By many counts, gold prices have increased far more than the prices of cars, houses, stocks, and other precious metals over the same time period. Gold prices may have had a good reason to rise, but prices have reached extremes—especially when compared to other asset classes.

Chapter 5 analyzes long-term gold prices, defines the stages of the bubble, and forecasts price targets for when the bubble collapses. Applying a heavy dose of technical analysis, Elliott Waves, Fibonacci time relationships, and seasonality patterns, Chapter 5 puts gold prices into historical context and shows why gold is nearing the end of a growth and decay cycle dating back to 1934. It should be shocking how well gold prices conform to the typical structure of a bubble.

Having established why gold is in a bubble, why it is set to burst, and what stage of the bubble we currently find ourselves in, Chapter 6 discusses the many outside factors that gold depends on, from stock markets to the U.S. dollar to emerging market troubles to Middle East and European upheavals. Since every investment ultimately relies on, or reacts to, outside factors and events, pinpointing all the determinants of gold's future price-moves helps us better predict when the bubble will pop. Since gold's popularity has soared to such a great extent due to poor stock market performance, Chapter 6 asks whether the fate of the stock market strongly influences gold prices, and why a fall in stocks or the onset of a recession could trigger the end of gold's run. Moreover, since gold's massive rise has coincided with huge declines in paper currencies and arguments of the U.S. dollar's demise, Chapter 6 presents the case of a dollar comeback and its implications for gold prices.

Perhaps the largest determinant of the fate of the global economy and the future of commodity prices, the strength of emerging markets is vital to the continuation of the bull markets in stocks, commodities, and gold. However, a multitude of signs have been surfacing that show weakening emerging markets, especially in China and Brazil. Expectations have been so high for emerging market growth and demand that these highly troubling signs of a slowdown could mean the beginning of a global recession and the end of the gold bubble. Add to that the giant upheavals and revolutions in the Middle East and the European banking crisis, which could spiral out of control and drag the entire global economy into recession (or worse), and it is clear that severe risks stand in our way. Chapter 6 explains why gold will be affected.

After having established that a bubble is nearly certain and that its collapse is inevitable, Chapter 7 searches for the signs of reversal that warn of an impending peak. Up until then, the book discusses why there's a bubble, why it will collapse, and what factors will influence gold prices; Chapter 7 discusses the signs that point to a developing peak—signs that show up as the bubble loses steam and prepares for a collapse.

Chapter 8 represents perhaps the most important aspect of this book for investors: ways to profit from the collapse of the gold bubble. Chapters 1 to 7 are extremely important for understanding why gold is in a bubble and how to best predict gold's future prices, but Chapter 8 puts it all together to form a coherent plan for turning knowledge into money. By presenting simple short-selling strategies, complex options strategies, pair trades, and alternative investment ideas, Chapter 8 offers a substantial number of methods and approaches for profiting from gold's collapse.

Chapter 9 looks beyond the gold bubble. Having presented readers with a very thorough description of the gold bubble, I offer Chapter 9 as an examination of other potential bubbles on the horizon: technology stocks, the IPO mania led by Facebook and the social media revolution, and Netflix, which has already seen a huge collapse. The case studies in Chapter 9 provide insight into how to apply the characteristics of a bubble to any popular theme. Readers can use what they learn from this book by applying it to future investment themes, spotting bubbles, and avoiding or even profiting from their demise. Gold is just one example of a bubble.

As You Begin

I have thoroughly enjoyed the arduous, yet very rewarding, process of writing this book. Taking a broad idea of "gold bubble" and developing it from start to finish, with a huge range of information, charts, and theories, has been tremendously gratifying. Not all accomplishments allow a person to look back and physically see tangible proof. I consider writing a book to be one of my lifelong goals, and I do not intend to stop here. This is just the beginning.

Please do not dismiss the gold bubble argument if you disagree with or find fault with one of my claims—there are so many different reasons and indicators of a bubble that you're almost guaranteed to be more effective in your trades from reading this book. You will likely find a number of reasons that will at least make you question gold.

Enjoy the read.

Yoni Jacobs
November 11, 2011

Disclaimer

Nothing in this book constitutes or should be construed as either an offer to sell or the solicitation of an offer to buy or sell securities. In the United States, offers to sell and solicitations of offers to buy any securities may be made only by a prospectus (as defined in the Securities Act of 1933, as amended) delivered to the prospective purchasers. This book contains various forward-looking statements based on the author's projections, hypotheses, forecasts, estimates, beliefs, and prognoses about future events. All forward-looking statements contained herein reflect solely the author's opinions about such future events and are subject to significant uncertainty. Actual events may differ from those described in such forward-looking statements.

CHAPTER 1

Why Gold?

Once a certain indicator or investment approach works for a while, word of its money-making capabilities spreads like wildfire. Then, when everyone is aware of its potential, it becomes factored into the price and the relationship breaks down.[1]

—Martin Pring

To set the record straight, I am not arguing with the fundamental reasons behind gold's move. I agree that the reasons why gold prices have increased make sense. Gold is a tangible store of value: It provides protection against inflation, and some even say it protects against deflation. Gold is also a *fear trade* during times of uncertainty or panic. These are fundamental reasons that explain why gold prices should go up. The problem, however, is that while these characteristics justify the rise of gold prices, they do not justify the *extremity* of the current gold prices. In other words, gold went up for a reason, but it has gone up too far. The individuals who have invested in gold may have acted rationally, but their actions are not as favorable if so many others are persuaded to behave in the same way. Therefore, using these arguments to justify further increases in gold prices is no longer useful because these fundamental reasons are already priced-in.

It is speculation of further price increases that runs the price of gold far beyond fair value. The fair market value of gold may be hard to pinpoint, but by definition, a bubble trades at prices well beyond where they should be based on historical average—or fair value.

Understanding Gold's Surge

The reasons behind the gold surge are understandable.

- **Gold has historically been a store of value.** Because people will always want more gold, it has been used as a form of exchange for

1

thousands of years. With global acceptance and negotiability, gold is a first choice for many as a noncurrency form of wealth. The more gold you own, the richer you are.

■ **Gold is a tangible asset.** At a time when the stability of stocks, derivatives, and other financial instruments are in question, gold offers a tangible and supposedly "stable" alternative. Gold is a hard asset you can actually hold in your hands.

■ **Gold has limited supply.** In order to increase the amount of gold in circulation, we have to mine it. Mines are obviously not limitless; there is a specific amount of gold in the earth's crust, and when we deplete all of the earth's gold reserves, supply will cease to grow. And if demand is continuous while supply is limited, gold prices are expected to keep rising. In other words, if more people demand gold and gold is a limited resource, the price of gold should rise.

■ **Gold acts as a currency hedge.** As the U.S. dollar has plummeted and as fears over the euro have escalated, because of uncertainties of the future of the Eurozone's economy, gold has been perceived as a way to avoid the potential disaster that unfolds if "paper" money becomes worthless. When investors buy gold, they assume that should world economies fail, gold will still be accepted as currency.

Figure 1.1 shows how weak fiat currencies have been versus gold since 1999.

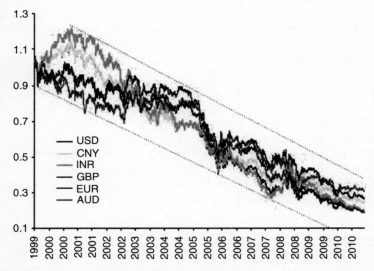

FIGURE 1.1 Various Currencies versus Gold since 1999
Source: Datastream, Erste Group Research.

- **Gold as a *fear hedge*.** Massive debt levels, high market volatility, and a constant looming threat of economic collapse have all spurred the buying of gold as a protection against the worst possible outcomes. With the United States experiencing the worst unemployment situation since the Great Depression, it's easy to understand why many investors have come to expect the worst. See Figure 1.2.
- **Gold as an alternative to equities.** Following the stock market devastation we have lived through, from the bursting of the dot-com bubble in 2000 to 2002 and the collapse of the housing bubble in 2007 to 2009, many investors have almost completely lost faith in stocks. But with a desperate need to increase their wealth in order to support their own lifestyles, pay for their childrens' education, and/or fund their retirements, investors continue to search for some form of investment that will meet their needs. Out go stocks, in comes gold—if stocks haven't worked, maybe a historically valuable, tangible, limited, and protective asset such as gold can.

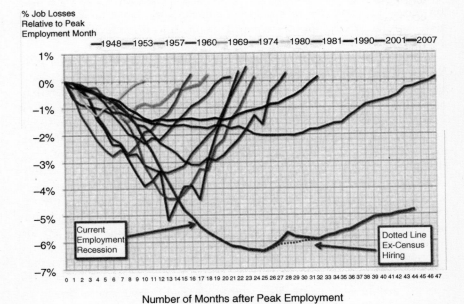

FIGURE 1.2 Percentage of Job Losses in Post–World War II Recessions, Aligned at Maximum Job Losses

Source: Business Insider, calculatedriskblog.com (6/3/11).

Why the "Gold Bugs" Are Wrong

While these reasons are understandable, they don't necessarily support the extent of gold's surge. Yes, they do support gold prices going up. But who says they support a 600 percent move?

Rapid price run-ups tend to diverge from the underlying fundamental reasons for their move. In other words, as people start getting overly excited about a certain investment theme, they actually run the price up too far, too fast. Their reasons for jumping in may be accurate, but their enthusiasm pushes investors to actually get ahead of themselves. Prices can't go up forever, and they eventually start to drop. And as more and more people start to realize this, prices plummet even faster. This marks the bursting of the bubble that will eventually see prices crash and many people worse off than before. And if gold is the current bubble, this fate awaits many people now investing in it.

Gold has a laundry list of great reasons to buy it. Gold bugs, apocalyptic doomsayers, and those who are discontent with government policy and volatile markets have all relied on gold's historical value as a reason to own gold. Fearing the worst outcomes—the collapse of the dollar or a stock market crash—investors and much of the financial world have put their faith in gold, assuming its significance will provide them with a "safe haven" if markets and currencies collapse.

Rationally speaking, however, there is likely no such thing as a "safe haven" that could protect investors from plunging asset prices. Some assets, such as growth stocks or complex derivatives, are riskier than other assets, such as defensive stocks and high-rated, secure bonds; but if stocks and economies fall, all asset prices will fall together with them, including gold. Using history as a benchmark is a necessary and smart investment approach, but only when viewed by the perspective of price changes and sentiment. In other words, using gold's historical significance as a reason to buy it makes a lot of sense, but not if prices have soared to unsustainable levels or if those buying gold are too euphoric. Once an investment theme becomes "overcrowded," it is no longer supported by history and fundamentals—it has become dependent on the psychology of crowds.

In the next chapters, we will explain which outside factors have enabled gold's surge, why using gold's historical significance is tremendously misleading, and how so many clues point to a gold bubble that is driven by fear, greed, and the need for stability.

CHAPTER 2

Bubble Enablers and Precipitating Factors

It is not enough to say that the markets in general are vulnerable to bouts of irrational exuberance. We must specify what precipitating factors from outside the markets themselves caused the markets to behave so dramatically.[1]

—Robert J. Shiller

In order to spot the gold bubble, we must first understand what a bubble is and what precipitating factors have caused a bubble to form *specifically* in gold.

Bubbles are generally the result of a number of contributing factors; they are usually not brought about by any one clearly distinguishable cause. The factors involved can range from monetary policy to popularity to technological shifts to emotions such as fear and greed and even to the lack of other investment alternatives. Understanding which factors have contributed to the formation and inflation of a bubble greatly increases our chances of correctly spotting, defining, and predicting that bubble. And in the case of gold, there are plenty of factors, enablers, arguments, and clues that make a bubble claim hard to dismiss.

A number of factors and causes have made a bubble in gold possible and perhaps partly inevitable.

Removal of the Fixed Price for Gold in 1968

The price of gold was fixed by the government for a significant period until 1968, when the process that allowed for gold price fluctuation—and eventually free-market pricing—began. This structural change, which allowed for

FIGURE 2.1 Gold Prices since the Removal of a Fixed Price
Source: goldprice.org.

gold prices to fluctuate based on supply and demand, can be regarded as a precipitating and an indirect causal factor of our current bubble. With gold prices exposed to market behavior and now susceptible to mass investor psychology, a bubble is increasingly possible. Even the historical importance of gold did not protect it from forming a bubble; on the contrary, its historical importance was one of the fundamental reasons that enabled it to form a bubble, as investors used its historical importance as a reason to buy gold. It is almost as if the arguments made by those buying gold are the exact reasons why gold is in a bubble.

Figure 2.1 shows how much gold has soared since the removal of a fixed price.

Poor Market Performance and Capital Diversion

The "lost decade" in the stock market, which began with the dot-com bubble era of the late 1990s through 2000, convinced many investors to look elsewhere for investment returns. With the market's volatility and bottom-line flat performance, stocks haven't been as appealing as real estate, oil, or gold at different stages over the same period. When the dot-com bubble burst, many investors lost faith in the stock market, thinking that there must be other investment opportunities that provide growth but limit the risk.

They had thought that stocks were generally safe, but the collapse of the NASDAQ and tech stocks in general, followed by a drop in the broader markets, proved them wrong. It was time to look for something else. That something else turned out to be real estate.

But the housing market grew too quickly and turned into a bubble as well. Together with oil, commodities, and many emerging markets, housing utterly collapsed in 2007 to 2008, sending stock markets and financial powerhouses crashing down and once again losing money for investors. Similar to the argument now made by gold investors (that gold is a physical, tangible asset), the fact that houses and real estate are real, tangible assets did not save them from the implosion of the housing bubble.

Now that almost any investment choice had proved itself to be ineffective and dangerous, it was time for another try. Stocks kept falling, housing was now a black hole—it was time to bet on two of the biggest themes of the decade: the growing emerging markets such as China, Brazil, and India, and the constant threat of economic collapse and stock market panic. Ironically, gold makes sense as an investment both for sustained emerging market growth—as increasing wealth in growing countries will demand more gold—as well as for protection in case the market falls. In other words, it appears that gold prices can benefit from both global growth and economic collapse—but that is likely not the case.

I refer to this transfer from one hot investment theme to the next as "capital diversion." As one investment collapses, individuals look for the next big thing; but as they move from one theme to the next, they simply transfer their speculative bets to a different asset and form a new bubble. Capital diversion is easily seen as investors move from technology stocks to housing to oil and now to commodities and gold. This capital diversion was warranted, since investors had to flee from plunging asset prices; but by diverting their money to the new theme, they have enabled a bubble in gold.

Uncertainty

With the ups and downs of the stock market and economy since 2000, investors simply can't be certain of anything. Their investments aren't necessarily safe; the economy could come crashing down any day. Unemployment is not only the worst it's been in the post–World War II era, it is also not improving. U.S. debt is at an extreme, and U.S. domination as a world economic power is slowly deteriorating.

So what's the solution to this unending uncertainty? Invest in something that has a long track record of stability: gold. Gold has been used as a form of currency and value for thousands of years. Gold investors therefore claim that since gold has been a steady and globally accepted form of wealth, it will always be a worthwhile investment—especially in times of economic turmoil and uncertainty.

The problem with this argument, however, is that gold may never become *worthless*, but if billions of dollars of speculative money are invested in gold and send the price soaring, it could easily one day be *worth less* than it is today. In other words, it may not drop to zero (worthless), but it could easily lose half of its value or fall back down to its historical average—which is far below where we are today. Gold is an illusion of certainty in an uncertain world.

Currency Troubles

Stock market drops are not the only troubling concerns that encourage the buying of gold. Massive government debt and seemingly unsafe government actions when it comes to fiscal and monetary policy are also threatening the stability of world economies and markets. It appears that even governments have acted dangerously and frivolously, and have tremendously increased their risk of spiraling out of control.

All of this financial irresponsibility translates into highly at-risk financial systems. And if a country's financial system is at risk, so is its currency—especially if debt levels keep rising and more money keeps getting printed. Once again, gold seems to be the best solution for tumbling markets and unstable currencies. If fiat currencies are so easily manipulated and rely so heavily on countries with such unsafe financial behavior, gold may be the only true currency (though, as we will see, gold is a commodity, not a currency).

Emerging Market Growth and Demand

Emerging countries like China, Brazil, and India are expected to grow at tremendous rates over the coming years, far outpacing those countries already in the developed world. The growth taking place in these emerging markets will bring about the growth of a large and powerful middle class in these countries, which will in turn increase demand for goods and services.

In many ways, the fate of global economies relies on the success of the emerging markets. And so, too, on the price of gold, since the growing middle class will be able to afford and demand more gold and jewelry. The argument for continuing rising prices in gold sounds plausible, but are expectations too high? What if emerging markets don't grow as quickly as most investors expect them to? What if the price of gold has soared to a level at which it already prices-in the expected future demand? Would the price then correct itself to represent a more reasonable forecast?

Hard to Value

The lack of true historically established methods of valuing an asset increase the probability of mispricings tremendously. Time and time again, bubbles have formed around assets that have no strong predecessors in valuation—tulip bulbs in the 1600s, Internet technology in the 1990s, and real estate in the first decade of the twenty-first century. Without an established, globally accepted method of valuing an investment, the doors are wide open for misunderstandings, false arguments, and costly mispricing.

Gold has no dividend, has its price based on fickle supply and demand, depends on multiple markets and currencies, and has seen such fluctuations over the past few decades that it is simply too difficult, if not impossible, to accurately predict its value. And that lack of more concrete pricing analysis greatly increases gold's chances of becoming highly mispriced.

Introduction of Gold ETFs

The more widespread an investment becomes, the greater its chances of forming a bubble. Perhaps nothing has helped gold prices soar more than the introduction of gold exchange-traded funds (ETFs). Before ETFs, the main ways to invest in gold were limited to buying physical gold and jewelry, or through real commodity trading. The introduction of gold ETFs, most notably the GLD (the largest gold-holding ETF in the world), has made it much easier, more accessible, and more liquid to invest in gold. With gold now traded similarly to stocks, the number of investors and degree of speculation has increased exponentially. With the proper tools for investment now at the disposal of gold investors, a speculative bubble has become drastically more likely. Figure 2.2 shows gold's massive rise since the introduction of gold ETFs

Former UK Prime Minister May Be Responsible for Gold Bubble

With the sale of over half of the UK's gold reserves from 1999 to 2002, when gold prices were at their lowest in 20 years, the man who later became Prime Minister prompted one of the worst financial blunders in recent history and launched the gold bubble that has lasted for over 12 years.

FIGURE 2.2 Gold's Rise since the Introduction of Gold ETFs
Source: www.kitco.com, Chart Prophet LLC.

The gold bubble has undoubtedly involved a number of precipitating factors that have made the bubble possible—such as poor stock market performance, currency troubles, soaring debt, and even the introduction of gold ETFs. But at the core and source of every bubble is an initial boost that launches it. And in our case of the gold bubble, that initial boost was the decision made by former UK Prime Minister Gordon Brown to sell over half of the UK's gold reserves while gold was at its lowest prices in 20 years.

After a nearly 20-year bear market in gold, from the $850 an ounce high in January 1980 to a low of nearly $250 an ounce in mid-1999, UK Chancellor of the Exchequer Gordon Brown decided to sell more than half of the country's gold reserves and reinvest the proceeds in foreign currencies—including euros and dollars. The official reason given for this decision was to "achieve a better balance in the portfolio (the UK's reserve holdings) by increasing the proportion held in currency."[2] Although Brown's intention may have been to diversify the UK's reserves away from the tremendous weakness in gold that had persisted for over 19 years, his decision to sell the gold reserves was made at the worst possible time!

Announcing the UK government's plan on May 7, 1999, when the price of gold was $282.40 an ounce, Brown not only sold at almost the lowest price possible, but his advance notice of the significant upcoming sales drove down the price an additional 10 percent by the time of the first auction on July 6. Prices bottomed out at $252.80 on July 20, 1999 and have since soared to over $1,900. Gordon Brown's terrible decision, which saw the United Kingdom sell approximately 400 tons of gold in 17 auctions from July 1999 to March 2002—at an average price of $275 an ounce—has been called the Brown Bottom,[3] since his plans to sell triggered "hysteria and a negative sentiment in the market,"[4] drove gold prices even lower, and marked the lowest gold prices since 1979.

Moreover, Gordon Brown's exit from gold in order to reinvest proceeds into foreign currencies has been a terrible failure on both fronts. Not only is gold up over 600 percent since the United Kingdom sold its gold, but the currencies that Brown simultaneously decided to invest in are down tremendously over the same period.

Currencies have been in a clear and steep downtrend in comparison to gold since 1999, as shown in Figure 2.3. Meanwhile, the U.S. dollar has lost nearly 40 percent of its value since 2001, while gold has soared (see Figure 2.4).[5]

Brown's decision even went against the advice of the financial experts, who warned that the price of gold was nearing a multidecade low and that announcing the timing and amounts of gold sold through auction would plunge the price even further. Martin Stokes, former vice-president at JP Morgan, was surprised that the auction method was chosen, saying "it indicated they did not have a real understanding of the gold market."[6]

The announcement of the upcoming gold sales also prompted a response from the most respected bank governors of other leading economies—Alan Greenspan and Jean-Claude Trichet. Greenspan, chairman of the U.S. Federal Reserve, defended gold, saying "gold still represents the

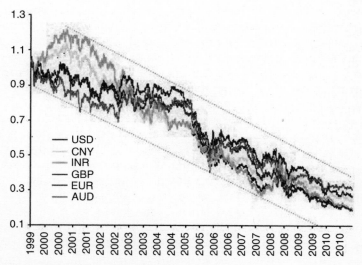

FIGURE 2.3 Currencies versus Gold since 1999
Source: Datastream, Erste Group Research.

FIGURE 2.4 Twenty Years of the U.S. Dollar and Gold

Source: StockCharts, Doug Short/*Twenty Years of the U.S. Dollar and Gold*, *Seeking Alpha*.

ultimate form of payment in the world." Trichet, governor of the Bank of France and later head of the European Central Bank (ECB), also defended gold, saying that according to France, Germany, Italy, and the United States, "the position is not to sell gold."[7]

To make matters worse, 15 European central banks signed the Washington Agreement on Gold in September 1999, limiting the sale of gold to 400 tons per year. This pivotal decision by a powerful group of central banks to support gold prices marked a critical structural change in gold policy. In response to Gordon Brown's ill-timed and poorly executed announcement to sell the UK's gold reserves, the Central Bank Gold Agreement offered protection for gold prices, and even triggered a surge in gold prices from approximately $260 an ounce to around $330 an ounce in two weeks; prices have not dropped below their July 1999 lows.

Brown was the final large seller of gold after a 19-year gold bear market. Normally, using supply and demand logic, we'd expect the price of gold to drop due to the increased supply on the market. But since Brown's advance notice of large selling caused the bottom in gold prices as the last wave of panicked sellers sold their gold, Brown's large selling—rather than buying—was the initial boost that marked the beginning of the bubble. Moreover, Brown's actions caused other central banks to band together and support gold prices, essentially creating a floor and allowing the price of gold to consistently rise over time. This structural shift bolstered gold's price increases and allowed for the gold bubble to take off.

Started by Gordon Brown and confirmed by central banks around the world, the "Brown Bottom" (seen in Figure 2.5) marked the end of the gold

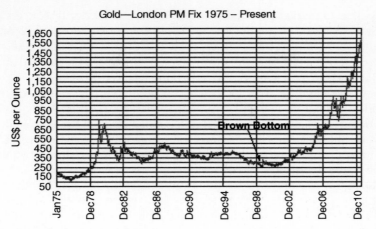

FIGURE 2.5 The "Brown Bottom" in Gold
Source: www.kitco.com, Chart Prophet LLC.

bear market and the beginning of the gold bubble, which has been accompanied by parabolic price increases, overspeculation, and extreme expectations.

Illusion of Safety

Perhaps the most dangerous of all of gold's qualities is the illusion engendered among investors that gold is a steady asset and store of value with a high degree of safety. It is assumed that since gold has always been a store of value throughout centuries, and through rises and falls of civilizations, that it is therefore stable. It is assumed that gold performs well during both inflationary and deflationary times. But as we will see in future chapters, it is largely ignored that the value of gold can and has dropped significantly in the past, and has done so both in inflationary and deflationary times. Gold may never lose its *entire* value, but it can surely lose a significant chunk of it. For those who define "safe" as "safe from severe losses," however, gold is by no means safe.

Conclusion

We have discussed why gold's historical significance and related outside factors enabled the justification for buying gold in order to protect and profit. The removal of the fixed price for gold enabled free-market pricing that is vulnerable to market psychology, poor stock market performance caused investors to lose faith and look to gold for protection and return, economic uncertainty prompted investors to falsely rely on a surefire and "certain" asset backed by history, massive devaluation of currencies created a panic and loss of faith in paper currency, emerging market growth and the huge expected demand for commodities has inflated gold prices, the lack of true historical valuation metrics has greatly increased the probability of costly mispricings, the introduction of gold ETFs has sparked vast speculation in gold and allowed a monstrous-sized wave of new investors to buy gold, and structural changes have turned gold into an unsafe haven driven by misconceptions and delusion.

Now that we understand the arguments made by gold investors and what factors have caused them to view gold as the solution, we can point out all of the clues and warning signs that indicate a massive gold bubble on the verge of collapse.

CHAPTER 3

Signs of a Gold Bubble

Bull markets are born on pessimism, grow on skepticism, mature on optimism, and die on euphoria.

—John Templeton, mutual fund pioneer

Indications of a bubble in gold encompass a very wide range of symptoms. More than just the extreme price movement, the signs of a gold bubble include overspeculation, extreme expectations, and massive publicity. This chapter explains why gold is in a bubble.

Parabolic Price Increases

Economists use the term bubble to mean any deviation in the price of an asset or a security or a commodity that cannot be explained in terms of the "fundamentals."[1]

—Charles Kindleberger

Since bubbles are defined by the tremendous and parabolic price movements in the underlying asset of speculation, the first place to spot a bubble is in a price chart. When prices rise at a steady rate, they are more sustainable than when they show sharp, sudden, or steep price increases, which are accompanied by greater risk and unsustainability. In other words, you generally do not want to buy a stock or asset that has soared in a dramatic fashion, where a sharp fall or collapse is increasingly likely. The steeper the angle of ascent, the sharper the fall.

In our case of gold, the parabolic price increase is clear in the charts. While gold has soared over 600 percent from the 1999 lows, the stock market has seen severe ups and downs and zero gains in over 11 years. See Figure 3.1.

15

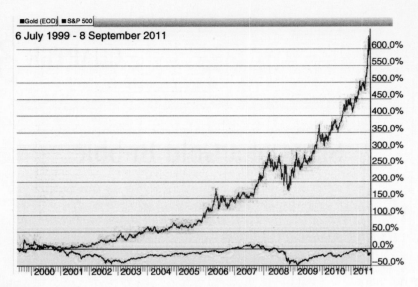

FIGURE 3.1 Gold versus S&P 500 since the Start of the Gold Bubble
Source: StockCharts.com.

Gold prices have exploded upwards from near $250 an ounce to above $1,900 an ounce in 11 years! For an asset that has been the main source of value for thousands of years and throughout the history of civilization, such a massive move requires a radical shift in circumstances. We do potentially have that radical shift underway, but it's unlikely that the chaos of our current state of affairs is any more extreme than the massive upheavals that have been encountered throughout history—such as World War I or II, the Great Depression, or other major financial panics. And even if a radical shift is underway, mainly in a currency-system collapse, who says gold will become the default currency? If anything, gold's massive rise has been fueled by excess liquidity and unwarranted money-printing, which has turned gold into a speculative commodity rather than a stable form of currency.

Some have even claimed that the 600 percent move for gold isn't extreme. These gold enthusiasts have attempted to refute the similarity between the current gold bull market and other bubbles such as the dot-com bubble of the late 1990s or the housing bubble that peaked in 2006 to 2007. One of the arguments presented by gold bugs is that the price of gold has not yet increased in parabolic form. Perhaps they are waiting for a move of a few thousand percent, but they fail to realize that gold has not only moved parabolically since 1999, but is up thousands of percentage points since the early 1970s.

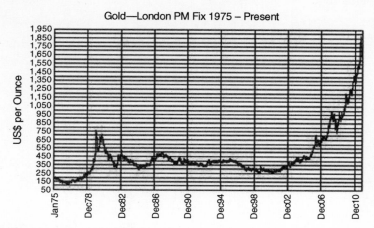

FIGURE 3.2 Gold ($ per Ounce): 1975 to Present
Source: kitco.com.

How is Figure 3.2 *not* a parabolic move? It's almost vertical—and definitely not sustainable.

Moreover, gold may be up *only* 600 percent in U.S. dollar terms since 1999, but it is up over 5,000 percent in U.S. dollar terms since 1968, over 2,700 percent in Canadian dollar (CAD) terms, over 3,400 percent in Australian dollar (AUD) terms, over 4,000 percent in British pounds sterling (GBP), and over 16,000 percent in Indian rupee (INR) terms! The claim that we haven't seen extreme price increases is absurd. Notice the nearly vertical price surges in Figure 3.3.

If we compare the current commodity price surge to the tremendous moves over the past 200 years, can we really say with certainty that this time will be different? Every other time commodity prices have risen this quickly, they have seen sharp declines. There appears to be a cyclical pattern in commodities, as in economies and markets; and we may be at the top of the current cycle. See Figure 3.4.

Just take a look at the recent massive outperformance of gold and commodities over the stock market, shown in Figure 3.5. Are these increases sustainable?

For another example of how the commodity space has soared in a drastic fashion, take a look at Figure 3.6 to see how dramatically cotton and silver prices rose in 2010 and early 2011. With such a basic material as cotton increasing 190 percent in a little over a year, and an important metal such as silver rising over 140 percent, the commodity space definitely looks frothy. And gold may be the biggest player in this theme. Note that cotton is represented by the top line, and silver by the bottom line.

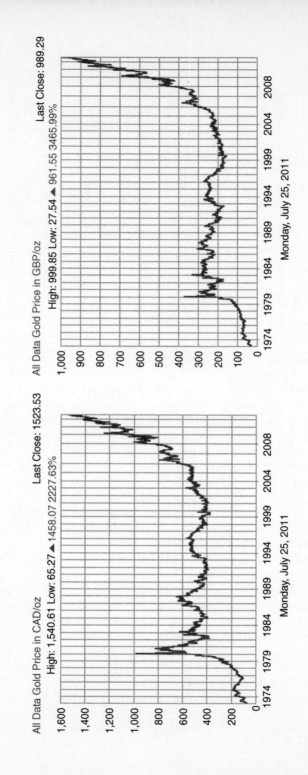

All Data Gold Price in CAD/oz   Last Close: 1523.53
High: 1,540.61 Low: 65.27 ▲ 1458.07 2227.63%

Monday, July 25, 2011

All Data Gold Price in GBP/oz   Last Close: 989.29
High: 999.85 Low: 27.54 ▲ 961.55 3465.99%

Monday, July 25, 2011

18

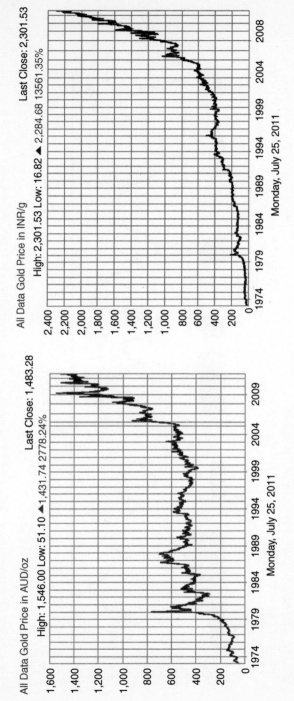

FIGURE 3.3 Gold's Massive Surge in Various Currencies
Source: goldprice.org.

At no time in the past 200 years have commodity prices risen as fast and as high as in the last decade without a sharp decline

 = Price of All Commodities
(10-year average rate of return)

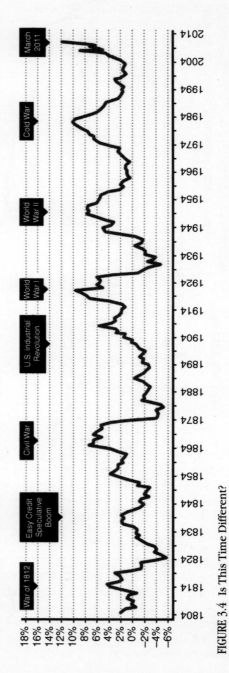

FIGURE 3.4 Is This Time Different?

Source: Hackett Financial Advisors; Maclean's (www2.macleans.ca/wp-content/uploads/2011/03/commodity-chart11.jpg).

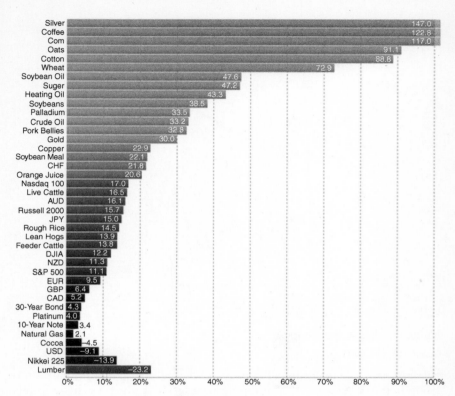

FIGURE 3.5 Commodity Mass Outperformance
Source: www.finviz.com.

Massive Publicity

> *Because the print and electronic media are midwives to the birth of*
> *investment crowds, we have the opportunity to watch crowds develop*
> *from toddlers to mature adults just by monitoring media content.*[2]
> —Carl Futia

For a speculative bubble to form and expand, a few core requirements must be met. First, there must exist a small number of individuals or investors who profit from a specific investment. Then, a second wave of investors must see the profits made by the first group and invest in the same asset in hopes of realizing profits similar to group one. The longer the speculative bubble lasts, the higher the number of waves or groups of investors that will participate. Most important, however, is that each successive wave of

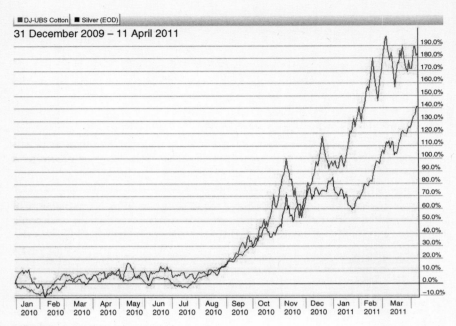

FIGURE 3.6 Cotton and Silver Soar

Source: StockCharts.com.

investors sees smaller and smaller profits and is accepting more risk than the group before it. In other words, the first ones to hear about or invest in this investment theme were the true leaders whose potentially big profits convinced many investors to follow in their footsteps and attempt to repeat their success; but the attempt to repeat the successes of previous investors is often met with failure, and those individuals who jump on the train too late can suffer huge losses.

It is therefore the transfer of investing enthusiasm from one individual to the next that makes the bubble develop and expand. The expansion is accomplished through what has been termed an "information cascade": As stories of profits proliferate via personal accounts or media coverage, information regarding the investment theme is transferred; and as that information transfer continues and grows, it sparks a lot of interest and enthusiasm among potential investors, thereby expanding the bubble.

This transfer of enthusiasm from one individual to the next is also known as a psychological feedback loop: One person's gains and excitement convince another person to attempt person number one's investment, which in turn convinces another person, and so on. This psychological feedback loop is the carrier of speculative bubbles, transmitting speculative fever from one person to the next.

In the words of Yale professor and highly acclaimed speculative-bubble spotter, Robert Shiller:

> *Irrational exuberance is the psychological basis of a speculative bubble. I define a speculative bubble as a situation in which news of price increases spurs investor enthusiasm, which spreads by psychological contagion from person to person, in the process amplifying stories that might justify the price increases and bringing in a larger and larger class of investors, who, despite doubts about the real value of an investment, are drawn to it partly through envy of others' successes and partly through a gambler's excitement.*[3]

Psychological feedback loops are not present only in the expansion of the bubble; they also exist as the bubble collapses, spreading fear and panic as prices tumble even below long-term averages. In other words, just as the feedback loop made investors overreact to the upside, so too will it make them overreact to the downside.

So how does this apply to gold?

Since the bull market in gold has lasted for over 11 years now, there has been plenty of time for success stories of the initial investors in gold to proliferate throughout the rest of the investing world. After a period of relative success, the next wave of investors joined the gold bandwagon. Then came the introduction of gold ETFs, which made investing in gold easier and more accessible to the average investor. With the addition of factors such as financial turmoil, plunging stock prices, and increasing media attention, gold has been able to continually expand as a "surefire" investment theme. But with the possibility that investor and media enthusiasm is at an extreme, the gold bubble could be reaching its peak.

Here's how Carl Futia, self-described contrarian, explains the influence of first-investor success stories:

> *This is a nearly universal characteristic of investment crowds. Any social group's growth is fed by the success of its founding members. An investment crowd's growth is stimulated by the financial success of its early adherents. They have gotten rich from a dramatic upward move in the price of some asset.*[4]

It is exactly these success stories combined with human greed, in attempting to copy others' success, that keep these speculative bubbles going:

> *Crowds develop and grow during a communication process called an information cascade. During an information cascade the print and electronic media focus public attention on recent, dramatic movements*

in markets and the associated profits and losses of investors. This in turn encourages people to put aside their natural skepticism and adopt the investment theme the media are highlighting. As the investment crowd thus grows larger, it pushes the market even further away from fair value and toward a substantial valuation mistake.[5]

Moreover, it is the big price change in the asset that the crowd then relies on as proof of further gains. And although betting on future price increases based on large run-ups that have already occurred is counter-intuitive and risky, the speculative bubble crowd uses these faulty arguments as proof of its correctness.

The crowd then continues to grow as institutional investors, investment gurus, and average investors join. The continuous coverage of success stories, hopes of extreme future profits, and the comfort of being part of an investment crowd with numerous and prominent members, all contribute to these investors' false beliefs that their investments are sound and that their arguments are well-supported.

But the crowd cannot be right forever. At some point there just aren't any profits to be made because everyone has attempted to profit from the same thing. The arguments that were made in support of the investment may have been based on true statements and forecasts, but the high prices to which the underlying asset has been pushed are no longer justified. In other words, investors were correct in that what they invested in should rise; but the excitement and frenzy over their investments pushed prices to extremes—which were no longer justified by their original arguments in support of those investments.

It is at this time that the speculative bubble is at risk of deflating. So long as the crowd's success continues, and money is still being made, the bubble can continue to grow by attracting new investors. But once profits begin to wane or there are few if any investors left to join the crowd, the bubble begins to implode. Not much different from a Ponzi scheme, the end of new-investor participation marks the end of the run, and it is many of the last investors to get in who suffer the greatest losses.

The collapse of the speculative bubble picks up steam on the way down just as the bubble picked up steam on its way up.

Because an information cascade is so fragile, the growth of an investment crowd is likely to halt as soon as the above-average returns to its investment theme fail to materialize. This will happen as a natural consequence of the significant divergence of the market price from fair value that has resulted from the crowd's investment activities. And as soon as the crowd's growth stops, there will then be a trickle of members who lose faith in the crowd's theme. As they leave the crowd, the market price will slowly begin to drift back toward fair value. At that point the information cascade that built the crowd will begin to run in reverse and the trickle of disillusioned members will become a flood.[6]

So, if Figure 3.7 maps the stages of a bubble, where do we currently stand with gold?

We have undoubtedly passed the "stealth" phase in which the first smart-money investors bought gold over 10 years ago. We have also passed the "awareness" phase, in which institutional investors jumped on board before the majority of the public; the introduction of the gold ETFs approximately six years ago probably took place during this phase. We then entered the "mania" phase, in which increasing media attention, public enthusiasm, and—likely—greed and delusion have taken place. There is still a possibility of a rapid "blow-off" phase where prices will shoot up for a short period, tricking the final investors to get in before the bubble ultimately collapses. It is still unsure if the top has been reached; but we are nearing or have already reached the arguments of gold investment as a "new paradigm." Caution is highly warranted.

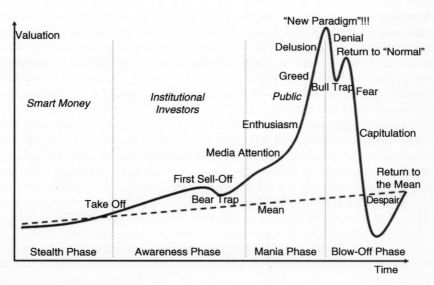

FIGURE 3.7 Stages of a Bubble

Source: Jean-Paul Rodrigue, http://canadianfinanceblog.com/is-the-current-market-a-return-to-normal/.

Media Frenzy

*Even more significant are new TV series that appear just as an asso-
ciated crowd is about to begin its disintegration process.*[7]

—Carl Futia

There is no doubt that gold has become the focus of much attention
over the past couple of years. The price has soared, it has become the number one source of "protection" from currency devaluations and economic
turmoil, and it is the center of discussion in much of the financial media. It is
by following the exuberant media coverage of gold that we can better understand the psychology and speculative behavior of the crowd.

Huge publicity may signal the top. If widespread media coverage is a
sign of investment saturation and peak of popularity, gold may be nearing
the top. Gold has made the front page of the *Wall Street Journal*, has become the topic of much financial media discussion, and has even been the
subject of a popular TV show entitled *Gold Rush: Alaska*.

IS TV SIGNALING A TOP IN GOLD?   Television may be signaling a top in gold in
a similar way it signaled a top in housing.

At the height of the housing craze, with the "unlimited potential" involved in rising real estate prices, some investors pocketed huge gains by
"flipping" houses. By purchasing houses that either needed repair or were
simply selling at a discount to market valuations, investors were able to ren-
ovate the houses or quickly resell them for considerable gains. This method,
or strategy, became so lucrative for some investors, that buying houses to
actually live in or sell years down the road no longer proved necessary;
"flipping" was the new fad.

And flipping was not only deemed lucrative for the few who had real
estate expertise. Starting in July 2005, with home prices already up a few
hundred percent in many areas, television networks began documenting and
promoting the flipping process for those who hadn't yet caught on. First, on
July 14, the Discovery Channel premiered *Flip That House*, documenting the
renovation of a Las Vegas home that was to be flipped. Next, on July 24, *Flip
This House* (note the very original title) was aired on A&E, following a
Charleston-based real estate company focused on doing the same. It seemed
as if the doors were opened for the next generation of real estate speculators.

But as is the case with most lucrative investment themes—they don't last
forever. And not only do they not last forever, but they can also prove to be
highly damaging for those who miss the boat and get in too late. In fact, the
week that *Flip That House* made its premier was the exact top in the housing
market! Not just a warning signal or a precursor to the ultimate peak, but the
exact top!

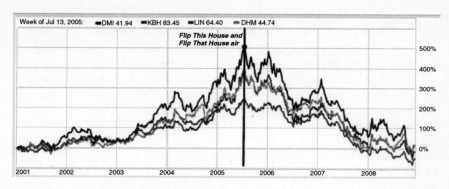

FIGURE 3.8 TV Signals Housing Bubble Peak
Source: Yahoo! Finance, Chart Prophet LLC.

Take a look at Figure 3.8. As you can see, homebuilders such as DR Horton (DHI), KB Home (KBH), Lennar (LEN), and PulteGroup (PHM) saw gains as large as 500 percent in less than four years as the housing market uproar sent real estate prices soaring. But after the massive gains, the ultimate top was reached the week of July 18, 2005—the exact time that flipping became the "norm." The rest we are familiar with: those who failed to get out in time saw their investment value nearly disappear, the housing bubble collapsed, and the market spiraled downwards as investors fled to the exits. Television, with its focus on informing the masses, had signaled the top; flipping was no longer a secret.

If the media craze about housing was a model for any future fads, we may be in the midst of another bubble yet to be popped—the gold bubble. Never mind the slew of reasons why gold looks dangerous here. But if you weren't concerned until now, maybe the TV bubble-signals will convince you.

On December 3, 2010, the Discovery Channel premiered its new show *Gold Rush Alaska*. Just like their 1849 California Gold Rush predecessors had done, the men portrayed in this new show will leave their homes and risk their lives in search of big profits as they dig for gold in Alaska. Yet while they may end up turning a considerable profit, especially since the show has already been recorded while the gold bubble was still raging, the "Gold Fever" may soon be over. And that's not to say that operating a mine is equal to flipping a house, in that it is probably much easier for the average person to flip a house than to mine for gold; but the portrayal of potential profits to be had by getting involved in the gold theme is definitely akin to the potential profits that were presented in the housing shows.

If *Flip This House* and *Flip That House* signaled the peak of the speculative bubble-hunting in the housing market, *Gold Rush Alaska* may prove to do the same for the gold bubble, which may have started for the right funda-mental reasons and which has made a considerable profit for a numerous bunch, but which may ultimately end in disaster for those who have joined the party too late.

As I've mentioned above, the housing bubble peaked and began its col-lapse at the exact time that TV shows were portraying the "house-flipping" process to the masses. If *Gold Rush Alaska* is our second TV bubble-signal, the gold bubble is near its peak.

WALL STREET JOURNAL WARNING SIGNAL   In addition to TV media, the print media has embraced the gold theme as well. And with the *Wall Street Jour-nal* displaying gold as the cover story in late 2010, the end may be near.

> *In the early 1970s Paul Macrae Montgomery observed that when* Time *magazine had a cover story about a prominent business personality, about the stock market, or about some other finance-related matter, one could often infer that an important move in the markets was imminent, a move that was likely to be in the direction opposite to what the cover suggested. Optimistic covers led to unexpected drops in prices, while pes-simistic covers had the opposite effect.*[8]

Though the study by Montgomery involves *Time* magazine, the same ob-servation could be made about the *Wall Street Journal:* when a story makes the front page of a well-known newspaper or magazine, it signals widespread recognition of that story or theme. Since heavily distributed newspapers and magazines tend to reflect the widespread sentiment of its readers and the gen-eral population, a front-page headline signals broad acceptance of that idea.

It's been a fairly long-standing negative omen for the market when major cover stories marvel at the wondrous bull-market run-ups and, inversely, a positive omen for the market when cover stories mourn the death of markets. That said, positive cover stories regarding investment themes are bad omens, signaling an upcoming pause or correction, if not an end to that theme.

A simple book search would reveal the massively one-sided bullish sen-timent in gold. Since 2007, numerous books have been published about gold and its tremendous potential for profits. Yet while all of these books have been encouraging investors to buy gold for the long-term, and have been written by industry-leading economists, investment professionals, and even government officials (such as Robert Kiyosaki, author of *Rich Dad, Poor Dad*; financial historian and economist Peter Bernstein; former Chair-man of the Federal Reserve Paul Volcker; commodity icon Dennis Gartman; congressman and presidential candidate Ron Paul; author and investor Peter Schiff), there are currently *zero* books warning investors about the tremen-dous risks involved in gold.

If mass mood in this case is extreme optimism regarding gold, it may be nearing the end of its run. At the very least, the TV series and heavy media attention signal that the mania phase is well underway.

Overspeculation

There is nothing as disturbing to one's well-being and judgment as to see a friend get rich. Unless it is to see a nonfriend get rich.[9]
—Charles Kindleberger

Aside from the gold price itself, we can measure and observe speculative fever in a number of ways:

"We Buy Gold" Everywhere

In the past two years, there have been more "Sell Your Gold" commercials and "We Buy Gold" stores than ever before—not to mention all the gold and silver ads located all over the Internet. It seems as if everywhere I go I see some kind of reference to gold. The prevalence of these stores and commercials not only points to market saturation and mass public awareness, but also to the massive spotlight that has been shining on gold. Massive publicity of a profitable investment theme or business model generally signals oversaturation and the end of profitability. If "We Buy Gold" and "Cash for Gold" are an indication of mass public awareness, we may be nearing the end of the run for profitability in gold. And since the end of profitability means sideways price movement or a decline, gold prices are at high risk of reaching a peak and falling. The addition of overspeculative bubble behavior makes the potential fall exponentially more devastating.

Famous stories have been told about Joe Kennedy avoiding the Wall Street Crash of 1929 because receiving stock tips from a shoeshine boy signaled to him that it was time to sell. Other stories have been told about taxi drivers recommending technology stocks at the peak of the technology bubble. Recently, my barber started buying and selling gold. I am not saying that shoe-shiners, taxi drivers, and barbers are incapable of making good investment decisions, but when people who generally have little or no financial and investment background start buying and selling gold, warning signs should be flashing.

Coin Sales

Authorized under the Gold Bullion Coin Act of 1985, and first released by the United States Mint, American Gold Eagle coins have been sold to the public since 1986. Together with American Silver Eagles, the sales of these

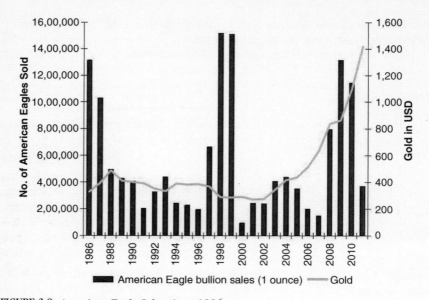

FIGURE 3.9 American Eagle Sales since 1986
Source: Erste Group Research, "Special Report Gold: July 2011," 38.

coins have fluctuated widely and may offer us some insight into the amount of speculation and interest in precious metals, as well as future prices.

As you can see in Figure 3.9, sales of American Gold Eagle coins show three distinct peaks.

- The first peak, in 1986 to 1987, can be attributed both to a spike in interest due to the introduction of these coins, as well as high interest due to the rise in gold prices from 1985 to 1988. Notice, however, that as gold prices continued to rise in 1987, the higher prices and/or declining interest in gold resulted in a lower number of sales of coins. The lower sales number as prices of the underlying gold actually rose may have forewarned of an upcoming fall in gold itself.
- The second peak, 1997 to 1999, came as gold prices reached a multidecade low. After collapsing since the early 1980s, gold fell to $252 an ounce in 1999. The huge number of coin sales, as seen by the spike, is likely the result of tremendously cheap prices—those who purchased the coins could afford much more with gold at $250 an ounce than they did when gold was at $400 or $500 an ounce a few years earlier.

     Once again, the massive spike in coin interest could have signaled a reversal in gold prices. With a sudden spike and higher sales in 1997 than any year in the more than 10-year history of these coins, the renewed spike in interest was a sign that the bottom may be close. 1997 was not the bottom, just as the 1987 divergence was not the exact top. But the spike in 1997 and the huge follow-up interest in 1998 and 1999 were strong signals that the end of the drop in prices was near. Gold did in fact bottom-out near $250 both in 1999 and early 2001 and has never looked back—yet.

- The third peak, where we find ourselves now, has taken place since 2008. After falling considerably throughout 2008, gold has more than doubled from its sub-$700 low in late 2008 to above $1,900 in 2011. Yet though the 2008 spike in coin sales may have signaled renewed buying interest in coins and the underlying gold itself, we are again seeing negative divergences with 2010 sales being lower than 2009 sales. Again, the sales number is likely affected by the higher gold prices in 2010—which has made gold less affordable; but if history has shown us a pattern, in the case of sudden spikes and divergences in coin sales, when the sales of coins fails to follow the trend in actual gold prices, a significant gold price reversal may be due.

An even more extreme example of coin sales signaling a bubble is that of silver coins, shown in Figure 3.10.

Silver coin sales have fluctuated widely as well, but showed an outlandish and almost ridiculous spike from late 2007 until early 2011. Silver coin sales may have soared to such higher levels largely due to their much more

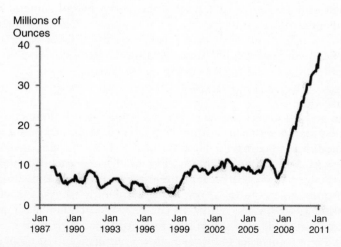

FIGURE 3.10 American Eagle Silver Coin Sales (12 Months Rolling)

Sources: U.S. Mint, Deutsche Bank (March 2011). Retrieved from Business Insider.

affordable prices in comparison to gold. However, the huge spike—nearly four times greater than any since the coins started selling in 1987—should have been a grave warning signal to silver investors. Not only did the tremendous spike forewarn of a potential upcoming silver price reversal (which took place a few months later, in May 2011, and sent silver prices down 40 percent); but the huge speculative fever visible in silver coin sales should forewarn us of a broader speculative bubble in precious metals—especially gold.

Investment Demand

One of the clearest measures of the rise in speculative interest in gold could be the amount of gold demanded for investment. Investment demand could be seen as a measure of popularity and speculative interest, since investment demand rises or falls with the popularity of gold. And since highest investment demand generally comes near peaking popularity, a very large and disproportional rise in investment demand may signal that popularity is peaking and prices may soon drop. In simple terms, if investment demand for gold rises substantially and to fairly extreme levels, it may be time to get out of gold.

In 2000, when the gold bubble was just starting, investment demand was only 4.8 percent of total demand. By 2010, it accounted for nearly 40 percent.[10] With a huge yearly increase of 35 percent in investment demand for 2010 and a dramatic surge in investment demand as percent of total demand from 2000 to 2010, the gold space appears to be highly speculative. Gold bugs would tell you that a huge surge in investment demand is a bullish sign that means investors are finally embracing gold. But with investment demand now making up 40 percent of total demand, it is, in my opinion, far clearer that the huge rise in investment is a sign of mass speculation.

The Dangers of Physical Gold and Silver

The huge growth in physical gold and silver buying is both a sign of mass speculation and an indication of much greater risk taken by investors. With the option of investing in gold either through ETFs or through physical gold, many have chosen to buy the physical kind. Physical gold provides the investor with the actual gold, rather than just some number appearing on his or her computer screen. However, an investment in physical gold can be costlier (due to premiums charged by the sellers) and much less liquid than an ETF investment. If gold prices start to plunge, an investment in the gold ETF would be much easier to dispose of than physical gold (though not necessarily easy). ETFs provide liquidity since the exchange between buyer and seller is much easier and the seller has access to an entire world of buyers through the stock exchange. On the other hand, someone trying to sell physical gold as gold prices plummet would have a much more difficult time finding buyers and fair prices. Though a collapse of gold ETFs is possible due to shady ETF prospectuses and insufficient gold holdings to back up the funds, physical gold and silver could leave many investors stuck with an asset that is falling in price with no one to sell it to.

The University of Texas has taken physical delivery of $1 billion worth of gold, and countries like Mexico, South Korea, and Russia have been large net buyers of gold in 2011. Though these actions are an attempt to capitalize on a continued increase in gold prices, the decision to buy gold or accept physical delivery may have been made too late. If the gold bubble collapses, these gold holdings will lose a large percent of their value. The buying of gold near the peak may be a poorly timed decision similar to former UK Prime Minister Gordon Brown's decision to sell over 50 percent of the UK's gold reserves at the end of the 19-year gold bear market in 1999.

How ETFs Have Spurred the Gold Bubble

The introduction of gold ETFs, and the ease with which the average investor can now invest in gold, has made gold much more accessible—and, in turn, has fueled more speculation than ever before.

The more widespread an investment becomes, the greater its chances of forming a bubble. Perhaps nothing has helped gold prices soar more than the introduction of gold exchange-traded funds (ETFs). Before ETFs, the main ways to invest in gold were limited to buying physical gold or jewelry or through real commodity trading. The introduction of gold ETFs, most notably the GLD (the largest gold-holding ETF in the world), has made investing in gold much easier and more accessible. With gold now traded similarly to stocks, the number of investors and degree of speculation has increased exponentially. With the proper tools for investment now at the disposal of gold investors, a speculative bubble has become drastically more likely.

The first gold ETF to be launched was Gold Bullion Securities, listed on the Australian Stock Exchange on March 28, 2003. The largest and most well-known gold ETF, the SPDR Gold ETF (GLD), was launched in November 2004. Recently holding over $75 billion in gold,[11] the GLD officially became the largest ETF in terms of assets (even bigger than the SPY) and holds more gold than China.[12] A multitude of gold ETFs has since emerged, and continues to ignite speculative interest in the precious metal, as shown in Table 3.1.

Though the speculative interest in gold has coincided with the growth of the gold ETF industry, and is not necessarily caused by the ETF, it is still easy to see how the introduction and availability of the gold ETFs has tremendously supported the rise in gold prices, and may even have acted as a multiplier.

TABLE 3.1 Top Gold-Backed ETFs by Size (June 2011)

Fund	Volume (tones)	Value (US$ million)	% of Total	Exchange	Region
SPDR Gold Shares (GLD)	1,208.2	58,481	56.1%	NYSE	North America
ZKB Gold ETF	196.0	9,489	9.1%	SIX Swiss SE	Europe
iShares Gold Trust	144.3	6,983	6.7%	NYSE	North America
ETFS Physical Gold	131.5	6,367	6.1%	London SE	Europe
Gold Bullion Securities—UK	115.3	5,583	5.4%	London SE	Europe
Julius Baer Physical Gold	95.4	4,618	4.4%	SIX Swiss SE	Europe
XETRA-Gold	49.0	2,371	2.3%	Deutsche Boerse	Europe
NewGold	48.1	2,328	2.2%	Johannesburg SE	Africa
CS II Gold ETF	42.4	2,051	2.0%	SIX Swiss SE	Europe
ETFS Physical Swiss Gold Shares	28.6	1,383	1.3%	NYSE	North America
UBS Index Solutions—Gold ETF	25.0	1,209	1.2%	SIX Swiss SE	Europe
Source Gold ETC	24.6	1,190	1.1%	London SE	Europe
db Gold ETC	23.6	1,143	1.1%	Deutsche Boerse	Europe
Gold Bullion Securities—Australia	14.7	714	0.7%	Australian SE	Asia-Pacific
ETFS Physical Swiss Gold Shares	6.2	298	0.3%	London SE	Europe
GOLDIST	1.4	70	0.1%	Istanbul SE	Middle East
RBS Physical Gold	0.8	40	0.0%	Deutsche Boerse	Europe
Dubai Gold Securities	0.2	7	0.0%	Nasdaq Dubai	Middle East
Total	2,155.3	104,325	100.0%		

"SE" stands for "stock exchange."
Only fully gold-backed gold ETFs are included.
Tonnage as of June 30, 2011.

Source: Respective ETF/ETC/ETP providers, Bloomberg, LBMA, World Gold Council.

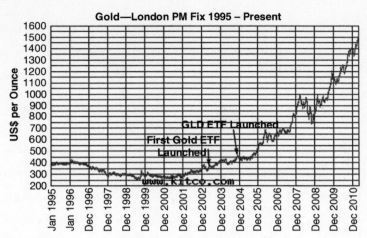

FIGURE 3.11 Gold's Rise since Introduction of Gold ETFs

Source: www.kitco.com, Chart Prophet LLC

Just take a look at Figure 3.11 to see how far gold prices have gone since the introduction of gold ETFs.

DID GOLD ETFs MULTIPLY THE GOLD PRICE? In describing the precipitating structural factors that had led to irrational exuberance and the market bubbles of the late 1990s and 2000s, Shiller points to the "proliferation of equity mutual funds with the effect of encouraging speculative price movements in stock market aggregates, rather than in individual stocks." Furthermore, the psychological aspect of new investment vehicles led to "the emerging popular concept that mutual fund investing is sound, convenient, and safe" and "has encouraged many investors who were once afraid of the market to want to enter it, thereby contributing to an upward thrust in the market."[13]

The eerie similarity between the mutual funds that led to the bubbles of the late 1990s and the ETFs that have led to the gold bubble of the past decade is uncanny. The introduction of the gold ETFs has increased awareness, created the illusion that investing in gold through ETFs is sound and safe, and has encouraged many investors who were once afraid of gold investing to buy gold and thereby contribute to the "upward thrust" of the gold bubble.

The price of gold is up over $1,500 since the introduction of the gold ETFs. And though it is hard, if not impossible, to truly measure the effect of ETFs on investment demand, it could very well be argued that ETFs have sparked a lot of interest in gold, both by allowing new investors a way to invest in gold and by involving a multitude of market participants who would otherwise never come across gold as an investment idea. Notice the high correlation between ETF volume and the rising gold price in Figure 3.12.

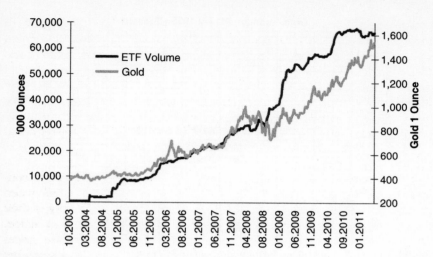

FIGURE 3.12 Total ETF Volume in Ounces versus Gold Price
Sources: Bloomberg, Erste Group Research.

FURTHER ETF RISKS: PROPER STORAGE AND PHYSICAL BACKING Although the
GLD ETF is supposedly backed by gold bullion in London, there has been
concern over the assurance of quantity, quality, and safety of the fund's
holdings. One example of questionable and potentially fraudulent practices:
According to the SPDR Gold Trust prospectus, "Gold bars allocated to the
Trust in connection with the creation of a basket may not meet the London
Good Delivery Standards."[14] Other questionable provisions in the prospectus that should raise red flags are ones that limit the liability of custodians
and subcustodians responsible for the safekeeping of the gold in cases of
fraud, damage, or theft.

The accusations[15] and potential fraud have not been proved, but the
ambiguous prospectus might be showing signs of speculation and questionable practices normally associated with risky asset bubbles. Furthermore, if
such fraud does turn out to be true, the gold market will tumble. This is just
another reason to watch out with gold.

Gold Miners Not Hedging

The lack of hedging by the mining companies, at the exact time when protecting themselves from declining gold prices is most important, stands as
another warning signal of a speculative bubble in gold.

Dealing largely and almost exclusively with gold, gold mining companies are highly exposed to risk from gold price fluctuations. Since their

profits depend heavily on the price of gold, and since they own gold for most months if not all year-round, gold miners would be correct and financially responsible in protecting their gold exposure risk. In fact, mining companies have historically protected themselves from sudden declines in gold prices by hedging their gold holdings with put options or other forms of derivatives that would limit their losses in case of such declines. And the higher the price of gold, the more dangerous the price decline is for the miners. Therefore, as the price is at an all-time historic high, the need for hedging should likewise be at an all-time high in order to protect the miners from sudden drops.

But because most of the miners think that gold prices are going to continue rising, they have recently stopped hedging themselves. At a time when protection is actually more important than at any time in the history of their businesses, they've joined the gold craze and essentially ceased to hedge. This is as counterintuitive as it gets; hedges are protections "just in case" prices go down. Miners seem to have forgotten that "just in case" is a small bet compared to the potential devastation they may be setting themselves up for.

As you can see in Figure 3.13, the trend in hedging has been a steady and steep decline since 2001. But with hedging near a multidecade low and gold prices at all-time highs, a reversal is likely. If the massive collapse of the homebuilder stocks during the housing bubble crash is a similar example,

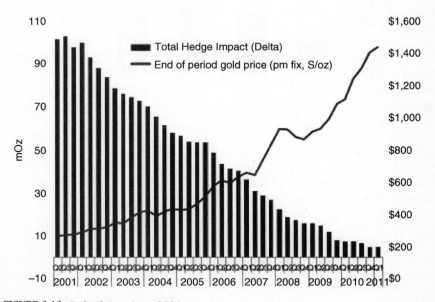

FIGURE 3.13 Dehedging since 2001

Sources: VM Group, Haliburton, ABN Amro, Erste Group Research.

the fate of the gold mining companies looks very bleak with the coming of the gold bubble crash.

Huge Profit-Cost Gap

A large gap between the cost of mining and production (around $600 an ounce) and the actual selling price of gold ($1,900) points to overspeculative gold prices. As production costs stay relatively low in comparison to the market price of gold, mining companies are seeing large profits from the very wide spread between the cost of production and sale price. But such disparities between the production costs and market price may be signaling overextended and frothy gold prices.

While production costs have risen over 50 percent since 2007 (see Figure 3.14), mining companies are still seeing soaring profit margins, up nearly double since 2009 (see Figure 3.15).

With mining companies seeing profits of over 100 percent, a big shift may be underway.

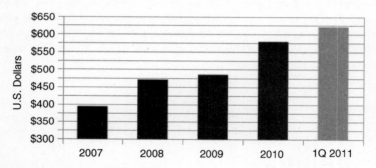

FIGURE 3.14 Gold Production Cash Costs
Sources: VM Group/Haliburton Mineral Services.

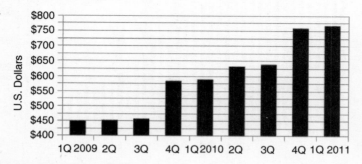

FIGURE 3.15 Average Profit Margin
Sources: VM Group/Haliburton Mineral Services.

In one scenario, the massive profit margins could entice new competitors to enter the gold mining space, which would increase costs of production, increase supply, and/or lower demand. If new competitors see the opportunity and increase the supply of gold by increasing production, the price of gold would drop.

As a second possibility, the huge profit margins brought about by the soaring gold prices could be signaling an overheated market for gold, since the price of production is so far below market price. Regardless, the wide gap between production costs and market price is not sustainable—either production costs must rise or gold market prices must fall.

Speculative Takeovers

Another sign of speculation and overreliance on future gold price increases is the number and size of takeovers by mining companies. Acquisitions are a good way for mining companies to grow their businesses and increase their gold exposure. But when gold prices are already at extremes, excessive takeover volume could signal a buying frenzy driven by the fear of losing out and the greed of wanting more. Excess takeover may signal the peak of popularity and an upcoming reversal. And with 2010 seeing the highest dollar volume in takeovers in decades, the speculative peak may be near. Notice the rising takeover volume in Figure 3.16.

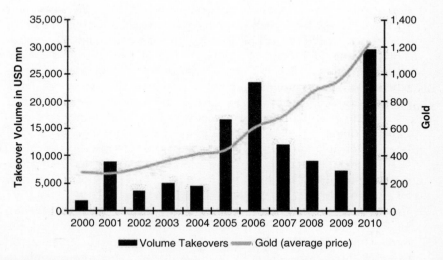

FIGURE 3.16 The Illusion of Opportunity Leads to Excessive Buying: Takeover Volume since 2000

Sources: Metals Economics Group, Bloomberg, Erste Group Research.

The one-year period from June 2010 to June 2011 saw 69 takeovers with an average deal of $881 million and an average premium of 40.98 percent.[16] I am unsure of the average deal size and premium historically, but I would be willing to bet it is nowhere near as speculative as current levels. Moreover, the massive volume of takeovers and the dehedging we discussed earlier are signs of speculation by the mining companies themselves, not just the investors. With speculation on the part of investors, gold companies, financial institutions, and even some governments, the risks of a gold bubble threaten a wide range of potential victims.

Three striking examples in the mining sector highlight the mass overspeculation in gold.

1. **Taxi Company Attempts to Buy a Mining Company:** Perhaps one of the most shocking pieces of evidence that a bubble has formed is the attempt by Wah Nam, a Hong Kong taxi company, to buy an Australian mining company in April 2011.[17] When a completely unrelated business attempts to enter a hot market, in our case a foreign limo service company attempting to buy a publicly traded Australian miner, red flags should appear. Such stories don't come out when a bubble is beginning; they come out when sentiment is at a positive extreme, near the peak.

2. **Large Gold Miner Buys Copper Miner:** One of the largest gold mining companies, Barrick Gold (ABX), recently announced a nearly $8 billion acquisition of copper miner Equinox. Since gold miners generally stick to gold, the large takeover of a copper miner could signal that the outlook for copper is very bullish going forward, and could also serve as a diversification for their gold holdings: "Barrick like other gold companies (is) looking to diversify their operations to some degree into metals where growth opportunities are not as expensive, but where commodity prices are still high and where the demand outlook is strong."[18]

   On the other hand, a large takeover of a copper miner by a gold mining company that has had 90 percent exposure to gold and has been largely a gold-only play may signal more than just diversification: "Barrick might be actually signaling to the market place that gold prices might be a little bit too high, and now it's starting to look to diversify away from gold."[19]

3. **Baby-Formula Producer Attempts to Enter Metals Market:** Similar to the Hong Kong taxi company that attempted to enter the mining business, a Hong Kong–listed baby-formula producer attempted to enter the metals sector by loading up on loans and lending to metals companies. This is a sure sign of overspeculation, "when companies neglect their core business and start speculating in 'hot' sectors

they know nothing about, especially with borrowed money."[20] These are blatant signs of a bubble.

Gold Vending Machines

It wasn't enough for gold to be bought at jewelry stores or through distributors directly. German company Ex Oriente Lux has now manufactured "Gold to Go" ATM vending machines and placed them across the globe, with 10 machines in Germany, two in Italy, one in the United Kingdom, six in the United Arab Emirates, and, ironically, even one in the gambling center of the world—Las Vegas.[21] When coins or bars of gold can be purchased through vending machines, speculation has reached an extreme.

Unemployment Picture Points to Gold Bubble

While the United States is barely, if at all, coming out of the worst recession since the Great Depression, it is no wonder our current unemployment situation is the worst in over 60 years. And to make matters worse, with the United States and global economies showing signs of slowing, our menacing unemployment issues could escalate.

Yet one, and only one, industry has actually added jobs since the beginning of the recession in December 2007: mining. See Figure 3.17.

Understandably, the construction industry, most closely related to housing (which was the industry most severely hurt in the recession), has lost

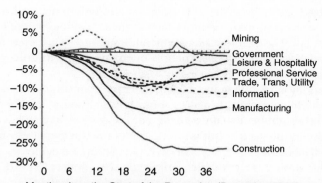

Months since the Start of the Recession (December 2007)
Construction employment declined the most during the recession.

FIGURE 3.17 U.S. Employment Change from December 2007
Source: Business Insider (www.businessinsider.com/category/chart-of-the-day).

most of its jobs since December 2007. Likewise, our weak manufacturing sector, much of which has been shifted overseas, has lost more jobs than other industries.

But the mining sector, which has tremendously benefited from soaring prices in gold, silver, copper, platinum, palladium, oil, and other resources, has seen gains.

If every other industry in the economy is *losing* jobs, there has to be a good reason why mining would be *gaining* jobs. That reason, of course, is the massive increases in the price of gold and other precious metals—which have increased profits in the mining sector and therefore increased the requirement for hiring, as more employees are needed in the growing industry. In other words, mining companies are seeing bigger profits because they are selling their gold, silver, or whichever metal they work with for much more than before.

Then, to increase profits further, the mining companies hire more employees as they expand their operations or mine for more metal. At the same time, new mining companies are emerging because they've seen the soaring gold and metals prices, and want to profit from the theme by mining it themselves. There is no doubt then, that the increased hiring in the mining industry is pointing to an increase in optimism about the future profitability of mining, and in turn the underlying metals—gold, silver, and others. Based on this data then, we can safely say that, on the whole, the market and the mining companies themselves are expecting continued increases in metals prices.

Yet the soaring expectations by both mining companies and investors will not be met. World markets are entering recessions, commodity prices and demand are falling, the U.S. dollar is strengthening, and deflation is more likely to occur than inflation. Due to these conditions, gold and other metals will fall. The excess hiring in the mining industry is therefore a sign of overspeculation, overenthusiasm, and overconfidence in gold, silver, and other metals.

The addition of jobs in the mining industry points to overinflated prices in the underlying metals. It makes sense why mining would benefit more than the other industries, since rising gold and silver prices have boosted profitability in the sector. But with mining being the *only* industry gaining jobs since December 2007, signs of overspeculation are evident.

Mining should be a "relative outperformer." It should be doing *better* than the other industries, but not necessarily doing *well*. In other words, if every part of the economy is getting hit hard, mining should at least get hit. Mining would therefore be a "relative outperformer" if its job losses were not as massive as the other industries. When mining is the *only* industry that gains jobs, however, unjustified metals prices may be to blame. Gold and precious metals have deserved an increase in prices as fears over the global economy spread; but such massive increases, with gold reaching nearly $2,000 an ounce, are very risky and unsustainable.

Gold bugs would say the increased hiring in the mining industry is a sign of higher future prices and a continuation of the gold and precious metals theme. But considering slowing global economies, a strengthening dollar, deflationary concerns, and tremendously unsustainable commodity and precious metals prices, the excess hiring in the mining industry points to extreme speculation and overconfidence in gold, silver, and precious metals.

Gold Is Not Enough

First, investors flocked to gold through the GLD ETF. Then, they jumped into the gold miners ETF (GDX) for higher returns. Then they dove into the junior miners (GDXJ). The further down the line investors go, the higher the speculation and, in turn, the risk.

But the gold and gold miners weren't enough, so investors have moved on to other derivative plays on gold—silver (SLV), platinum (PPLT), palladium (PAL), copper (JJC), rare earth elements (REE), Molycorp (MCP), and the GLTR ETF, just to name a few. These moves by investors are not only evidence of the extreme belief that gold prices will continue to rise, but are also signs of massive risk-taking and a potential expansion of the gold bubble, as investors flock to these stocks and ETFs simply due to the fact that they are related to gold.

Rare-Earth CEO "Mistakenly" Calls It a Bubble[22]

The contagion of the gold and precious metals bubble has been highly visible in the run-up in other metals, commodities, and even rare-earth elements. And if my opinion isn't enough to convince you, maybe the CEO of Molycorp calling the rare-earth space a bubble will.

On CNBC's *Fast Money* on October 21, 2010, the CEO of Molycorp (a rare-earth producer) mistakenly called the rare-earth space a bubble. I say "mistakenly" because no CEO wants to call his business a bubble. Rather, CEO Mark Smith was just completely unprepared and perhaps even foolish when he said:

> *I also don't think that these short-term prices are things that people ought to be counting on because they are really spiked right now and we think there may be a form of a bubble occurring because of all of the news and the frenzy that's occurring.*[23]

Such a misstep, in calling his own business a bubble, could have proved to be devastating. It was true that Smith thought there was a bubble underway, but revealing that to the public could send Molycorp's stock plunging as investors would quickly sell their positions to avoid the upcoming drop. So with the right public relations strategy behind him, Smith attempted to take back his real opinions by telling Bloomberg seven days later:

> *I don't believe there is a bubble. . . . These prices are absolutely sustainable and that's really based upon the very simple facts of supply and demand.*[24]

Then, appearing again on CNBC's *Fast Money* on December 21, Smith explained his completely contradictory statements (probably choosing to keep his real opinions to himself and protect his company's stock from falling). When asked what happened that would cause him to completely change his outlook on what he had called a bubble, Smith responded:

> *Well, I got a lot smarter, number one. And I learned how to do interviews a lot better. . . . We are absolutely bullish on prices. We think these prices are absolutely sustainable and we think that the simple supply and demand fundamentals support the prices that we are bullish on.*[25]

A complete change of opinion, from thinking a bubble is occurring to saying prices are "absolutely sustainable," are blatant signs of manipulation and irresponsibility on Smith's part. It is almost obvious from his comments that he was told what to say in order to protect his company, even at the cost of lying to investors. Furthermore, the initial acknowledgment of a "frenzy" and bubble occurring in the space is an additional signal that the gold mania had spilled over to other precious metals and commodities, and has highly increased the speculation and risk involved in the growing bubble.

Rare earth metals have shown other signs of overspeculation and potential fraud. First, the name "rare earth elements" is a misnomer since most of these 17 elements are actually not so rare. Second, much of the exorbitant price increase can be attributed to the misconception that China has a near-monopoly on rare-earth minerals. However, there exist a number of other rare-earth mines in the United States and elsewhere. China only appears to control the industry because it employs cheap labor that has made it economically inefficient for Western-world mines to compete until now. Moreover, the shock that put rare-earth minerals at the forefront of investor attention and caused a huge increase in prices was China's ban of rare-earth exports to Japan in September 2010. The dispute between China and Japan brought massive publicity to rare-earths and has further fueled the speculative mania for these minerals.[26]

Several signs of potential fraud and manipulation have surfaced as well. Other than Molycorp's CEO calling the sector a bubble and then mysteriously retracting his claims, another rare-earth company appears to be engaged in some shady business. Rare Earth Elements (REE), which has also benefited tremendously from rare-earth overspeculation, is not even in operations mode until 2015 when it opens its mine. Moreover, its management seems to be engaged in highly suspicious activity. First, the CEO, CFO, and Corporate Secretary are involved as managers or directors for 12 additional companies. These three individuals are interconnected and intertwined through a number of similar companies—none of which has moved beyond the exploration phase of the business. Not only do these companies operate at a deficit, but management has been paid hundreds of thousands of dollars through fees and stock-based compensation at the expense of the shareholders. Furthermore, management has failed to adequately disclose the major conflicts of interest that exist between the companies in which they have a vested interest—and to which over $1,000,000 in fees has been billed from shareholder investment.[27]

With gold's massive run, investors have flocked to silver, copper, palladium, rare earth elements, and other precious metals for the "next big thing." What many fail to realize, however, is that if we are currently in a gold bubble, many of the precious metals will also collapse as the gold bubble deflates.

Extreme Expectations

At the source of a speculative bubble are lofty and unrealistic expectations that support the parabolic price increases and justify the mass overspeculation that fuels the bubble. These extreme expectations by investors are the result of flawed valuations, faulty historical comparisons, and a high degree of emotion.

Extreme expectations for gold can be linked to a number of reasons and rationalizations.

Lack of Traditional Investment Valuations

A major characteristic of speculative bubbles is the lack of ways to correctly value the underlying asset. Many bubbles, such as the technology bubble of the late 1990s, develop and grow due to giant expectations of the future success or appreciation of the often-misunderstood asset.

> *So it is natural to expect that an information cascade is especially likely to develop in response to a genuinely new and different investment opportunity, one that is completely outside the realm of most investors'*

personal experience. And this is exactly what is happening when we
hear talk about new industries and new technologies that promise to
revolutionize the economy.[28]

With the tech bubble, investors thought the Internet was the future and
their investments would only keep rising in value. Spurred on by the growing use of the Internet and the speculation that this new technology was the
wave of the future, stock prices soared as investors piled into Internet-based
companies, sometimes simply based on the fact that they included an "e-"
prefix or a ".com" ending to their names. And though investors were correct
in assuming that the Internet and technology were the future of business, the
exorbitant prices they were willing to pay for companies that hadn't even
turned in a profit should have stood as a stark warning.

But what could investors have done? The Internet was rapidly gaining in
popularity, stock prices were soaring, and the argument that this was a
"new age," where old valuation measures no longer applied, was becoming
the norm. Things were "different this time," and you'd be crazy not to join
the party.

Yet while investors were correct in asserting that the Internet and technology companies were the wave of the future, their expectations got a little
ahead of themselves, and their blind faith in almost any company in the
technology space was unwarranted. If you joined the party too late, you
would have lost almost everything.

Similar to the technology bubble, gold also involves an asset that is hard
to truly value. It has been the main source of wealth for thousands of years
and throughout the globe, yet it is hard to determine what it's truly worth. Its
value is affected by inflation, deflation, war, economic crisis, and so forth—
factors that are nearly impossible to evaluate or determine with certainty.
Instead, gold prices have been highly influenced by speculation about
upcoming world events, as well as uncertainty and fear.

Appeals to Fear and Emotion

Human psychology and its extreme opposition to fear make gold an almost
perfect candidate for a bubble that preys on emotion.

> *Affirmative messages that build crowd unity are not usually appeals to*
> *the intellect of crowd members. Instead they are appeals to emotion, to*
> *stereotypes, to dreams or fears. The language of persuasion and crowd*
> *solidarity is the language of drama, not science.*[29]

Gold prices have skyrocketed largely due to the intense fear and uncertainty about the future of the economy and the speculation that we're

approaching a time of massive turmoil. Buying due to such passionate fears makes gold's appeal to emotion a strong enabler for a speculative bubble.

> *Fifth wave advances in the stock market are propelled by hope, while fifth wave advances in commodities are propelled by a comparatively dramatic emotion, fear: fear of inflation, fear of drought, fear of war.*[30]

These "fifth waves" are the final moves before sharp and devastating declines.

"It's Different This Time"

As in most bubbles and overly euphoric investor behavior, the argument that "this time things are different" has surfaced once again. In the dot-com bubble the argument was that the "new age of technology and the Internet" was here. In the housing bubble, land values were going to continue to soar because land was only to continue to be scarce as population grew and people needed homes; the extravagant prices were seen as a result of new valuations for homes. Now, gold's value is considered to be "different this time" because global markets are interconnected, economies are at high risk, and currency systems are seen as highly unstable. But are things really so different now? Arguments of a "new paradigm" and "new era" are many times accompanied by peaks in asset prices or ends of popular themes.

Faulty Historical Comparison

Originally published November 23, 2010: "Why Inflation Isn't Affecting Gold Prices," *Seeking Alpha*.[31]

The often-used argument by gold bugs has been that the gold price, if adjusted for inflation, is still considerably below the record highs of the early 1980s. And since we are still below the early 1980s prices when we adjust for inflation, we should not be concerned about a gold bubble. Even more, the argument claims that since we are well below inflation-adjusted record prices in gold, we can expect gold prices to continue to run up significantly before a peak is in place. In other words, they claim that $2,000 an ounce gold is still not expensive because $2,000 in 2011 is worth less than $700 in the early 1980s.

However, I have four issues, at least, with these claims.

1. **Rampant inflation in 1970s, not now.** Gold price records of 1980 came at a time of soaring inflation. Inflation was at 13.5 percent in 1980! Compare that to 2009 where we had negative inflation, and to 2010 and 2011 when we are averaging less than 5 percent inflation—nowhere near

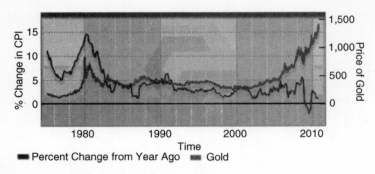

FIGURE 3.18 Inflation, CPI All Items (Seasonal Adjustment)

Source: U.S. Department of Labor, Bureau of Labor Statistics; Chartfacts.

the 13.5 percent as in 1980. Even in China and fast-growing emerging markets, inflation is closer to 6 percent. Since inflation "inflates" prices, it is understandable why gold prices skyrocketed in the early 1980s in order to reflect the surge in overall prices. But at a time when inflation is far from soaring (at least in comparison to the early 1980s), much of the speculation in gold today is due to uncertainty and fears about the *future*, rather than the *reality* that supported gold's rise in the late 1970s.

As you can see in Figure 3.18, the 1980 gold price high was accompanied by huge percentage increases in the Consumer Price Index (CPI), which tracks price changes in a broad basket of goods and services, as a measure of inflation. Over the next 25 years, gold prices were generally stable as the CPI grew between 1 and 6 percent annually. But starting in 2005, we all of a sudden have a huge divergence between gold prices and the CPI. In other words, we would expect gold prices to rise and fall in accordance with changes in the CPI—if the CPI soars we would expect gold prices to rise as well, and if the CPI falls we would expect gold prices to fall or at least grow modestly. But that's not the case here; the gold price surged together with CPI in 1980, but is completely diverging from CPI since 2005. If anything, we should be seeing gold prices stagnate or even drop a little to match the lower inflation rates of the past few years.

2. **Largest divergence between real gold prices and inflation-adjusted gold prices.** Not only are gold prices diverging from the yearly CPI changes, but they are also diverging from themselves (see Figure 3.19).

   While real gold prices and gold prices adjusted for inflation have generally remained close, they have diverged from each other to a huge extent since 2005. In the early 1980s, the two prices were almost identical, and even overlapped. But in 2010, we had real prices at $1,400

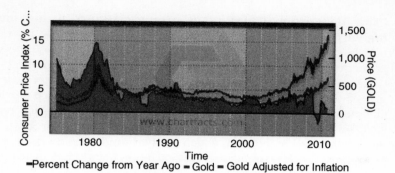

FIGURE 3.19 Inflation, CPI All Items (Seasonal Adjustment)

Source: U.S. Department of Labor, Bureau of Labor Statistics; Chartfacts.

while the inflation-adjusted price of $644 lagged by over 50 percent. Either the inflation-adjusted price has to catch up, or the $1,500-plus real gold price has to drop. With such a massive and unprecedented divergence between the two, I'd bet on option B.

3. **Gold is up way more than inflation.** As CPI is up less than 30 percent since 2000, gold is up over 500 percent. If CPI is a good measure of overall inflation, we'd expect prices of most items to increase, or decrease, in accordance with changes in the CPI. Therefore, if the CPI increases by 30 percent, we'd expect most items to increase in a range around that 30 percent; prices of food may rise 35 percent, but prices of energy could rise only 25 percent, for example. But when we see the price of one item increase by 500 percent, as gold has in this case, we should question whether such a move is justified, as prices of the rest of the things we could buy are not even close to moving that rapidly (see Figure 3.20). As CPI has essentially flat-lined since 2005, gold is up almost threefold.

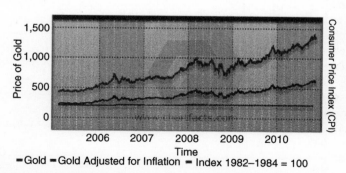

FIGURE 3.20 Inflation, CPI All Items (Seasonal Adjustment)

Source: U.S. Department of Labor, Bureau of Labor Statistics; Chartfacts.

4. **Price highs from 1980 stand as strong resistance against much higher prices.** Since gold lacks intrinsic value, unlike stocks, and relies mainly on supply and demand, previous high prices play an even greater role. In our case, the inflation-adjusted price highs of the 1980s (between $1,700 and $2,400) could present heavy selling pressure, as investors reconsider their gold investments as prices approach previous all-time highs. Not only is the $2,000 level a major psychological resistance level, where many investors would likely sell their gold; but the lack of soaring inflation, which justified surging gold prices in the 1970s, poses major barriers to a continuation of gold price increases at current times.

In conclusion, though we have not surpassed the record high price of gold in 1980 when we adjust for inflation, we have certainly doubled the record in real prices, we currently have no soaring inflation that would justify the huge price moves (as it did in the 1970s), and we have the largest divergence ever between real prices and inflation-adjusted prices. In other words, gold is moving much faster than inflation, and maybe even too fast.

There has been concern over the reliability and accuracy of the inflation data provided by the CPI (see Figure 3.21). Some have claimed that the CPI is fundamentally flawed and that inflation is higher than shown by the CPI. But in my opinion either outcome supports a gold bubble:

If CPI is flawed, we've had higher inflation, and therefore it makes sense that gold is up. But the extent of gold's rise and the upcoming deflation will hurt gold and commodities.

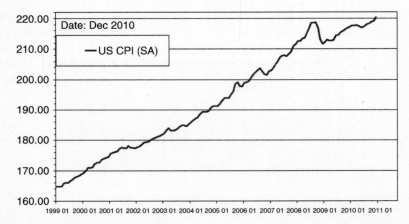

FIGURE 3.21   U.S. CPI Inflation Index

Data source: BLS. © Marketoracle.co.uk 2010.

On the other hand, if the CPI is right, we've had low inflation, which should not have caused such huge price increases in gold (as was the case in the late 1970s).

The price of gold has risen over 600 percent since 1999, but the CPI, which measures inflation, is up only around 30 percent. Gold has been bought due to inflation expectations, but with the increase in gold prices heavily outweighing actual inflation, extreme speculation may have pushed gold way beyond reasonable levels.

A similar scenario played out in the 1970s, when gold surged hundreds of percent to the 1980 high of $850 an ounce before starting a collapse and a 19-year bear market in gold. In the words of financial-crises expert, Charles Kindleberger:

> *The 1970s was a decade of accelerating inflation, the largest sustained increase in the U.S. consumer price level in peacetime. The market price of gold surged initially because some investors relied on the cliché that "gold is a good inflation hedge" as the basis for their price forecasts; however the increase in the gold price was many times larger than the contemporary increase in the U.S. price level. Toward the end of the 1970s investors were buying gold because the price of gold was increasing—and the price was increasing because investors were buying gold.*[32]

Not only does our current gold bubble show remarkable similarities to the one during the 1970s, where gold prices far outpaced inflation and eventually imploded; but our current situation is even more dangerous, because current inflation is nowhere near the high levels that were present in the 1970s. If anything, the threat of recession may be signaling an upcoming deflationary phase, in which inflation is negative. And if inflation is negative, asset prices will fall and gold will not gain as investors are expecting it to.

From 1971 to 2001, gold and bonds moved together. But since 1999— when I claim our current gold bubble began—gold has skyrocketed while bonds have continued to decline. The failure to move together, as was the case historically, could be pointing to an irrational price for one of them— either gold is too high, or bonds are too low. They will likely converge again, and chances are that gold has formed a bubble and will soon collapse in order to resume historical correlation to bonds.

Intolerance of Opposing Views

One of the strongest signs of herd mentality is the fear of taking the opposite view. So far, I have yet to see strong opinions in opposition to gold— someone who puts his money where his mouth is. And when I do see individuals claiming gold to be a bubble, their claims are met with heavy opposition and ridicule. This ridicule and scorn (visible in the comment sections of many antigold articles on the Internet) are undoubtedly signs of intense bias and strong emotional ties to the gold theme; and breaking from these biases or emotions is extremely hard to do—especially when one's money is invested.

We therefore can understand why gold-bubble claims are met with heavy opposition: because those invested in gold have a high interest in continued price increases. But when the ridicule becomes so one-sided and intense, especially when it's backed by faulty logic or extreme expectations, signs of a speculative crowd emerge. Strong and vehement opposition to antigold individuals is therefore substantial proof that the gold bubble is nearing saturation.

Herd-Like Price Targets

Originally published March 30, 2011: "The Impending Collapse of the Gold Bubble," *Seeking Alpha*[33]

Gold price-targets range from $1,000 to $15,000. Who is right?

Virtually no one is willing to bet against gold. Even among those who think gold is a bubble or risky investment, there are very few, if any, people actually willing to bet against it. Though it's generally a very smart move to avoid betting against a stock or investment theme with a lot of momentum behind it, the fact that even gold bears are shying away from betting against it may signal that it is a bubble with extremely high bullish sentiment. If the gold bears won't bet against it, is there really much room left for gold to run? What happens if these gold bears finally gather the courage to start betting against it?

Moreover, if we look at the huge number of price-target estimates made by institutions, investment professionals, analysts, and the gold mining companies themselves—only 2 out of over 100 estimates are below $1,400! And most of them are far beyond the current price. Such extreme bullishness should be met with severe caution at the very least. The lack of dissenting opinion is highly unsettling.

But—I could be wrong. At least that's what almost every analyst, bank, mining company, investor, and financial institution thinks. Gold price targets for 2011 range from anywhere near $1,000 to as high as $15,000. The larger financial institutions are clustered near $1,500 though. And considering that gold is currently selling near $1,500, does it really pay to take on the potentially large risk when consensus estimates have already been reached? If you do think it is worth it, you should hope some of the individuals predicting $2,000 or $15,000 gold are right.

Here is a comprehensive and exhaustive list of gold price projections (as of March 30, 2011):

Analyst/Company	2011 Gold Price Target
Morgan Stanley	$1,512
Goldman Sachs	$1,650
JP Morgan	$1,650–$1,700
Jeffries	$1,400
Barclays	$1,850
Bank of America	$1,500
UBS	$1,400
Citigroup	$1,450
Deutsche Bank	$1,600
Société General	$1,425
Jim Rogers	$2,000
CIBC	$1,600
Jon Nadler, Kitco	$1,150
IBIS World	$1,150–$1,210
Scotia Capital	$1,400–$1,500
Mark Bristow, CEO Randgold Resources	$1,500
Chuck Jeannes, CEO Goldcorp	$1,500–$2,300
Sean Boyd, CEO Agnico-Eagle	$1,600
Mark Cutifani, CEO AngloGold Ashanti	$1,300–$1,500
Aaron Regent, CEO Barrick Gold	$1,500
Jeff Pontius, CEO International Tower Hill	$1,500
Jochen Hitzfeld, Unicredit	$1,500
Bretton Woods Research	$1,500
Harmony Gold	$1,500

The following is a full list of gold price projections, with extreme expectations clearly noticeable.[34]

Higher Than $10,000

1. Mike Maloney: $15,000
2. Ben Davies: $10,000–$15,000
3. Howard Katz: $14,000
4. Dr. Jeffrey Lewis: $7,000–$14,000
5. Jim Rickards: $4,000–$11,000
6. Roland Watson: $10,800 (in our lifetime)

$5,000–$10,000

1. Bob Kirtley: $10,000 (by 2011)
2. Arnold Bock: $10,000 (by 2012)
3. Porter Stansberry: $10,000 (by 2012)
4. Tom Fischer: $10,000
5. Shayne McGuire: $10,000
6. Eric Hommelberg: $10,000
7. Anonymous: $6,410–$10,000 (by 2012–2016)
8. David Petch: $6,000–$10,000
9. Gerald Celente: $6,000–$10,000
10. Egon von Greyerz: $6,000–$10,000
11. Peter Schiff: $5,000–$10,000 (in 5 to 10 years)
12. Patrick Kerr: $5,000–$10,000 (by 2011)
13. Peter Millar: $5,000–$10,000
14. Roger Wiegand: $5,000–$10,000
15. Alf Field: $4,250–$10,000
16. Peter George: $3,500 (by 2011–2013); $10,000 (by Dec. 2015)
17. Jeff Nielson: $3,000–$10,000
18. Dennis van Ek: $9,000 (by 2015)
19. Dominic Frisby: $8,500
20. James Turk: $8,000 (by 2015)
21. Joseph Russo: $7,000–$8,000
22. Michael Rozeff: $2,865–$7,151
23. Martin Murenbeeld: $3,100–$7,000
24. Jim Willie: $7,000
25. Dylan Grice: $6,300
26. Chuck DiFalco: $6,214 (by 2018)
27. Aubie Baltin: $6,200 (by 2017)
28. Murray Sabrin: $6,153
29. Samuel "Bud" Kress: $6,000 (by 2014)
30. Robert Kientz: $6,000
31. Harry Schultz: $6,000
32. Lawrence Hunt: $5,000–$6,000 (by 2019)
33. Martin Hutchinson: $3,100–$5,700
34. Jeremy Charlesworth: $5,000+
35. Przemyslaw Radomski: $5,000+

$5,000

1. David Rosenberg: $5,000
2. Doug Casey: $5,000
3. Peter Cooper: $5,000
4. Robert McEwen: $5,000

5. Martin Armstrong: $5,000 (by 2016)
6. Peter Krauth: $5,000
7. Tim Iacono: $5,000 (by 2017)
8. Christopher Wyke: $5,000
9. Frank Barbera: $5,000
10. John Lee: $5,000
11. Barry Dawes: $5,000
12. Bob Lenzer: $5,000 (by 2015)
13. Steve Betts: $5,000
14. Stewart Thomson: $5,000

Up to $5,000

1. Pierre Lassonde: $4,000–$5,000
2. Willem Middelkoop: $4,000–$5,000
3. Mary Anne and Pamela Aden: $3,000–$5,000 (by February 2012)
4. James Dines: $3,000–$5,000 (in June 2011)
5. Goldrunner: $3,000–$5,000 (by 2012)
6. Bill Murphy: $3,000–$5,000
7. Eric Janszen: $2,500–$5,000
8. Larry Edelson: $2,300–$5,000 (by 2015)
9. Luke Burgess: $2,000–$5,000
10. Jeff Nichols: $2,000–$5,000
11. Jim Sinclair: $1,650–$5,000

$3,000–$4,000

1. Mike Knowles: $4,000
2. Ian Gordon/Christopher Funston: $4,000
3. D.P. Baker: $3,000–$3,750 (by Jan./Feb. 2012)
4. Adam Hamilton: $3,500 (by 2010–2011)
5. Christopher Wood: $3,360
6. Eric Roseman: $3,500+
7. John Henderson: $3,000+ (by 2015-2017)
8. Hans Goetti: $3,000
9. Michael Yorba: $3,000
10. David Tice: $3,000 (by 2012)
11. David Urban: $3,000
12. Mitchell Langbert: $3,000
13. Brett Arends: $3,000
14. Ambrose Evans-Pritchard: $3,000
15. Trader Mark: $3,000 (by mid-2011)
16. John Williams: $3,000
17. Louise Yamada: $3,000 (by 2016-2017)

18. Byron King: $3,000
19. ThumbCharts.com: $3,000
20. Bob Chapman: $3,000 (by 2011)
21. Ron Paul: $3,000 (by 2020)
22. Chris Weber: $3,000 (by 2020)

$2,500–$3,000

1. Ian McAvity: $2,500–$3,000 (by 2012)
2. Graham French: $2,000–$3,000
3. Joe Foster: $2,000–$3,000 (by 2019)
4. Sascha Opel: $2,500+
5. Rick Rule: $2,500 (by 2013)
6. Daniel Brebner: $2,500
7. James DiGeorgia: $2,500

Conclusion

Signs of a gold bubble are numerous and even shocking. Aside from the classic and quantitative sign of a bubble—the massive and parabolic run-up in price—investors' extreme enthusiasm and euphoria over gold have been accompanied by massive publicity, media frenzy, overspeculation, surging and unsustainable investment demand, a multitude of ETF investment vehicles, highly risky behavior by the miners, a huge gap between the low cost to produce gold and the high selling price, irrational expectations about the future, and herd-like behavior.

These warning signs are out there, but the bubble continues because gold investors refuse to accept them. Led by many talking heads who make passionate arguments supporting gold, the herd that invests appears to have great reasons to do so. The herd also has strength in numbers, which it uses as another reason to support its speculative behavior; ironically, many gold investors also claim that *not enough* people have bought gold and that many more will do so in the future. Moreover, expectations about future prices reach extremes because gold does not have a traditional way of being valued; almost any price could be argued, as long as believable reasons are given. Prices also surge because gold investing appeals to fear and emotion, which can cause panic buying and justify nearly any price. This strong emotional component of the bubble also allows for faulty historical comparisons that make gold prices appear to be reasonable and even cheap. Investors claim that "things are different this time" and buying gold is the smart thing to do.

But one does not have to look so hard to see how widespread and speculative the gold theme has become. "We Buy Gold" stores are everywhere, gold is a major focus on TV and news, gold advertisements fill websites and magazines, and nearly all banks and financial institutions think gold prices will continue to rise. Most shockingly, gold speculation has filtered through to nearly all sectors of the market—with examples of a taxi company and a baby-formula maker attempting to enter the metals business; and gold is even being sold in vending machines. Profitable and safe investments do not involve such massive media attention and extreme enthusiasm. Instead, gold investing is extremely risky and misleading.

In the next chapters, we show how overvalued gold has become by comparing it to other asset classes and presenting the case for why gold is not recession-proof. We also present an in-depth analysis of gold's massive price increases over the past 40 or more years, and discuss the number of factors that gold's future relies on. Now that we have seen the many warning signs pointing to a bubble, we can attempt to predict exactly at what stage of the bubble we currently find ourselves and what circumstances could trigger its collapse.

CHAPTER 4

Gold Takes On . . .

O ne argument commonly made by gold investors is that gold is both an inflation and a deflation hedge. The argument essentially claims that gold will benefit if inflation spirals out of control or if deflation materializes due to a recession. In other words, these gold investors basically claim that gold will never go down—an obviously logically incorrect argument.

But in order to truly test the claim by many gold bugs that gold benefits from both inflation and deflation, we must look back at history to see how gold has performed in different scenarios.

Deflation

As Robert Prechter of Elliott Wave International points out, the claim for gold outperformance during deflationary times stems from the 1930s. Gold stocks generally performed better relative to the market during the 1929–1932 downturn and Depression. However, a few special-case scenarios were involved in the 1930s that may invalidate the claim that gold or gold stocks outperform in deflationary times.

First, gold stocks barely moved in the 1929 to 1932 market. It was actually during the bull market that followed that the gold stocks soared. Second, gold stocks outperformed in the 1930s mainly because the federal government fixed the price of gold at $20.67 per ounce and then $35 per ounce starting in 1934. Gold stocks outperformed in this time period because the fixed gold prices kept it at a steady level while all other commodities and stocks suffered due to deflation. In other words, since the price of gold was not dropping, as was the value of many other assets, there was no reason for gold stocks to suffer; gold served as a safe haven only because its price was fixed while everything else was falling. Moreover, when the government raised the fixed price of gold to $35 an ounce in 1934 (and further devalued the dollar), mining companies actually benefited from the increased profits associated with gold, despite a scenario of extremely low inflation. But since the price of gold is no longer fixed, gold and gold stocks are no longer artificially protected from a deflationary period or fall in commodities and stocks. Rather, a deflationary scenario will likely hurt gold and gold mining stocks to a similar extent that it hurts the rest of the commodity space. The deflationary argument based on the 1930s therefore does not apply to our current situation.[1]

Is Gold a Safe Haven During Recessions?

Another big reason why people have bought gold over the past decade is because they believe gold will outperform the market, and even soar, if the economy returns to recession. However, other than the 1930s, where the fixed gold price protected gold stocks from falling, gold has not performed exceptionally well and has not even outperformed the market in recessions dating back to 1945. Robert Prechter tracked the performance of gold and the Dow Jones Industrial Average during those recessions,[2] as shown in Tables 4.1 and 4.2.

As you can see, aside from its impressive performance from 1973 to 1975, gold has shown negative or low returns in recessions since 1945 (excluding 2002 to 2011, where the gold bubble has ignored this historical correlation). Since gold has historically not performed exceptionally well on average during recessions, we do not expect gold to perform exceptionally well in case of an upcoming recession. Moreover, the appearance and escalation of the gold bubble since 1999 has further increased the risks and chances of a severe drop in gold prices if that recession does come.

In fact, as Prechter points out, the three biggest gains in gold over the past century have been while the economy was expanding! The first, a gain against the dollar of 69 percent, followed the raising of the fixed price of gold by Congress from \$20.67 to \$35 an ounce in 1934—during an economic expansion. The second, and huge, gold bull market from 1970 to 1980 occurred during an economic expansion as well. Of the \$815 rise in gold from 1970 to 1980, \$725 of it came during economic expansion. And thirdly, of the \$748 rise in gold from February 2001 to March 2008, \$726 occurred during an economic expansion as well.[3] Additionally, gold is up from approximately \$900 to \$1900 since the official "end of the recession" in 2009; that makes gold prices essentially flat if we take out economic expansions. Therefore, even though this third gold bull market is ideologically and substantially based on an upcoming economic meltdown and recession, most of the price rise has actually taken place during expansionary times. Based on this, we can't claim that gold would benefit from an economic contraction. Gold investors may be wrong in buying gold as a safe haven.

TABLE 4.1 Gold's Performance during Recessions

GOLD

Recession Start (15th of month)	Recession End (15th of month)	Length in Months	Start Value	End Value	Capital Gain/Loss	Income	Total Return	Total Return with 2008 Transaction Costs
Feb 1945	Oct 1945	8	35	35	0.00%	0.00%	0.00%	−4.00%
Nov 1948	Oct 1949	11	35	35	0.00%	0.00%	0.00%	−4.00%
Jul 1953	May 1954	10	35	35	0.00%	0.00%	0.00%	−4.00%
Aug 1957	Apr 1958	8	35	35	0.00%	0.00%	0.00%	−4.00%
Apr 1960	Feb 1961	10	35	35	0.00%	0.00%	0.00%	−4.00%
Dec 1969	Nov 1970	11	35.35	37.95	7.36%	0.00%	7.36%	3.36%
Nov 1973	Mar 1975	16	91.5	178.25	94.81%	0.00%	94.81%	90.81%
Jan 1980	Jul 1980	6	684	619.5	−9.43%	0.00%	−9.43%	−13.43%
Jul 1981	Nov 1982	16	412.25	403.25	−2.18%	0.00%	−2.18%	−6.18%
Jul 1990	Mar 1991	8	363.6	366	0.66%	0.00%	0.66%	−3.34%
Mar 2001	Nov 2001	8	260.9	275.6	5.63%	0.00%	5.63%	1.63%
Average		10.18182				**Average:**	8.80%	4.80%
						Median:	0.00%	−4.00%

Source: © Prechter, Robert R. Jr. *Robert Prechter on Gold & Silver*. Elliott Wave International, 2009. Pages 15, 23, 28.

TABLE 4.2 DJIA Performance during Recessions

DJIA

Recession Start (15th of month)	Recession End (15th of month)	Length in Months	Start Value	End Value	Capital Gain/Loss	Income	Total Return	Total Return with 2008 Transaction Costs
Feb 1945	Oct 1945	8	158.2	185.5	17.26%	2.55%	19.80%	19.78%
Nov 1948	Oct 1949	11	176	186.4	5.91%	5.86%	11.77%	11.75%
Jul 1953	May 1954	10	268.7	322.5	20.02%	4.22%	24.24%	24.22%
Aug 1957	Apr 1958	8	487.3	447.5	-8.17%	3.03%	-5.13%	-5.15%
Apr 1960	Feb 1961	10	630.1	648.8	2.97%	2.93%	5.90%	5.88%
Dec 1969	Nov 1970	11	784	759.7	-3.10%	3.85%	0.75%	0.73%
Nov 1973	Mar 1975	16	874.5	773.4	-11.56%	7.03%	-4.53%	-4.55%
Jan 1980	Jul 1980	6	868.6	901.5	3.79%	2.96%	6.75%	6.73%
Jul 1981	Nov 1982	16	954.1	1021.4	7.05%	8.20%	15.25%	15.23%
Jul 1990	Mar 1991	8	2980.2	2948.5	-1.06%	2.47%	1.40%	1.38%
Mar 2001	Nov 2001	8	10031.3	9872.4	-1.58%	1.21%	-0.37%	-0.39%
Average		10.18182				Average:	6.89%	6.87%
						Median:	5.90%	5.88%

Source: © Prechter, Robert R. Jr. Robert Prechter on Gold & Silver. Elliott Wave International, 2009. Pages 15, 23, 28.

Gold versus Various Asset Classes: Ratio Analysis

In order to fully see and understand where gold stands historically, we compare how expensive or cheap it is in relation to other asset classes. For example, if one ounce of gold bought you one watch 10 years ago but buys you 10 watches today, it could be overvalued. See Table 4.3.

As you can see, gold's purchasing power has greatly increased in relation to other assets and items. It would be understandable if gold prices rose slightly more than car, home, food, and gasoline prices over the same time period. But gold is up way more than most other assets and items. The comparison of purchasing power of gold over the years should grab our attention and leave us thinking whether or not it has become overvalued.

Since 1900, the Dow has had a median 6x multiple of gold, with huge spikes in the late 1920s, 1950s to mid-1960s, and through the dot-com bubble of the late 1990s (see Figure 4.1). When the market is outperforming gold, the ratio gets bigger; and when gold is outperforming the market, the ratio gets smaller. In our case, gold has outperformed since around 2000 when the bubble began. The market had reached the highest multiple in comparison to gold, and it started a long drop that has lasted over 10 years. To sum it up, the market tremendously outperformed gold from 1980 until around 2000, but gold has tremendously outperformed the market from 2000 until now. As we approach the 1980 ratio low, we have to wonder whether we're near gold price extremes. And since both the market and gold are at significantly high levels historically, the fact that gold prices have outperformed the market by such a wide margin further adds to the possibility that gold prices are near extremes. In other words, the market is overvalued and gold is even more overvalued.

Gold's relationship with other asset classes can help us predict future movements in other commodities, bonds, the dollar, and stocks. If history provides any insight into the future, historical correlations between asset

TABLE 4.3 Gold Purchasing Power Then and Now (as of 9/1/11)

Purchase	1999 (source below)	2011	% Change
Ounce of Gold	$275	$1,800	554.5%
Gallon of Gas	$1.30	$3.56	173.8%
Coca-Cola	$1.14 (1 liter)	$1.79 (2 liter)	57.0%
Average House	$119,600	$156,100	30.5%
Gallon of Milk	$2.88	$3.75	30.2%
Car (Toyota Camry)	$17,518	$19,820	13.1%
Dow Jones	11,000	12,000	9.1%

Source: www.dailyfinance.com/2009/12/29/then-vs-now-how-prices-have-changed-since-1999/.

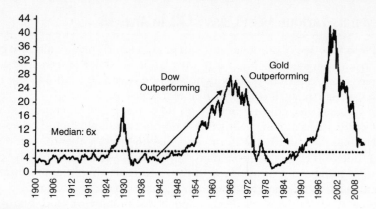

FIGURE 4.1   Dow/Gold Ratio

Sources: Erste Group Research, Bloomberg.

classes can reveal their future direction of prices. In our case, if gold goes up or down, how would silver, oil, stocks, or the dollar react? And vice versa.

Gold's direction has been highly correlated with that of precious metals such as silver and platinum (.6 to .8), fairly correlated to oil prices (nearly .5), and inversely related to stocks, bonds, and the dollar (See Figure 4.2). From this data, we can be fairly confident that gold, precious metals, and commodities will tend to move together in the opposite direction of the dollar.

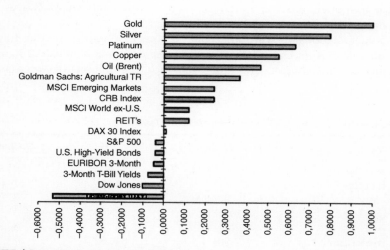

FIGURE 4.2   Gold vs. Other Asset Classes

Source: "Special Report Gold: July 2011." Erste Group Research 28.

Much of gold's future price may also rely on the strength or weakness of the U.S. dollar. With the dollar "near extinction" according to the big fiat-currency bears, it is no wonder gold has soared so high over the past 10 years. Since the dollar falling means gold rising, the huge drop in the dollar since 2001 has helped gold skyrocket. However, with bearish sentiment regarding the dollar at an extreme, an upcoming dollar reversal and come-back could kill the gold bull market.

Conclusion

As this chapter has shown, gold is extremely overvalued when we compare it to other asset classes and will likely not serve as a safe haven in the case of a recession. Gold has not performed well during recessions, and has actually fallen together with the market and other asset classes. Those who claim that gold is a safe haven during recessions are relying on faulty claims that no longer apply—gold outperformed during the Great Depression only because gold prices were fixed at the time, which prevented prices from falling while most or all other asset classes fell; gold was therefore artificially protected, which no longer applies today. Moreover, throughout its tremendous run, gold has seen nearly all of its gains during bull markets in stocks—which bolstered gold's price (even though so many gold investors believe gold will gain during *down* markets). Perhaps most shocking, however, is gold's massive outperformance over other asset classes since 1999. Gold has risen nearly 600 percent while home, car, and food prices haven't even risen more than 100 percent, and have barely gained more than 30 percent. At the same time, the stock market is up less than 10 percent, and gas prices—which consumers have worried and complained about so much—are nearly 400 percent behind. When we look at the big picture and compare gold to other assets, we see how extremely overvalued it really is. And its correlation to the U.S. dollar warns us of an impending reversal.

Now that we have discussed the causes behind gold's surge, the multitude of signs pointing to a speculative and highly risky asset bubble, gold's performance during recessions, and its historical relation to other asset classes, we are finally ready to determine where gold currently stands in the scheme of history, what stage of the bubble we currently find ourselves in, and whether we're approaching or have reached the peak.

CHAPTER 5

Price Analysis and Forecasts

Adapted from material published in Unsafe Haven, September 2011[1]

One of the most defining characteristics of a bubble is the parabolic shape of the rise in prices as the bubble develops and reaches a peak. Prices can rise at an extremely steep angle and show increases of hundreds of percent before the bubble bursts and prices fall. The problem, however, is that what is considered to be "parabolic" or "extreme" price movement is left to the discretion of investors—what one person considers outrageous price rises may not satisfy the criteria of another person. Plus, a person involved in the bubble may think that there is plenty more parabolic rise left in the underlying asset to justify the investment. In other words, most people don't know when the price will stop rising, and their gambling-like behavior will lead them to justify parabolic price rises in order to not "miss out" on the even sharper price rise that is, in their minds, upcoming.

Parabolic rises tend to be followed by disastrous falls. If gold prices have been in a parabolic rise, they are setting up for a major fall. But the question that may be hardest to answer is "Exactly where are we in this bubble?" If we have already seen the most intense price rises and the most euphoric phases of the bubble, now would definitely be a dangerous time to invest; but if the "speculative mania" phase, which pushes prices to stratospheric extremes, is still not here, prices could soar even more. A final blow-off phase may still be upon us.

Gold Bubble Anatomy: Is a Parabolic Spike Coming?

Looking at the anatomy of a bubble and a diagram of its progression, we can track how the gold bubble has developed, grown, and approaches its ultimate peak. Compare the progression of a theoretical bubble to our current gold bubble, shown in Figure 5.1.

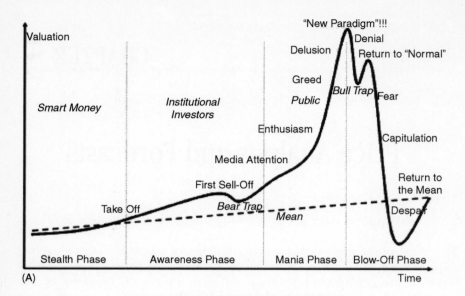

(A)

(B)

FIGURE 5.1 (A) Stages of a Bubble[2] and (B) a Gold Bubble

Sources: (A) Jean-Paul Rodrigue; (B) www.kitco.com.

If we compare the anatomy of the theoretical bubble to gold prices since 2000, we can see very similar price movement. And if we compare the specific phases of bubbles by matching the proper examples in the case of gold, we can better identify where we currently stand within the bubble.

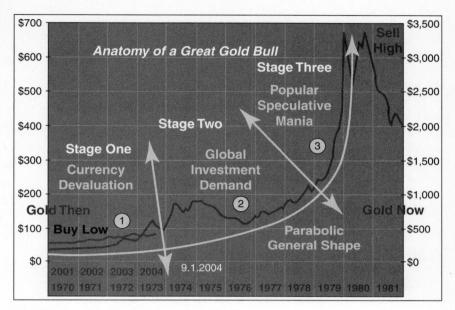

FIGURE 5.2 Gold Bulls' Three Stages
Source: www.ZealLLC.com.

Matching up the stages of the bubble to the progression of gold prices, 2000 to 2003 was the "Stealth Phase," during which the "Smart Money" investors bought gold. Smart Money investors generally precede the major price movement by being the first to catch on to a strong investment theme. They in turn lead the rest of the investment community to do as they did, and invest. Price increases during the Stealth Phase, but nowhere nearly as steeply as it does in the later stages.

With the introduction of the first gold ETF in March 2003 and then the largest gold ETF (GLD) in late 2004, the bubble transitioned to the "Awareness Phase" as large institutional investors such as mutual funds, hedge funds, banks, and others invested in gold. This phase also saw a selloff in 2008 that may have scared some investors away but did not end the bull market in gold.

Most gold bugs would argue that gold has not yet progressed through the parabolic "Mania Phase" since mass public attention over gold has not yet appeared. But with gold having made the front page of many magazines and newspapers (including the *Wall Street Journal*); rising to the forefront of financial news and media (CNBC, Fox Business, etc.); becoming the focus of a TV show (*Gold Rush Alaska*); inviting a tsunami of "We Buy Gold" stores; and welcoming euphoric price targets reaching $15,000 an ounce—it is hard to truly argue that we have not already seen the public engage in media attention, enthusiasm, greed, and possibly delusion on the way to the gold bubble peak.

If we were to update Figure 5.2, to match it with the gold bubble of 1970 to 1980, it appears that our current gold bubble fits almost perfectly together with the stages of the bubble. 2000 through 2004 was the smart money and beginning of the currency devaluation; 2005 through 2008 was the global investment demand phase triggered by the introduction of gold ETFs and other institutional investment; and from the 2008 bottom until 2011 we may be in the midst of a popular speculative mania, led by the media and the common investor, and approaching a final peak before the upcoming collapse. Though a final parabolic blow-off (which could see rapid price increases) is possible, the dangers of the subsequent bubble collapse and the rapidity with which prices will suddenly plummet make investing in gold highly risky and ill-advised for average and sophisticated investors alike.

Gold's Place in History: Elliott Waves

Must we, from this appalling and repeated record, draw once more the despairing conclusion that the only thing man learns from history is that man learns nothing from history?[3]

—Hazlitt

The price of gold may fall to its long-term average—well below $700 an ounce.

Looking further back in time, in order to see where the current gold bubble stands in the big picture of history, could help us predict when the top may come as well as the magnitude of the upcoming price collapse.

Stocks and commodities do not move straight in one direction; they swing up and down as optimism and pessimism take hold at different times and various magnitudes. In fact, the market's progression unfolds in waves, or "patterns of directional movement,"[4] and may actually be fairly predictable. Since people are ultimately the source of price movement in stocks and commodities as they buy and invest, it is human behavior that guides the change in prices that takes place over time. And because human behavior, especially regarding investments, involves an alternation between optimism and pessimism, fear and greed, growth and decay, knowing where the mass psyche currently stands reveals a lot of information as to the current position within the up-and-down cycle. In other words, if we can assess the intensity of human optimism or pessimism at a given point, we can predict future price moves.

The Elliott Wave Principle

In 1978 Robert R. Prechter Jr. and A. J. Frost released their revolutionary book *The Elliott Wave Principle,* based on the 1930s works of Ralph Nelson

Elliott. Applying a mathematical pattern that exists in nature—from pine cones to hurricanes to DNA—Prechter and Frost proved how "the same law that shapes living creatures and galaxies is inherent in the spirit and activities of men *en masse.*" And since the stock market is "the most meticulously tabulated reflector of mass psychology in the world,"[5] applying the Elliott Wave Principle to the stock market produces a very accurate recording of mass investor psychology and trends. Using this method, Prechter called the 1982 bottom in stocks before the tremendous bull market that ensued; he also predicted the 2000 top that marked the beginning of the "Lost Decade," and has been warning about a deflationary period that will see the Dow Jones drop well below its current level.

Gold undoubtedly has a massive psychological and emotional component among investors and people all over the world. Gold is not only used for jewelry or coins; it has become a go-to store of value and protection against worst-case scenarios. Its role as a "fear hedge" makes its psychological effects distinctively clear. Since gold is an historical reflector of mass psychology, the Elliott Wave Principle is an ideal match for explaining gold price movement and predicting its future course. But in order to apply the Elliott Wave Principle to gold, we must first understand how the principle works.

The market progresses in cycles of growth and decay, ups and downs. To the Elliott Wave practitioner, ups and downs are considered *waves.* The Wave Principle points to a five-wave structure of growth—with waves 1, 3, and 5 contributing to the rise in prices, and waves 2 and 4 moving counter to the trend, as a pause before the next price rise (see Figure 5.3). The Elliott

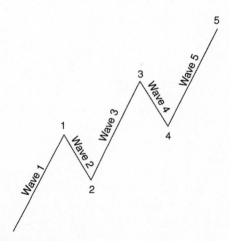

FIGURE 5.3 The Basic Pattern

Source: A. J. Frost and Robert R. Prechter Jr., *Elliott Wave Principle: Key to Market Behavior*, 10th ed. (Gainesville, GA: New Classics Library, 2005), 22.

Wave states that "progress takes place in a 'three steps forward, two steps back' fashion, a form that nature prefers."[6]

After reaching the end of the growth—or "motive"—phase that ends at the peak of wave 5, the market must then correct itself before continuing its upward direction. That "corrective" phase takes form in a three-wave structure, as opposed to the five-wave structure in the growth phase. Instead of the number format of waves 1 to 5 in the growth phase, the corrective phase is labeled A-B-C, with waves A and C contributing to the decline and wave B moving countertrend between the declines of waves A and C (see Figure 5.4).

Moreover, the Elliott Wave Principle shows that each wave can then be broken up into subdividing waves in fractal form, so that waves exist in all time-frames—from minutes to days to weeks to months to years and even to millennia (see Figure 5.5).

Suffice it to say that the Elliott Wave Principle has much more to it than this book can present. I will, however, present you with my wave count for gold.

Elliott Wave Principle Applied to Gold

Our first question when applying the Wave Principle is "where exactly does the motive, or growth, phase begin?" Once we find the beginning of the move, we can count the waves and assess our current position within the

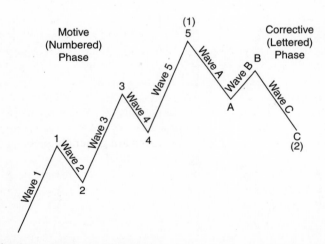

FIGURE 5.4 Motive and Corrective Phases

Source: A. J. Frost and Robert R. Prechter Jr., *Elliott Wave Principle: Key to Market Behavior*, 10th ed. (Gainesville, GA: New Classics Library, 2005), 23.

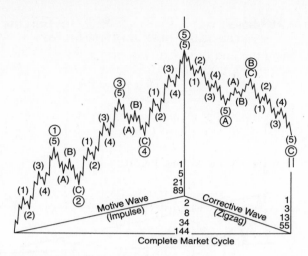

FIGURE 5.5 Complete Wave Broken Down into Fractals

Source: A. J. Frost and Robert R. Prechter Jr., *Elliott Wave Principle: Key to Market Behavior*, 10th ed. (Gainesville, GA: New Classics Library, 2005), 25.

pattern. In simple terms, where is the bottom and how close are we to the top?

1968 TO 1999 In a long-term view, we can trace the beginning of the gold price move either to 1934, when the government raised the fixed-price of gold from $20.67 an ounce to $35 an ounce, or to 1968 when the gold price began to respond to supply and demand factors rather than a fixed price. 1968 is more likely, since the structural factors of a free-flowing market price are likely to have enabled the gold bubble. Regardless of whether 1934 or 1968 was the beginning (though I think 1968 is more likely), the 1980 high of $850 an ounce clarifies our count, as we will soon see.

Assuming the 1968 bottom was the beginning of our long-term gold bull market, we must now count the highs and lows of the five-wave structure leading to 2011 (see Figure 5.6). First waves are generally small in comparison to ensuing waves, since they are the initial bursts that launch further price moves. In our case, the first wave can be seen from 1968 to 1975, where gold prices rose from $35 an ounce to $185.25 an ounce (February 24, 1975). In the ensuing wave 2, however, prices dropped from $185.25 an ounce to $103.50 an ounce (August 25, 1976)—a fairly deep correction of 44 percent. Following the wave 2 correction, gold saw an extremely sharp increase from the 1976 low to the $850 an ounce peak of 1980. Prices had increased from just above $100 an ounce to $850 an ounce in little over three years—a nearly 750 percent increase!

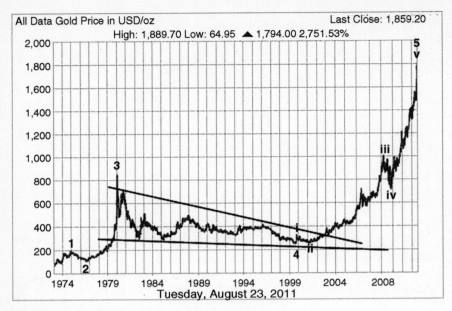

FIGURE 5.6 Gold Bubble, Wave Count 1968 to 2011
Source: www.goldprice.org, Chart Prophet LLC.

After reaching the $850 an ounce peak in 1980, however, gold prices entered a bear market that lasted nearly 20 years until 1999, and prices dropped to nearly $250 an ounce. Then came our current gold bull market, starting in 1999, with prices rising from a $252.80 an ounce low to over $1,900 an ounce in August 2011.

Putting it together, wave 1 lasted from 1968 to 1975, wave 2 corrected prices until 1976, wave 3 carried prices back up until 1980, and wave 4 corrected prices until 1999. So far, it appears that the four waves starting in 1968 fit very well with the long-term picture of gold prices. In fact, our wave count fits perfectly with Elliott Wave rules and guidelines. Firstly, *wave 2 never moves beyond the start of wave 1*; since the count begins at $35 an ounce and wave 2 corrected to $103.50 an ounce, this rule stands. Secondly, *wave 3 is never the shortest wave*; since wave 3 was approximately a $750 move (750 percent) in comparison to a move of approximately $160 (450 percent) for wave 1, wave 3 is automatically not the shortest wave (in absolute dollar terms) and this rule fits as well. Thirdly, *wave 4 never moves beyond the end of wave 1*; since the top of wave 1 was $185.25 an ounce and the bottom of wave 4 was $252.80 an ounce, the two waves did not overlap and this rule fits as well. Furthermore, the nearly 20-year bear market in gold from 1980 to 1999 formed a large triangle pattern. Since the Elliott Wave guidelines state that "wave 4 is usually a flat, triangle, or flat combination," the wave 4 triangle from 1980 to 1999 fits in very well with the long-term picture.[7]

This brings us to our current gold bull market, from 1999 to now. If our wave count is correct, the move from 1999 to now is the fifth and final wave before a massive correction. And since many clues point to a gold bubble, the alignment of the wave counts with my claims for an upcoming collapse should add further strength to my argument. In fact, the nearly $1,700 move from the $252.80/oz bottom in 1999 to the August 2011 high near $1,900 an ounce points to a final extended wave that fits in perfectly with Elliott Wave rules. If the 1980 top to the 1999 bottom was a wave 4 triangle correction, our claims are further backed by the Elliott Wave Principle:

A triangle always occurs in a position prior to the final actionary wave in the pattern of one larger degree, i.e., as wave four in an impulse.[8]

Since the fifth wave from 1999 to now is the largest in dollar terms, the preceding fourth wave triangle predicted our current massive fifth wave:

Post-triangle advancing impulses in commodities at degrees above Intermediate are usually the longest wave in the sequence.[9]

Moreover, Elliott Wave rules and guidelines point to extended fifth waves in commodity bull markets:

Extended fifths are quite common in major bull markets in commodities.[10]
Commodity bull market extensions, moreover, often appear following a triangle in the fourth wave position. Thus, while post-triangle thrusts in the stock market are often "swift and short," triangles in commodity bull markets of large degree often precede extended blowoffs.[11]

It is therefore not surprising that our bull market in gold since 1999 has been so extended and so dramatic. The problem, however, is that not only are we currently in the fifth and final wave, but corrections following extended fifth waves are usually massive:

Fifth wave extensions, truncated fifths, and ending diagonals all imply the same thing: dramatic reversal ahead.[12]

From the evidence above, it is almost perfectly clear that we are currently in the fifth and final wave. But in order to predict when gold prices will reach the top, we must first apply the Wave Principle to the subdivisions of this final wave.

1999 TO NOW   We have established that 1999 until now has been the extended fifth and final wave of the gold bull market. This final move has been accompanied by arguments that "things are different this time," that the world is coming to an end, that gold will be the only source of value, and that gold serves as protection from almost any turmoil that may be upcoming. However, once again the investor psychology and behavior fits in perfectly with Elliott Wave Principles:

> *Fifth wave advances in the stock market are propelled by* hope, *while fifth wave advances in commodities are propelled by a comparatively dramatic emotion,* fear: *fear of inflation, fear of drought, fear of war.*[13]

The fifth wave in gold has coincided with the "Lost Decade" in stocks. Understandably so, since the 2000 peak in stocks, gold has soared (see Figure 5.7).

Within our current fifth wave, we can point out the subdividing waves. From the 1999 bottom, we can see wave 1 and wave 2, with wave 2 forming a very deep correction of wave 1—retracing 95.67 percent of wave 1. Once

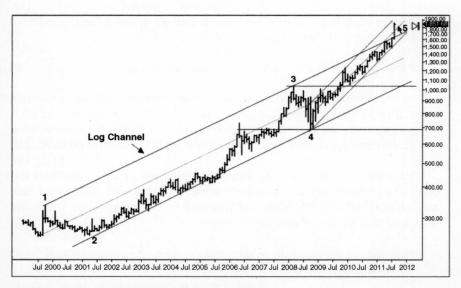

FIGURE 5.7   Gold Bubble, Wave Count 1999 to 2011
Source: www.studyofcycles.com; NinjaTrader, LLC.

again our wave count conforms to theory, as the deep retracement formed by wave 2 fits in with the Elliott Wave Principles:

> *As a rough estimate, about half of first waves are part of the "basing" process and thus tend to be heavily corrected by wave two.*[14]

From the wave 2 bottom on April 2, 2001, prices rose from $255.95 an ounce to $1,011.25 an ounce (March 17, 2008) before correcting back down to $681 an ounce (October 2008). The $750 move up and the ensuing $300 correction can be labeled as waves 3 and 4. Not only are waves 2 and 4 the most visible price corrections on the chart, but they also follow a very important Elliott Wave guideline:

> *Wave 4 will almost always be a different corrective pattern than wave 2.*[15]

Since wave 2 was more of a gradual, sideways correction than the much sharper decline of wave 4, this "alternation" between corrective waves 2 and 4 stands as further evidence that we are currently in the fifth wave (starting in late 2008) of a larger fifth wave (starting in 1999). And while this current final fifth wave may extend and even end in a parabolic "blow-off" that sees prices shoot up for a period of time, it will ultimately end in disaster as many investors lose a huge percentage of their investments as prices collapse. Some investors may be able to monitor their gold investments and may even see significant profits. But the majority of investors who fail to closely monitor prices, or simply fail to sell their gold before the peak, will see significant losses.

Price Target for Gold Collapse

Since gold prices are up from $681 in October 2008 to over $1,900 by August 2011, the tremendous $1,200-plus rise since the wave 4 bottom in October 2008 (of the larger fifth wave that began in 1999) makes our current fifth and final wave the longest wave within our current gold bull market and also signals a "Fifth Wave Extension" (see Figure 5.8).

Since large commodity bull markets tend to show extended fifth waves (as opposed to extended third waves in stocks), the extension of a fifth wave in our gold bull market (see Figure 5.9) fits in very well with our outlook.

The Elliott Wave Principle even offers a measurement for the upcoming correction: an extended fifth wave is usually followed by a sharp correction that finds support at the low of wave 2 of the extension (Figure 5.10).[16]

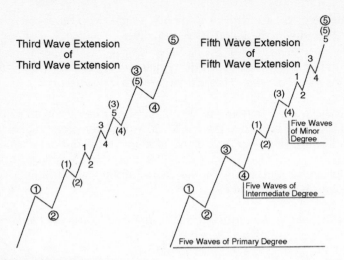

FIGURE 5.8 Wave Extensions

Source: A. J. Frost and Robert R. Prechter Jr., *Elliott Wave Principle: Key to Market Behavior,* 10th ed. (Gainesville, GA: New Classics Library, 2005), 69.

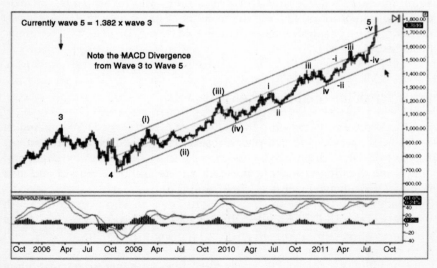

FIGURE 5.9 Fifth Wave Extension in Gold

Source: www.studyofcycles.com.

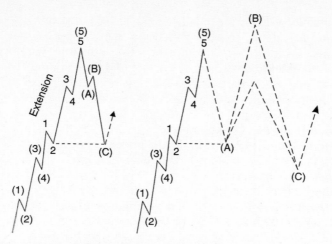

FIGURE 5.10 Price Target Following Extended Waves

Source: A. J. Frost and Robert R. Prechter Jr., *Elliott Wave Principle: Key to Market Behavior*, 10th ed. (Gainesville, GA: New Classics Library, 2005), 69.

Applying the Elliott Wave target, gold prices should drop to and find support near the $1,000 to $1,200 range, to wave 2 of the extension. However, if the entire move since 1999 has been a fifth wave of a larger wave count dating back to 1968, prices may drop to the low of wave 2 of our larger fifth wave (starting in 1999)—a much steeper plunge to the low of $252.80 an ounce.

Moreover, the existence of a speculative bubble in gold makes the upcoming price collapse much more dangerous. Since the implosion of a bubble tends to drag prices down even below long-term averages, as panicked investors overreact to the downside, we can forecast prices to drop to levels near gold's long-term mean ($500 to $700) and below.

Prices don't collapse and bottom out in a straight-downwards move though. Once a peak is reached, prices will fall sharply in spurts and bursts; but there are many ups and downs along the way. The ups and downs may be opportunities for experienced or expert traders to buy and sell. But the most important thing to remember is: once the bubble pops, the trend is down.

Fibonacci Time Relationships

Time cannot predict price changes by itself. But time relationships and durations between critical junctures in markets frequently reflect Fibonacci measurements and sequences. Applying Fibonacci time relationships to important years or periods can help us predict critical turning points in the future, especially if they coincide with wave counts or price targets.

The process involves first compiling a list of the important dates in the history of the market or investment theme and then adding Fibonacci sequences to the critical dates to see if a time relationship exists. First, let's compile the list of important dates in gold's history:

1934: Fixed price of gold is raised
1968: Beginning of free-market gold prices
1975: Peak of wave 1 of the larger gold bull market
1976: Bottom of wave 2
January 21, 1980: $850 an ounce, peak of wave 3
July 20, 1999: Bottom of wave 4, beginning of final wave 5
October 5, 1999: Peak of wave 1 within the larger wave 5
April 2, 2001: Bottom of wave 2 within the larger wave 5
March 17, 2008: Peak of wave 3 within the larger wave 5
October 24, 2008: Bottom of wave 4 within the larger wave 5

Next, we apply the Fibonacci sequence to the above dates to see if any time relationship appears:

1, 2, 3, 5, 8, 13, 21, 34, 55, 89, 144, 233, 377

(The sequence is formed by adding each number to the preceding number to derive the third number—for example, $1 + 2 = 3$, $2 + 3 = 5$, $3 + 5 = 8$, and so on.)

There are certainly a number of Fibonacci relationships I have missed, but here are some I have found:

1934 to 1968	$\rightarrow$	34 years
1968 to 1980	$\rightarrow$	12 years (13 +/− 1)
1968 to 2001	$\rightarrow$	33 years (34 +/− 1)
1980 to 2001	$\rightarrow$	21 years
1999 to 2012	$\rightarrow$	13 years
1968 to 1980	$\rightarrow$	144 months
January 21, 1980 to July 20, 1999	$\rightarrow$	234 months (233 +/− 1)
July 20, 1999 to July 2011	$\rightarrow$	144 months
1968 to July 20, 1999	$\rightarrow$	378 months (377 +/− 1)
January 21, 1980 to July 2011	$\rightarrow$	378 months (377 +/− 1)

Based on the above time relationships, it appears that 1968, 1980, 1999, and 2001 were significant years. The fact that these years coincide with our wave count and also display a measurable time relationship to each other highly increases the probability that our analysis is correct. Moreover, if we use these important years and project Fibonacci relationships into the future, we may be able to predict the upcoming turning points.

2023 (+/− 2) appears to be a significant year, though it is quite far away (1934 + 89 = 2023; 1968 + 55 = 2023; 2001 + 21 = 2022).

July 2011 also shows significant time relationships with the 1999 bottom and 1980 top. Since deviations of +/− 1 are allowed for durations of 21 and 34; deviations of +/− 2 for 55 and 89; and deviations of +/− 3 for 144, 233, and 377, July 2011 +/− 3 months could be a target for the top. In other words, the top may be reached between July and October 2011.

Seasonality

In addition to wave counts, technical analysis, and the multitude of reasons why gold is showing signs of an upcoming drop, gold's pattern of popularity and weakness during specific times of the year could reveal when gold prices have a high probability of falling. Otherwise known as "seasonality," the strength or weakness of an underlying asset or investment during specific time periods throughout the year can provide a considerable amount of momentum behind future price moves. If we really are nearing the peak of the gold bubble, when is the likely time for prices to begin to fall?

Interestingly, since our current gold bubble starting in 1999 is part of a larger gold bubble that began in 1968, we must compare yet differentiate between the seasonality patterns of both time frames. The gold boom of the 1970s encompassed a largely different set of circumstances—especially much higher inflation rates, which spurred the buying of gold as an inflationary hedge. Moreover, the gold bear market from 1980 to 1999 has affected the seasonality pattern in a much different way from our current bull market from 1999 to now. Therefore, we must look at seasonality patterns for two time periods—from the late 1960s and early 1970s to now, and from 1999 to now.

Our current gold bull market, starting in 1999, has been very strong near year-end (see Table 5.1). Out of the 12 years from 1999 to 2010, gold prices reached their highs six times in December, once in September, once in October, and once in November. Only 3 out of 12 years saw highs in the months before September—a February high in 2000, May high in 2006, and March high in 2008. As for the lows of the year—four times in January, two times in February, two times in April, one time in May, one time in July, and two times in October. As opposed to the yearly highs, yearly lows have been reached in the first half of the year, with half of the lows in January and February. Based on seasonality for the past 12 years, gold prices could see increasing strength as we enter year-end. However, the peaks and bursting of

TABLE 5.1 Gold Seasonality, 1999 to 2010

	Year Low	Year High
1999	July 20	October 5
2000	October 27	February 7
2001	April 2	September 17
2002	January 4	December 27
2003	April 7	December 31
2004	May 10	December 2
2005	February 8	December 12
2006	January 5	May 12
2007	January 10	November 8
2008	October 24	March 17
2009	January 15	December 2
2010	February 5	December 6

Source: Kitco, Bloomberg, Erste Group Research.

bubbles generally come almost unexpectedly and at the worst time for investors. If that is the case, the gold bubble could actually begin to collapse at what has been the most popular time during this bull market. Year-end will be either a strong push upward or a reversal of direction to mark the end of higher prices.

Looking at seasonality in gold prices from 1969 to 2010[17] (see Figure 5.11), we can see that September is the strongest month in terms of average

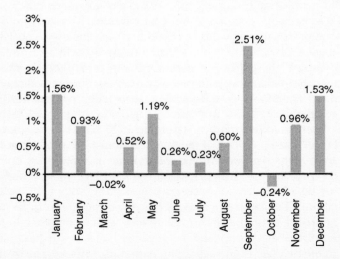

FIGURE 5.11 Gold Seasonality, January 1969 to July 2010 (average monthly returns)
Source: Bloomberg, *Seeking Alpha.*

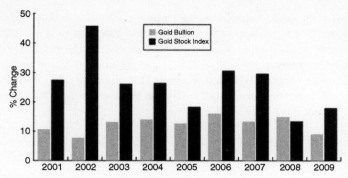

FIGURE 5.12 Late Summer Rally for Gold and Gold Stocks
Note: 2001 to 2003: TSE Gold and Precious Metals Index; 2004 to 2006: S&P/TSX Gold Index; 2007 to Present: S&P/TSX Global Gold Index.
Source: Bloomberg, Bank of America, Merrill Lynch Global Research.

monthly returns and October is the weakest. March through August tend to be quieter than the early months and year-end.

As Figure 5.12 shows, the late summer season has been very strong for gold and gold stocks since 2001, with consistent gains for 10 years.

We have passed the late-summer period that has been historically very strong for gold. Gold performed very well in August and beginning of September 2011, and may have reached a peak. If weakness emerges near year-end, the chances of a reversal are much more likely.

Conclusion

By tracing the gold bubble back to 1934, 1968, and 1999, we have presented a study of the anatomy of a bubble and the dire consequences that may soon befall gold. After presenting the various stages of a typical bubble, we have come to the conclusion that the gold bubble is likely intensely engrossed in the "mania" phase already and is near the peak. Aside from the long list of clues pointing to the overspeculative behavior generally associated with the popular mania phase, we have supported our claims of a gold bubble with a very thorough analysis of the technicals and price action in gold since 1968, when gold prices began responding to supply/demand factors rather than a fixed price. Applying the Elliott Wave Principle to gold, we have also put the gold bubble in historical perspective, pointing out that our current bull market in gold since 1999 is the longest and final wave of a larger bull market in gold starting in 1968. The gold bubble is at or near a peak, and is strongly confirmed by many Elliott Wave guidelines.

Moreover, based on its long-term average, gold is way beyond fair value. Instead of $1,900 an ounce, reasonable gold prices should be closer to $500 to $700 an ounce. Supported by Fibonacci time relationships and seasonality patterns, the likelihood that a peak in gold has already formed or rapidly approaching is almost certain. The possibility of a final blow-off phase is still not ruled out, but the risks in gold are enormous. Now is not the time to buy gold.

CHAPTER 6

What Does Gold Depend On?

Gold's future is highly dependent on the direction of the stock market, U.S. dollar, and global economies. Since gold's tremendous run has coincided with a period of volatile markets and sharp declines in stocks, a continuation of the gold bull market may hinge upon the persistent weakness in stocks and economies. Gold's popularity as a "fear hedge" has greatly benefited from weak markets and concerns over the future sustainability of the economic recovery. At the same time, however, gold prices have risen the most when stock prices increased as well. In other words, even though gold is viewed as a safe haven from falling stock prices, its growing correlation with stocks makes it increasingly likely that gold will move in the same direction as the stock market. Since gold is a commodity, it benefits from economic expansions that see rising asset prices; recessions, on the other hand, cause asset and commodity prices to fall, which should bring a decline in gold.

As I see it, gold's future direction relies on two main possible scenarios. The first—rising stock prices—could benefit gold, as asset prices continue rising and as gold benefits from continued commodity price increases. The major problem with rising stock prices, however, is that gold has soared due to fears over *falling* stock prices. Since many investors and institutions bought gold due to expectations of *falling* stock markets, a *rising* stock market would likely convince many gold investors to exit the gold trade and invest in stocks instead, as faith in the stock market returns. Rising stock prices would therefore end gold's run, as stability in stocks resumes.

A second scenario—falling stock prices—would likely hurt gold as well. Though gold is touted as a safe haven that would benefit from falling stock prices, it has become so overvalued and speculative that it would likely fall together with falling stock prices. As we've mentioned, gold is still a commodity, and is likely to fall as asset prices decline. At the same time, gold has seen nearly all of its gains during economic expansions and *rising* stock prices; falling stocks are actually a threat to gold. Moreover, gold has benefited from massive currency devaluation and excess liquidity. If stock prices fall, recession takes hold, or a liquidity crunch materializes, gold prices are more likely to fall as deflationary pressures bring asset prices down. Gold is increasingly correlated with stocks and benefits from *increasing* stock prices. Falling stock markets would therefore hurt gold.

I currently favor the outlook of a renewed recession and falling stock prices. This chapter will present the factors pointing to falling stocks, a rising U.S. dollar, and the fate of emerging markets—factors which the gold theme is highly dependent on and which signal a very likely drop in gold prices.

Herd Mentality in the Stock Market

A compelling piece of evidence that the market is full of euphoria: over 90 percent of analyst ratings were "buy" or "outperform" as of May 2011 (see Figure 6.1). This decisive number of bullish analyst opinion undoubtedly spurs extra excitement and optimism among investors, which in turn results in increased buying, until the point where buyers run out or reality sets in. When over 90 percent of analysts prepare for a well-performing market, investors should prepare for the worst-performing market.

If those analysts are right—and the market continues to rise—gold will fall, since the fear in the markets will subside and economies will get back on track. But more likely, markets will fall and gold will follow. Gold will not be able to fulfill its role as a safe haven; it will fall together with a

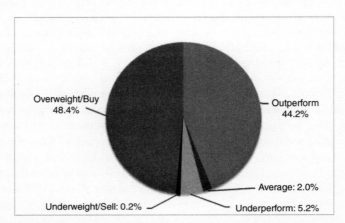

FIGURE 6.1 Consensus Analyst Ratings for the Stocks in the S&P 500
Source: Business Insider, Bloomberg, Catalpa Capital Advisers (May 2011).

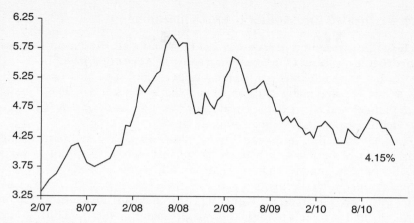

FIGURE 6.2 S&P 500 Short Interest (Percentage of Float)
Source: Bespoke Investment Group.

dropping market. Its failure to act as protection, as people had hoped, will cause them to sell gold. Gold will not serve as protection during an upcoming recession.

Analysts are not the only market participants displaying a heavy dose of euphoria. By December 2010, the total Short Interest for the S&P 500 (which measures bearish bets on stocks) was back down to 2007 levels.[1] With short interest at 2007 levels (see Figure 6.2), investors have signaled that they are as bullish as they were near the 2007 stock market peak. And since we are nowhere near 2007 levels in terms of economic strength, such a signal is a warning of excess and unwarranted optimism.

My response to a bullish investor is as follows.

The market is up about 100 percent from the 2009 lows. China and emerging markets are showing weakness. A large part of U.S. investments are based on growing emerging countries continuing to perform well. China and others will begin to fall as asset bubbles within their countries begin to pop. Credit will then dry up, and investors will sell in a panic. The falling emerging markets will cause investors to realize that any investment relying on Chinese and emerging market growth is no longer a good investment. Commodities will then fall since emerging market growth is much lower than expected. U.S. markets will inevitably be dragged into the turmoil, since the United States hasn't truly fixed its own economic and financial problems of the past decade. The risks are too large and the hurdles too numerous to be bullish right now.

Are We Headed for Another Great Depression?

Originally published March 11, 2011: "What Can the Great Depression Teach Us about Our Great Recession?," *Seeking Alpha*.[2]

Is the massive market rally of the past two years just a temporary recovery that has tricked many investors to jump back into stocks right before the next plunge? And how can the Great Depression reveal what may happen to the markets this year, more than 80 years later?

As we enter the third year of what has been a very impressive "bull" market, many are left wondering whether this incredible run of as much as 100 percent on the S&P 500 can continue—and for how long. Yet while the economy seems to have rebounded very strongly off its early 2009 lows, accompanied by improving fundamentals, increased company earnings, and a more optimistic consumer, many investors fail to at least consider the thought that this entire "recovery" could, in fact, be just an extreme overreaction to the 2008 market crash. In other words, the huge rally we have seen in the global stock markets since early 2009 could be just a temporary recovery and pause before the next—and possibly worse—market decline.

It was only recently that the fear of an economic "double dip"—a plunge back down to recession—intensely gripped the markets. The "flash crash," BP oil spill, European troubles, high unemployment, and potential derailment of the economy all posed a severe threat to the viability of our recovery. Yet while many parts of the economy seem to have been improving, there are still so many issues surfacing daily that most of the world is basically ignoring. I am not saying that all these issues are guaranteed to pull us back into recession, but with such a huge rebound in stocks accompanied by so many potential derailers, it is not so far-fetched to at least consider the possibilities of the tremendous upcoming turmoil.

The issues now: huge government debt, credit crisis, European troubles, high insider selling, Middle East turmoil, surging oil prices that threaten to hurt the economy, soaring commodity prices, surfacing inflation, uncertainty about the Fed's QE2 and QE3, billions of dollars of toxic assets on the balance sheets of many banks, emerging market weakness since the end of 2010, real estate bubbles from China to Singapore, rationalization of fundamentals and a strong complacency that things will continue to be just as positive as they have been, a very slowly improving unemployment picture, and perhaps one of the most telling points—the average investor is finally getting back in, and maybe right at the end of the rally.

So why should investors at least consider the possibility of a *double dip*? What are the potential scenarios if this tremendous market rally was, in fact, a *fool's rally*? And what can the Great Depression teach us about our current situation?

First, we must understand what a fool's rally is. Otherwise known as a *dead cat bounce*, the fool's rally is a corrective bounce or temporary rebound that follows a severe decline in an individual stock or broader market. Following a severe decline, stocks and markets can sometimes see sharp bounces off the lows as a rapid overreaction to the downside is followed by an overreactive bounce to the upside. In other words, a market crashes quickly and sharply but rebounds temporarily as much of the bad news takes some time to fully sink in.

This phenomenon has been termed the *dead cat bounce* based on the saying that "even a dead cat will bounce if dropped from high enough."

The dead cat bounce is just a temporary recovery, however.

The scenario follows five stages: (1) the market drops sharply; (2) after an extreme downturn, the market recovers as some investors buy up what they consider to be "value" stocks; (3) the market cannot make it all the way back up to where it started its down move, however, because the economy is nowhere near as healthy as it was; (4) the investors who have pulled their money out of the stock market or who have missed the recovery now jump back in, thinking the market is going back up; and (5) since this has been a dead cat bounce, and therefore is merely a corrective rebound before the dead cat falls back down, many investors were tricked into thinking the recovery was underway—but the market enters the next phase of decline or recession. A double dip takes place.

Think of a tennis ball dropped from the top of a building: as it drops, it gains momentum, hits the ground, and bounces up—but the bounce cannot be as high as its original point. And following that bounce, it will ultimately be pulled back down by gravity. So too with the dead cat bounce—the market drops from above, falls sharply, hits the "ground," bounces back up (but not as high), and ultimately falls back down.

I bring the Great Depression up because it is one of the best examples of a dead cat bounce. We often think of the Wall Street Crash of 1929 as the biggest event of the Great Depression, and perhaps also consider it to be the biggest drop in the market. But the Crash of 1929 was just the beginning. The following describes how the dead cat bounce played out in the Great Depression.

Following 17 years of sideways movement beginning in 1904, the market finally embarked on an uptrend from 1921 to the ultimate peak of 1929 (see Figure 6.3).

Compare Figure 6.3 to what we have recently seen in our market, shown in Figure 6.4.

Like the Dow from 1904 to 1921, the Dow of 1960 to 1983 was also stuck in a long sideways trend. It eventually broke out above the 1,000 level in 1983 and began one of the greatest bull markets we have ever seen. Like the 1929 top before the Great Depression, the 2007 peak marked the top before

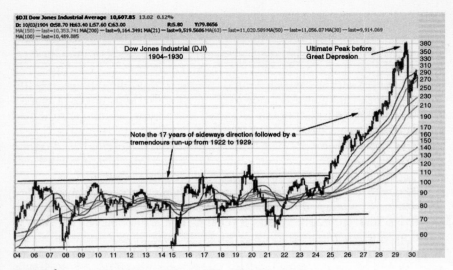

FIGURE 6.3 Dow Jones Industrial Average, 1904 to 1930
Source: thinkorswim, Chart Prophet LLC.

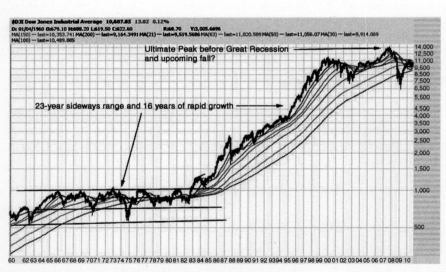

FIGURE 6.4 Dow Jones Industrial Average, 1960 to 2010
Source: thinkorswim, Chart Prophet LLC.

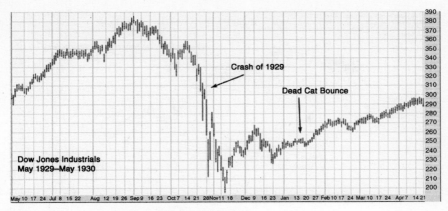

FIGURE 6.5 Crash of 1929 and Dead Cat Bounce
Source: thinkorswim, Chart Prophet LLC.

the Great Recession we find ourselves in. Figures 6.2 and 6.3 look eerily similar, and make dismissing the relationship between the Great Depression and Great Recession almost a fool's move.

Now take a look at Figure 6.5, showing the 1929 stock market crash.

After reaching a peak of 380-plus, the Dow tumbled to under 200 as the Crash of 1929 sent markets into a free-fall. Following the Crash, a dead cat bounce took place—raising the market approximately 50 percent.

Compare the Wall Street Crash/dead cat bounce scenario just described with our recent market (2006 to 2011), as shown in Figure 6.6.

After a bull market from 2003 to the end of 2007, the Dow reached a peak of over 14,000. As the housing market collapsed, so did the stock

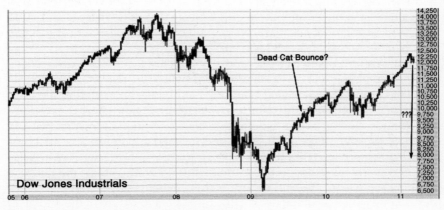

FIGURE 6.6 Crash of 2008 and Dead Cat Bounce
Source: thinkorswim, Chart Prophet LLC.

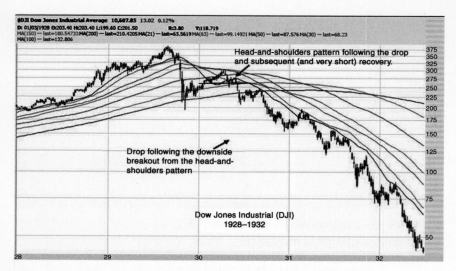

FIGURE 6.7 What Followed the Dead Cat Bounce of 1929 to 1930

Source: thinkorswim, Chart Prophet LLC.

market—sending the Dow below 6,500. As in the Dow of 1929 to 1930, a potential dead cat bounce has followed since 2009.

The question remains—what followed the dead cat bounce of 1929 to 1930, and will our market follow the same course? Figure 6.7 shows how it played out in 1930.

The Crash of 1929 was almost negligible in comparison to the Great Depression that followed. The crash sent the Dow tumbling from 380 to 200, and was followed by a dead cat bounce that recovered over 50 percent of the value lost in the crash; but the real damage was done beginning in April 1930 and lasting until late 1932, when the Dow toppled from nearly 300 to less than 50—a loss of over 83 percent.

The dead cat bounce in 1929 and 1930 was just a corrective overreaction to the steep plunge that the Crash of 1929 brought to the market. But as we can see, the crash and the ensuing bounce were nothing compared to the huge drop that followed and carried through until the end of the Great Depression.

We now find ourselves in perhaps a similar situation—a market that saw a very impressive bull run for years, and reached a lofty top followed by a severe downturn in 2008 and early 2009. It has since shown signs of improving, and many investors and economists are optimistic about the future—thinking the worst is behind us. But with so many negative and potentially devastating issues constantly surfacing, can it be that we are in the middle of a dead cat bounce before reality sets in and the market plunges back down into recession? I do not yet know the answer to that question, but with the very strong similarities between our market and that of the Great Depression, it would be very wise to at least pay attention.

Has the 500-Point Drop Confirmed a Great Depression 2.0?

This section is based on two articles, originally published August 5, 2011 and October 26, 2011: "Has the 500-Point Drop Confirmed a Great Depression 2.0?"[3] and "Stocks Are Approaching a Brick Wall?,"[4] *Seeking Alpha.*

After a two-year or longer "bull" market, the nearly 5 percent drop in the broad S&P 500 on August 5, 2011, may be confirmation that the bear market has resumed, and that round two of the recession is on its way.

The majority of the world is either optimistic or unsure about the future of the global economy. But with so many hurdles in the way and warning signals that point to a slowing, if not collapsing, global economy, the prudent and rational investor would be extremely wise to protect his or her portfolio, if not pull out of stocks completely.

After essentially crashing from late 2007 to early 2009 and losing nearly 60 percent of its value, the stock market (as represented by the S&P 500) bounced back and more than doubled from March 2009 to early May 2011. However, even though the "recovery" powerfully carried stocks back toward the 2007 all-time highs, the stock market failed to make *new highs*. The failure to make new highs is a warning sign that we have yet to truly recover, regardless of the relative improvements since the depths of the recession. Even worse, the tremendous upward thrust in the stock market could have been just an illusion of recovery right before the next—and worse—recession and stock market crash.

The two-year or longer "bull market" and "recovery" from the 2009 lows could be just a sharp bounce and counterreaction to the deadly economic situation the world is actually in. The bad news takes time to fully sink in, and this fact has allowed markets to rise on *hopes* of a sustainable recovery. Instead, the "recovery" in stocks and economies may have been just a pause before reality sets in and markets resume their downtrend.

As we warned in March 2011, this fake rally in stocks and economies may have been a fool's rally or a dead cat bounce—a sharp countertrend rally before the market falls back into recession. Even more, this dead cat bounce we have witnessed is very similar to the fake rally that took place following the stock market crash of 1929—before the Great Depression entered its worst stages. In other words, unless we resume the uptrend in stocks and sustain new highs, the global economy may be doomed to follow in a similar path to the Great Depression.

Forming a large head-and-shoulders reversal pattern since the beginning of 2011, the S&P 500, Dow Jones Industrial Average, and many other

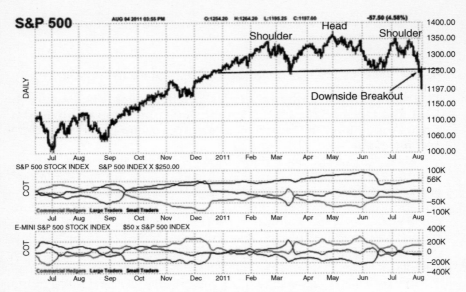

FIGURE 6.8 Does the Head-and-Shoulders Pattern Signal a Top?

Source: finviz.com, Chart Prophet LLC.

market sectors and stocks may have capitulated in August—signaling the beginning of a renewed downturn (see Figure 6.8).

Breaking down through the "neckline" (drawn *under* the head-and-shoulders pattern), the stock market has likely resumed its downtrend and confirmed an upcoming recession. We warned readers to get out of stocks on August 5.

Since the head-and-shoulders pattern is one of the best signs of a peak in stocks, long-term investors would be greedy and stupid (excuse my honesty) in staying invested. Yes, there is still a chance the market makes new highs; but why take such a huge risk after a 100 percent (or greater) move from the 2009 lows, when bad news continues to emerge, and when stocks just underwent one of the sharpest drops *ever* in August? The wise decision would be to pull out of stocks until we get some more clarity.

To emphasize how risky it would be to buy stocks at this point, take a look at Figure 6.9. The similarity between the "textbook" head-and-shoulders pattern and our actual, real-world situation (seen in Figure 6.10) is shockingly uncanny.

If, in fact, the S&P 500 has just formed and broken down from a head-and-shoulders top, an upcoming drop could be severe, and could usher in a very serious recession. To make matters worse, the tremendous bounce in October (which has been the best month for the Dow Jones in 10 years) may have tricked many investors to jump back into stocks right before the next plunge. Many investors who just read the headlines and see "Stock Market

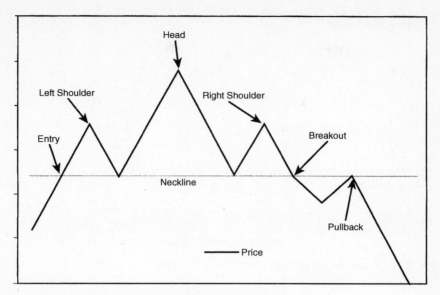

FIGURE 6.9 Textbook Head-and-Shoulders with Pullback

Source: **Charles D. Kirkpatrick and Julie R. Dahlquist,** *Technical Analysis* **(Upper Saddle River, NJ: FT Press, 2007), 333.**

Posts Best Gains in 10 Years" have jumped back in without realizing that even with the best month in years, the stock market is still down. If the head-and-shoulders pattern plays out, this tremendous bounce in October has just been a "pullback" to the neckline of the pattern—right before resuming the down-trend. We expect stocks to fail at the maximum range between 1,275 and 1,300 on the S&P 500 and between 12,250 and 12,500 on the Dow. If prices break through and sustain above, the head-and-shoulders pattern may be nul-lified. But regardless, the risks of going long at these levels are *tremendous.*

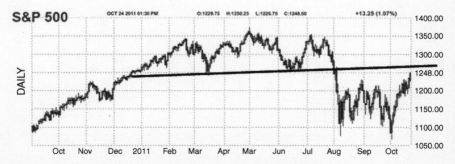

FIGURE 6.10 S&P 500 Head-and-Shoulders Pattern with Pullback

Source: finviz.com, Chart Prophet LLC.

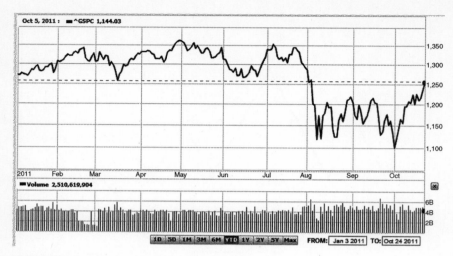

FIGURE 6.11 S&P 500 Approaches Break-Even Resistance
Source: Yahoo! Finance.

Even if you don't believe in technical analysis and chart patterns, here's a reason why we still may be approaching a very strong barrier: the bottom of the head-and-shoulders pattern that we pointed out happens to coincide almost perfectly with the level at which the stock market began in 2011 (see Figure 6.12). In other words, we are approaching the level where stocks began the year. Why is this such a big deal? Because as stocks approach that level, many investors and funds will begin to pull out of the market in order to break even. Considering we are approaching this break-even level from

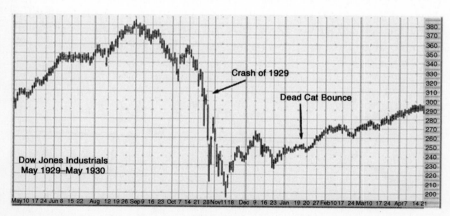

FIGURE 6.12 Dow Jones, May 1929 to May 1930
Source: thinkorswim, Chart Prophet LLC.

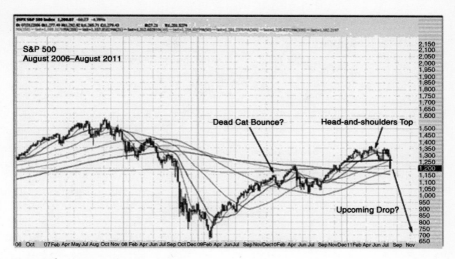

FIGURE 6.13 S&P 500, 2006 to 2011

Source: thinkorswim, Chart Prophet LLC.

below, it could act as very strong resistance. Prices may break above, but why take such a huge risk when we are right at that level and chances are greater that stocks will fail.

Comparing Figures 6.12 and 6.13, we can see that the market since the 2007 top is eerily similar to the market of the Great Depression.

The Crash of 1929 was nothing compared to the Great Depression that ensued. The dead cat bounce from November 1929 to May 1930 was just a temporary pause and trap before the next drop. If our current market from 2006 to 2011 is anything like the market preceding the Great Depression (see Figure 6.14), we may be setting up for a huge upcoming recession.

I'd prefer not to be such a doomsayer, but with our market currently behaving so similarly to that of the Great Depression, I can't help but at least present the possibilities.

Market Cycle Predicts Recession

Originally published April 18, 2011: "Sector Rotation: How Energy and Consumer Staples May Reveal a Contraction," *Seeking Alpha.*[5]

Paying close attention to which sectors are outperforming other sectors or the overall market can tell us a lot about which phase of the economic cycle we are currently in—and where we may be heading.

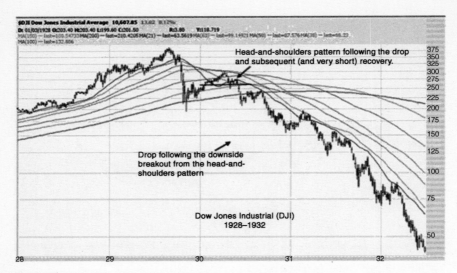

FIGURE 6.14 Head-and-Shoulders Pattern Tops the Dead Cat Bounce of 1929 to 1930 before the Great Depression
Source: thinkorswim, Chart Prophet LLC.

As the economic recovery and expansion progresses, leadership within and among the various market sectors and industries can tell us a lot about how the economy is truly behaving. Depending on the relatively defensive or aggressive nature of investors at a specific time, the economic and business environment, and numerous other factors such as interest rates, forecasted growth, and the overall cause-and-effect nature of what has become a "global" marketplace, certain sectors outperform others at specific stages of the economic cycle. And the outperformance of certain sectors over others may actually be predictable!

Sector rotation is not a new concept. The idea that some companies do better than others in certain economic environments is well established. For example, cyclical companies whose profits seesaw together with the strength or weakness of the economy perform much better during economic expansions that see a healthy, strong consumer with increased spending power to buy their products. At the same time, noncyclical companies whose profits remain relatively unaffected by the ups and downs—due to the fact that their products are essential to consumers regardless of the economic environment—show much steadier performance throughout the economic cycle. Cyclical and noncyclical are far from being the only two sectors in the market (as financials, utilities, energy, basic materials, technology, and others exist as well), but the ability to monitor and compare the performance of the specific sectors and industries at various times may help

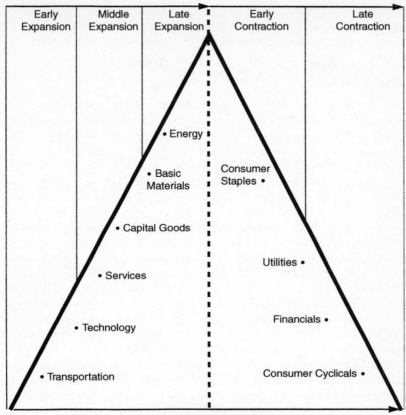

FIGURE 6.15 How Market Sectors Perform during the Business Cycle

Source: Sam Stovall, *Standard & Poor's Guide to Sector Investing*, (New York: McGraw-Hill, 1995).

us find future winners, improve asset allocation decisions, and even predict future market moves.

The rotation between the different market sectors is even predictable (see Figure 6.15).

As you can see, different sectors outperform the others depending on the stage of the economic cycle. Based on the chart, the beginning of an economic recovery sees transportation and technology stocks outperforming others due to a pickup in economic activity, an increased need to physically deliver more products, and higher investment and expenditure on new technologies for the new business cycle. The cycle continues from *early expansion* to *middle expansion* and, finally, to *late expansion*—with different sectors dominating as the economy recovers, grows, and approaches an economic contraction. As the cycle then enters the contraction phases (*early* and *late*), other sectors stand to benefit. And the cycle repeats.

So Where in the Cycle Are We Now?

Following a huge economic contraction and the onset of the Great Recession from late 2007 to early 2009, markets have rebounded tremendously—with the S&P 500 seeing returns of over 100 percent from the 2009 lows. But after nearly two years of historically record-breaking performance, many signs of potential trouble ahead are brewing. And according to the sector rotation theories we have discussed and presented, our current position within the economic cycle may have approached the end of the expansionary phase.

Following the huge economic contraction of 2008 and early 2009, we can see in Figure 6.16 that the financial and consumer discretionary (cyclicals) sectors led the way in early-to-mid 2009 as the economy was transitioning from *late contraction* to *early expansion* (note how these two sectors outperformed the others). The technology and transportation sectors also led the way since mid-2010, as the economic expansion continued (Figure 6.17). But starting in November 2010, energy and basic materials have outperformed the rest of the market, with energy massively outperforming the other sectors by 6 to 11 percentage points (Figure 6.18).

The massive outperformance of energy over the broader market over the course of five to six months may serve as a very important warning signal of a potential end to the expansionary cycle in the economy. Due to rising energy prices and the buildup of increasing inflationary pressures, the

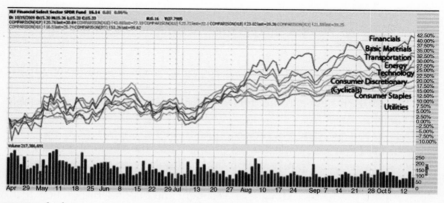

FIGURE 6.16 Financials and Cyclicals Lead the Way
Source: thinkorswim, Chart Prophet LLC.

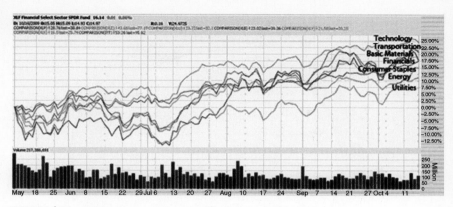

FIGURE 6.17 Technology and Transports Continue Expansion
Source: thinkorswim, Chart Prophet LLC.

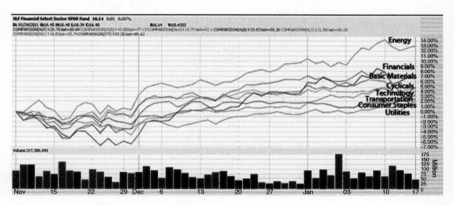

FIGURE 6.18 Energy Massively Outperforms
Source: thinkorswim, Chart Prophet LLC.

energy sector usually outperforms at the end of the cycle (see Figure 6.19). If the sector rotation theory is correct about the order of sector performance throughout the economic cycle, the onset of outperformance by the basic materials and energy sectors signals we have entered the *late expansion* phase and are nearing a contraction.

Actionable Investing Strategies

If the sector rotation is correct, then we can expect consumer staples (XLP) and utilities (XLU) to outperform in the next phase of the cycle. In fact, if we see consumer staples and utilities outperforming, it may even be signaling

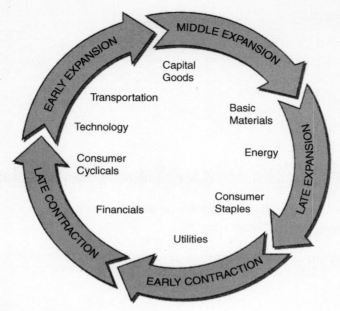

FIGURE 6.19 Sector Rotation and the Economic Cycle

Source: John J. Murphy, *Intermarket Analysis* (Hoboken, N.J.: John Wiley & Sons), p. 200.

the beginning of the contractionary phase in our economic cycle—and the potential beginnings of a new recession.

The first sign of a transition in sector strength, according to this theory, is the gradual weakening of the leading sectors and the strengthening of the next sector in line. In our case, the weakening of the energy sector in comparison to the consumer staples sector is our first sign of such a change.

From June 2010 until early 2011, energy and basic materials far outperformed the consumer staples sector, seen in Figure 6.20.

However, since early March 2011, consumer staples have been outperforming both basic materials and energy, as seen in Figure 6.21.

Such a shift in market leadership not only signals the need for a new investing strategy, but may also point to the beginnings of an economic contraction. Consumer staples stocks are generally safe stocks, and see heavy investor interest when economic downturns are on the horizon; since consumer staples companies (such as Procter & Gamble [PG], Phillip Morris [PM], Wal-Mart [WMT], and Coca-Cola [KO]) sell products that consumers must buy regardless of the economic condition, investors use these stocks as safe-havens and protection from the harmful effects that recessions have on most other companies. An increase in relative performance of the staples

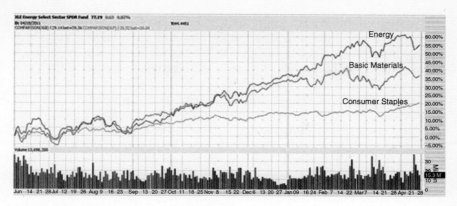

FIGURE 6.20 Energy and Basic Materials Outperform
Source: thinkorswim, Chart Prophet LLC.

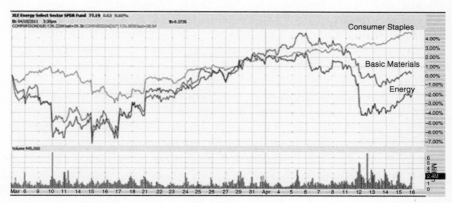

FIGURE 6.21 Consumer Staples Outperform
Source: thinkorswim, Chart Prophet LLC.

(XLP) in comparison to the other sectors, then, may be a signal that investors are beginning to decrease their risk exposure and that they may even be expecting a market downturn.

Our recommendation in April 2011 was to invest in the consumer staples sector. Investors could do so by either investing in the broad consumer staples ETFs (XLP) or through individual companies within the sector such as Procter & Gamble (PG), Molson Coors (TAP), General Mills (GIS), Kraft (KFT), and CVS (CVS) among others. The consumer staples not only offer relative protection in case of an economic downturn, but would also provide investors with income from dividends, because many consumer staples companies pay out dividends to shareholders. If our analysis is correct, the outperformance of the consumer staples not only provided a good investment opportunity, but also signaled the onset of an upcoming economic contraction. Slowing economic growth worldwide will mean falling stock prices, a decreased demand for commodities, and likely a drop in gold and other "safe" plays.

Another indicator that we may be nearing a contractionary phase: our economic recovery has been accompanied by a sharp pullback in industrial production after a steep drop during the recent Great Recession, but it is still below the late 2007 to early 2008 peak (see Figure 6.22). Company profits may be at record highs, but the country's industrial production and manufacturing are still about 10 percent lower than they were a few years ago.

The Dangers of ETFs

Originally published October 19, 2011: "Are ETFs To Blame For Overspeculation, Record-Correlations, and a Potential Crash?," *Seeking Alpha.*[6]

ETFs are huge enablers for soaring stock and commodity prices. And like their mutual fund predecessors, ETFs may have encouraged mass overspeculation that will ultimately result in a stock-market crash.

ETF investing continues to be a top choice for diversification, targeted exposure, and specific strategies; but ETFs have caused such mass speculation and have inflated prices to such an extent, that their intended benefits may actually be void and nullified by the tremendous risks and unintended consequences that they have posed. ETFs have increased speculation, massively inflated stock and commodity prices, and may be responsible for the unprecedented and hugely risky correlations across all stocks, sectors, and markets.

ETF Overview

Exchange traded funds (ETFs) are a revolutionary financial innovation, and provide many benefits for both individuals and institutions. Bought and sold much like stocks, ETFs are listed on exchanges and can be traded throughout the day. Like mutual funds, ETFs aim at providing diversification and exposure to a wider range of individual stocks or assets. Unlike mutual funds, however, ETFs can be traded all day, since their prices are instantaneously adjusted. Moreover, ETFs are cheaper and easier to invest in than mutual funds.

ETF USES   ETFs represent a portfolio of individual stocks, and provide an enormous number of uses—from tracking broad stock indices (like the S&P

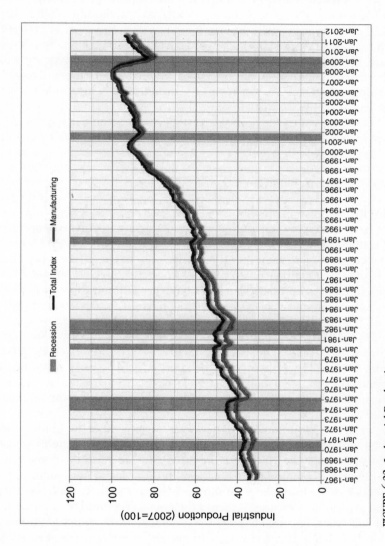

FIGURE 6.22 Industrial Production
Source: Federal Reserve.[7]

500 [SPY] or Russell 2000 [IWM], for example), to investing in specific themes or sectors (like technology [XLK], financials [XLF], housing [XHB]), to providing exposure to emerging markets and individual countries (emerging markets [EEM], China [FXI], Brazil [EWZ], etc.), to currency investment (U.S. dollar [UUP]), euro (FXE)), to volatility (VXX), to commodities (Oil [OIL], gold [GLD], natural gas [GAZ]), to bonds (TLT, TBT), and even to actively managed trading strategies. In other words, ETFs are exceptional tools for individuals and institutions to invest in commodities, sectors, countries, bonds, currencies, strategies, and just about any investment theme imaginable. ETFs provide a way for the average person to invest in a wide basket of stocks that he otherwise would not be able to.

ETFs offer many uses for portfolio strategy and asset allocation, including risk management and exposure to a wide range of markets and asset classes. They also provide a slew of reasons why investors should use them as part of their investment approach, including transparency, liquidity, diversification, and cost effectiveness.

ETF INDUSTRY   With so many innovative uses and benefits, it is no surprise that ETFs have grown at such a rapid and perhaps unprecedented pace. By May 2011, there were 2,747 ETFs offered by 142 ETF providers and traded on 49 exchanges—adding up to $1.446 trillion in assets! There were also plans to launch an additional 1,022 ETFs.[8] With such a huge number of ETFs being traded, there is no doubt that ETFs have revolutionized stock market trading—the question now, however, is "How have ETFs affected markets?"

MASSIVE ETF GROWTH   Since their introduction, ETFs have grown tremendously, from $0.8 billion in 1993 to nearly $1.5 trillion by May 2011 (see Figure 6.23). ETFs' popularity has soared largely because institutions have embraced them (see Figure 6.24). ETFs have also made it much easier and more accessible for individuals and institutions to invest in commodities (see Figure 6.25).

Prior to ETFs, investment in commodities such as oil, gold, grains, and others was limited to commodity traders, futures, or buying the physical commodities themselves. ETFs have provided a means for the common investor to buy these commodities from the comfort of his or her home, without any expertise or knowledge of the underlying asset. To make matters worse, the availability of these ETFs and the constant touting by the institutions that sell them, has greatly increased speculation in commodities and tremendously inflated prices. It is easy to understand why we've seen such massive rises in commodity prices over the past few years—investors have poured billions of dollars into commodity ETFs in order to profit from the shortage they expect, as China and emerging markets demand more and more commodities and raw materials for their growing economies. The

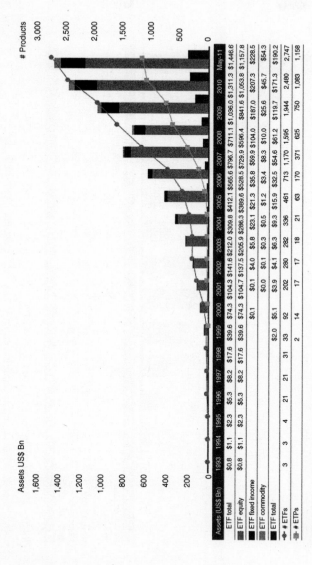

Assets (US$ Bn)	1993	1994	1995	1996	1997	1998	1999	2000	2001	2002	2003	2004	2005	2006	2007	2008	2009	2010	May-11
ETF total	$0.8	$1.1	$2.3	$5.3	$8.2	$17.6	$39.6	$74.3	$104.3	$141.6	$212.0	$309.8	$412.1	$565.6	$796.7	$711.1	$1,036.0	$1,311.3	$1,446.6
ETF equity	$0.8	$1.1	$2.3	$5.3	$8.2	$17.6	$39.6	$74.3	$104.7	$137.5	$205.9	$296.3	$389.6	$528.5	$729.9	$596.4	$841.6	$1,053.8	$1,157.8
ETF fixed income								$0.1	$0.1	$4.0	$5.8	$23.1	$21.3	$35.8	$59.9	$104.0	$187.0	$207.3	$228.5
ETF commodity									$0.0	$0.1	$0.3	$0.5	$1.2	$3.4	$8.3	$10.0	$25.6	$45.7	$54.3
ETF total							$2.0	$5.1	$3.9	$4.1	$6.3	$9.3	$15.9	$32.5	$54.6	$61.2	$119.7	$171.3	$190.2
# ETFs	3	3	4	21	21	31	33	92	202	280	282	336	461	713	1,170	1,595	1,944	2,480	2,747
# ETPs							2	14	17	17	18	21	63	170	371	625	750	1,083	1,158

FIGURE 6.23 Global ETF and ETP Asset Growth

Note: Data as of May 2011.

Source: Global ETF Research and Implementation Strategy Team, BlackRock, Bloomberg.

Number of institutions

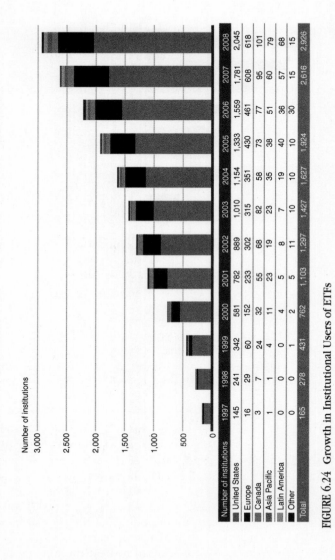

Number of institutions	1997	1998	1999	2000	2001	2002	2003	2004	2005	2006	2007	2008
United States	145	241	342	581	782	889	1,010	1,154	1,333	1,559	1,781	2,045
Europe	16	29	60	152	233	302	315	351	430	461	608	618
Canada	3	7	24	32	55	68	82	58	73	77	95	101
Asia Pacific	1	1	4	11	23	19	23	35	38	51	60	79
Latin America	0	0	0	4	5	8	7	19	40	36	57	68
Other	0	0	1	2	5	11	10	10	10	30	15	15
Total	165	278	431	762	1,103	1,297	1,427	1,627	1,924		2,616	2,926

FIGURE 6.24 Growth in Institutional Users of ETFs

Source: Global ETF Research and Implementation Strategy Team, BlackRock, Bloomberg.

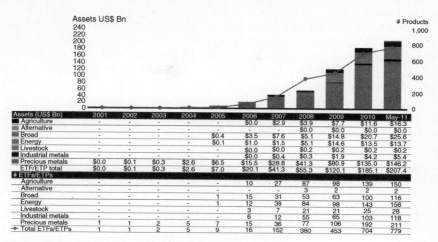

Assets (US$ Bn)	2001	2002	2003	2004	2005	2006	2007	2008	2009	2010	May-11
Agriculture	-	-	-	-	-	$0.0	$2.9	$3.9	$7.7	$11.6	$16.3
Alternative	-	-	-	-	-	-	-	$0.0	$0.0	$0.0	$0.0
Broad	-	-	-	-	$0.4	$3.5	$7.6	$5.1	$14.8	$20.7	$25.6
Energy	-	-	-	-	$0.1	$1.0	$1.5	$5.1	$14.6	$13.5	$13.7
Livestock	-	-	-	-	-	$0.0	$0.0	$0.2	$0.2	$0.2	$0.2
Industrial metals	-	-	-	-	-	$0.0	$0.4	$0.3	$1.9	$4.2	$5.4
Precious metals	$0.0	$0.1	$0.3	$2.6	$6.5	$15.5	$28.8	$41.3	$80.9	$135.0	$146.2
ETF/ETP total	$0.0	$0.1	$0.3	$2.6	$7.0	$20.1	$41.3	$55.3	$120.1	$185.1	$207.4
# ETFs/ETPs											
Agriculture	-	-	-	-	-	10	27	87	98	139	150
Alternative	-	-	-	-	-	-	-	3	2	2	2
Broad	-	-	-	-	1	15	31	53	63	100	116
Energy	-	-	-	-	1	12	39	84	98	143	156
Livestock	-	-	-	-	-	3	7	21	21	25	28
Industrial metals	-	-	-	-	-	6	12	55	65	103	118
Precious metals	1	1	2	5	7	15	36	77	106	192	211
Total ETFs/ETPs	1	1	2	5	9	16	152	380	453	704	779

FIGURE 6.25 Global Commodity ETF and ETP Asset Growth
Note: Data as of May 2011.

Source: Global ETF Research and Implementation Strategy Team, BlackRock, Bloomberg.

major problem, however, is that it has become extremely hard to track exactly how much of this commodity price surge is due to real demand—as opposed to the inflated demand that ETFs have caused. In other words, commodity prices could be severely out of whack with reality and way beyond where they should be.

ETFs may have offered tremendous benefits when they were introduced, and still continue to offer investors a way to pick specific sectors, themes, individual commodities, and so forth, but we are at a point where ETFs may have created such investor frenzy and overinvestment, that current prices for stocks and commodities may be highly overextended—and set for a sharp pullback.

MUTUAL FUNDS VERSUS ETFS ETFs have essentially made mutual funds obsolete. For decades, mutual funds were the number-one way for investors to diversify and gain exposure to specific strategies and professional money managers. The introduction of the ETF, however, has made it easier, cheaper, and more effective to invest. Mutual funds have therefore seen large outflows over the past decade, as investors who were disillusioned by terrible mutual fund performance have pulled out their money. Investors simply have no good reason to keep their money in mutual funds when so many funds actually *underperform* and fail to beat the market while still charging high management fees. ETFs are cheaper, easier to buy and sell, and allow investors to bet on whatever they choose.

In the dot-com bubble era, stocks rose to extreme levels because investors were piling into technology stocks and, most important, mutual funds. Mutual funds were seeing huge inflows of new investors, and the money that came into these "diversified money managers" was then being invested into the stock market—sending stock prices even higher.

Eventually, after millions of investors piled their money into these mutual funds and the stock market in general, the dot-com bubble collapsed, the stock market fell, and mutual funds lost their investors billions of dollars. Average investors, professionals, people with retirement accounts like 401(k)s or IRAs, and others lost a large chunk of their investment value.

Mutual funds are essentially an investment fund led by one or more portfolio managers. These managers accept investments, trying to invest the funds appropriately in order to make their investors a profit. Most funds, however, charge a management fee just for investing. Even if the fund does not gain for the year, the manager may still get paid for managing the investors' money. The investor is actually worse off in the mutual fund than if he owned a stock of the broader market. In other words, the fund manager did worse than the overall market, when he was actually hired by the investor to *beat* the market.

It is no surprise, then, that mutual funds lost a lot of their appeal when the tech bubble burst and when NASDAQ and stock markets fell during 2000 to 2002. A new financial instrument was about to launch into mass popularity—the ETF. Since so many mutual fund managers couldn't beat the market, why should investors keep their money invested there? If investors just bet on the overall market they could've beat the mutual fund's returns. Yet there were few if any ways for investors to invest in the broad markets; investors would have to buy a very wide selection of stocks that represented the whole market, and track each of those positions to closely monitor the portfolio allocations. The average, and even the professional, trader simply doesn't have the means to buy so many stocks and monitor them closely. Yet diversified exposure to the overall market was still available mainly through mutual funds.

The innovation of ETFs, however, largely cuts out the middle man (portfolio manager), lowers fees, and allows investors to invest in broad themes and overall stock indices that track markets. In other words, if the mutual funds were failing to beat the market, why not just bet on the market? ETFs were invented to very closely track the overall markets or sectors by buying a proportional share of stocks to mirror an index or sector. Investors now had an investment vehicle that was pretty much automated, cutting out the costly middle man and eliminating poor investment choices. Instead, investors could now just "buy the market" and expect the 8 percent return that the market averaged per year, going back 60 or more years.

Irrational Exuberance in ETFs?

ETFs are undoubtedly an amazing innovation in investing, but may have also helped create overspeculation and unwarranted price increases in the underlying stocks and commodities. By offering an easy, cost-effective, and highly intriguing way of investing, ETFs have created the illusion that investing is less risky than it really is. ETFs have also massively boosted stock and commodity prices, as investors who were once not able to invest in certain stocks or commodities now bid up the prices of the underlying stocks and commodities by buying ETFs.

ETFs are huge enablers for soaring stock and commodity prices. And like their mutual fund predecessors, ETFs may have encouraged mass overspeculation that will ultimately result in a stock market crash.

In his award-winning and best-selling book *Irrational Exuberance*, Robert Shiller warned of massive stock market and housing bubbles. In the book, he points to a number of precipitating factors that have allowed stocks to become so dramatically overvalued. One of them was the growth of mutual funds. Unfortunately for us, the points Shiller made regarding mutual funds can easily be applied to ETFs. In other words, mutual funds caused the stock market overvaluation in the late 1990s, and ETFs may have caused the stock and commodity overvaluation over the past few years. If the similarities are a sign, we may be setting up for a sharp drop in stocks and commodities.

Referring to mutual funds, Shiller says:

> *Another reason for the funds' explosive growth is that they have paid for a great deal of advertising. Television shows, magazines, and newspapers frequently carry advertisements for them, and active investors receive unsolicited ads in the mail. Mutual funds encourage more naïve investors to participate in the market, by leading them to think that experts managing the funds will steer them away from pitfalls.*[9]

Just like mutual funds, ETFs have grown so rapidly largely due to constant advertising on TV, magazines, newspapers, and the Internet. And just like mutual funds, ETFs encourage more naïve investors to participate in the market by leading them to think that the "diversification" offered by these ETFs will steer them away from losses.

> *The proliferation of equity mutual funds has therefore focused public attention on the market, with the effect of encouraging speculative price movements in stock market aggregates, rather than in individual stocks.*[10]

Somewhat different, but very much the same, ETFs appear to be offering "diversification" by investing in a wide range of stocks. However, this so-called "diversification" actually inflates the prices of a wide number of individual stocks—some of which may not be worthy of the investment. For example, an investor may choose an ETF that tracks "technology stocks." His total investment is then divided among a number of different stocks that aim to represent "technology." However, while the investor was aiming to gain exposure to technology stocks, he did not choose the individual stocks that made up the portfolio—some of his investment may have been invested in a "technology" stock that has no merit; in other words, some companies in an ETF are benefiting from a broader theme (like technology) when they aren't necessarily good investments.

Take "cloud computing" as an example. The cloud ETF (SKYY) was introduced for investors who would like to invest in cloud computing. Investors who wanted to capitalize on the popular theme would then buy SKYY. The money invested would then be allocated among a number of different individual stocks representing "cloud computing." An investor would therefore expect the money invested to be allocated among strong cloud-related companies like Salesforce.com (CRM), F5 Networks (FFIV), and Amazon (AMZN). However, looking at the list of SKYY's holdings (Table 6.1), we can see how ETFs tremendously overinflate the prices of companies that don't deserve the investment.

TABLE 6.1 Top 10 Cloud ETF (SKYY) Holdings (Ranked by Market Cap)

Company	Symbol	Weighting
Apple	APPL	2.46%
Microsoft	MSFT	2.55%
International Business Machines	IBM	2.51%
Google	GOOG	3.27%
Oracle	ORCL	3.35%
Amazon.com	AMZN	3.61%
Cisco Systems	CSCO	3.23%
Hewlett-Packard	HPQ	2.36%
SAP AG (ADR)	SAP	3.18%
EMC Corporation	EMC	3.32%
VMware	VMW	3.49%
Wipro Ltd. (ADR)	WIT)	0.78%
Salesforce.com	CRM	3.50%
NetApp	NTAP	3.42%
Juniper Networks	JNPR	3.21%
Adobe Systems	ADBE	0.80%
Netflix	NFLX	3.53%
Check Point Software	CHKP	0.87%
CA Inc.	CA	0.86%
Teradata Corporation	TDC	3.65%
BMC Software	BMC	0.85%

F5 Networks	FFIV	3.45%
Iron Mountain	IRM	0.88%
Informatica	INFA	3.53%
Rackspace Hostin	RAX	3.52%
Akamai Technologies	AKAM	3.35%
Polycom	PLCM	0.92%
TIBCO Software	TIBX	3.81%
Equinix	EQIX	3.36%
Acme Packet	APKT	3.42%
Open Text Corp	OTEX	3.54%
Aruba Networks	ARUN	3.71%
SuccessFactors	SFSF	0.79%
SAVVIS	SVVS	0.81%
Blackboard	BBBB	3.47%
j2 Global Communications	JCOM	0.83%
Financial Engines	FNGN	0.90%
Rightnow Technologies	RNOW	3.33%
OPNET Technologies	OPNT	0.87%
NetScout Systems	NTCT	0.70%

Source: Richard Bloch, "SKYY: What's in the Cloud? Smaller Stocks That Pack a Lot of Punch," July 7, 2011.[11]

The following are the best examples of ETF flaws: Why should Apple (AAPL) make up 2.46 percent of the ETF when Apple barely has any cloud exposure? Apple just introduced iCloud; when SKYY came out, Apple had almost no cloud capabilities. Then, Netflix (NFLX) is a media-based company and definitely not cloud-centric; even if Netflix did offer investors decent exposure to "cloud computing," giving the stock a massive 3.53 percent weighting (more than the actual cloud companies like CRM or FFIV) is completely insane. Netflix (NFLX) and Apple (AAPL) are benefiting from the "cloud computing" theme when they don't really deserve it. ETFs therefore cause price increases in stocks that should not be taking place.

Another example is the homebuilders ETF (XHB). Investors buying XHB should expect to gain exposure to "homebuilders" like PulteGroup (PHM), Toll Brothers (TOL), DR Horton (DHI), and Lennar (LEN). However, looking at XHB's holdings (see Table 6.2), we can see that some of its biggest holdings aren't even homebuilding stocks! Instead, companies like Aaron's (AAN) and Tempur-pedic (TPX)—which sell electronics and mattresses—are allocated over 4 percent each. AAN and TPX are part of the portfolio since increased homebuilding will likely result in more buying of electronics and mattresses; but their correlation to homebuilding in no way justifies 4 percent allocations! While companies like AAN and TPX gain so

TABLE 6.2 Top 10 Holdings, Homebuilders ETF (XHB)—42.74 Percent of Total Assets

Company	Symbol	% Assets
Aaron's, Inc. Common Stock	AAN	4.65
Sherwin-Williams Company (The)	SHW	4.56
PulteGroup, Inc. Common Stock	PHM	4.34
Aaron's, Inc. Common Stock	AAN	4.30
A.O. Smith Corporation Common Stock	AOS	4.24
Simpson Manufacturing Company	SSD	4.22
Armstrong World Industries Inc.	AWI	4.20
Tempur-pedic International Inc.	TPX	4.12
Masco Corporation Common Stock	MAS	4.07
D.R. Horton, Inc. Common Stock	DHI	4.04

Source: Yahoo! Finance.

much, the companies that really should be getting that investment (the actual homebuilders) are being ignored.

Since ETFs aim to diversify within either the broad market or specific sectors, they push stock prices up with little regard sometimes as to whether all of these individual companies deserve the investment. In other words, ETFs also "encourage speculative price movements in stock market aggregates, rather than in individual stocks." Yes, it is also true that ETFs allow for diversification by selecting *specific* sectors within the broad market; but, at the same time, even the sector-targeted ETFs are allocating the total investment capital among a number of individual stocks, some of which may not be individually worthy of the investment. It may just be much healthier for the market if investors chose individual stocks rather than trying to profit from a broader theme by investing through ETFs.

> *The emerging popular concept that mutual fund investing is sound, convenient, and safe has encouraged many investors who were once afraid of the market to want to enter it, thereby contributing to an upward thrust in the market.*[12]

Likewise, ETFs with their "diversification" and "protection" benefits encouraged many investors who were afraid of investing in stocks to enter the market again, and also increased the downside risks by inflating prices and "contributing to an upward thrust in the market."

This huge speculative growth in investment cannot be sustained forever. Eventually, stock prices must drop to accurately reflect economic conditions and future growth—not the extremely high expectations that investors have about the future. Recessions occur, growth cannot grow exponentially forever, and stock prices must fall to clean up some of the speculative excesses that these investment manias produce.

ETFs are a great innovative tool that allows individuals and fund managers to invest in a wide range of stocks while also making the process easier and more efficient; but ETFs have created so much speculation and unwarranted investment that they may be serving a very similar role to the market as mutual funds served in the late 1990s—before the markets tanked. ETFs have made it easier, but also tremendously riskier; their intended benefits may actually be void and nullified by the tremendous risks and unintended consequences they have posed.

Are ETFs to Blame for High Correlations?

Both ETFs and the growth of a "global economy" and interconnected markets are causes of the tremendous risks involved. Technology has advanced so rapidly, and financial instruments and derivatives are increasing the speed of trading as well as decreasing the transparency of what exactly is invested in. Investment leverage has increased tremendously, and banks and investors sometimes don't even know exactly what their money is invested in.

ETFs have increased "aggregate stock price movements" in which stocks move together more than ever before. Unlike in the past, when markets still had some independence and did not move so parallel to every other market, markets today are highly affected by what goes on around the globe. If the stock market in Asia falls, the U.S. stock markets will likely fall as well, and vice versa. Nothing displays this tremendous and unprecedented interconnectedness between markets, better than the extremely high correlations of the past year, seen in Figure 6.26.

The buying of ETFs has caused stocks to move together, since investors and high-frequency-traders (HFTs) are buying and selling large groups of stocks simultaneously. By buying large groups of stocks through ETFs, investors have greatly increased the risks—if one part of the market falls, other sectors are likely to be affected as well. Correlations have reached a higher level than they did in 1987, before the massive stock market crash.

And while foreign stocks have historically provided diversification benefits to investors, the extreme correlations now present between stocks all over the world may completely cancel out those benefits (see Figure 6.27).

Conclusion

ETFs provide leverage, cost effectiveness, ease of investment, liquidity, and the ability to invest in a huge range of themes, markets, and sectors. But they also highly increase speculation in the broad markets (rather than just

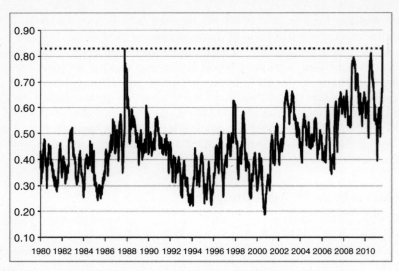

FIGURE 6.26 S&P 500 Member Correlation (Average Rolling 50-Day)
Source: *Business Insider* (August 2011), tickersense.

individual stocks); they inflate prices of all related companies, regardless of that company's real financial strength or weakness; and they present an "illusion of safety" when investors buy ETFs thinking they are getting "diversified" exposure with limited "market risk."

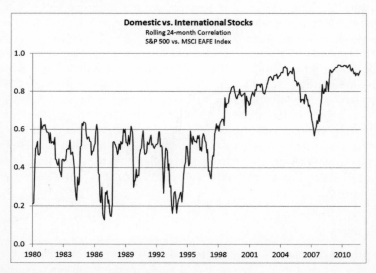

FIGURE 6.27 Foreign Stocks Correlation
Source: Jones & Company.

It is time to watch our investments more closely, know exactly what our ETFs are invested in, and keep in mind that there has been an extraordinary amount of speculative money invested in all forms of ETFs. The stock market may have reached a peak, and an upcoming drop or recession can severely hurt investors as the value of their ETFs drops sharply.

What about the Dollar?

Gold's massive rise has largely been fueled by the decade-long decline of the dollar and other currencies. Shaky economies and soaring debt have given fiat (paper) currencies the stigma of being highly risky and increasingly on the verge of becoming worthless as a measure of value.

With highly volatile markets over the past decade, and increasing fears regarding economic stability and future growth, it is no surprise that currencies have seen huge declines in relation to gold since the turn of the century (see Figure 6.28).

And with a strong negative correlation between gold and the dollar, we can expect the future of both asset classes to move, for the most part, in opposite directions (see Figure 6.29). In essence, the future of gold may be highly dependent on the strength or weakness of the U.S. dollar. While the dollar appears to be eternally doomed, the extreme despair and loss of hope for the dollar may be signaling a bottom and upcoming recovery. And that recovery in the dollar could be very bad news for gold.

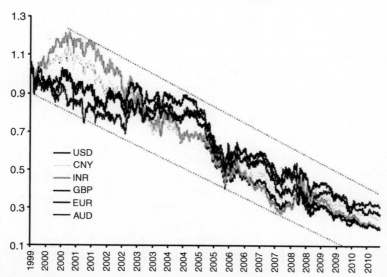

FIGURE 6.28 Various Currencies versus Gold since 1999
Sources: Datastream, Erste Group Research.

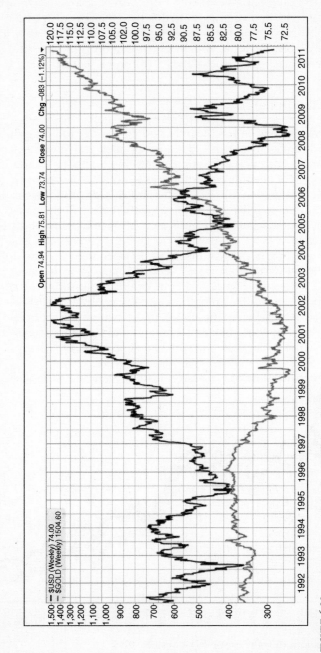

FIGURE 6.29 Twenty Years of the U.S. Dollar and Gold

Sources: StockCharts.com, *Seeking Alpha*/Doug Short.

Dollar "Demise" Looks Overblown

Originally published April 26, 2011: "Dollar 'Demise' Looks Overblown: Betting on a Short-Term Bounce or Medium-Term Recovery," *Seeking Alpha.*[13]

After plunging over 15 percent since June 2010, the U.S. dollar may be set for a short-term bounce if not a medium-term recovery.

With massive and extreme pessimism regarding the dollar and fiat currencies in general, driven by escalating fears over potential U.S. government debt defaults, soaring inflation, irresponsible money printing by the Fed, and the possible overthrow of the dollar as the global reserve currency, fears of the "demise of the dollar" may be overblown.

The dollar's strength or weakness has a much larger effect than many realize. It affects the stock market, bonds, commodity prices, debt levels, inflation, consumer confidence and behavior, foreign currencies, and even global policy. It is therefore crucial that investors, economists, analysts, politicians, and just about everyone else monitor the U.S. dollar's movement and potential effects on markets, economies, policies, gas and food prices, standards of living, and numerous other factors.

NEGATIVE VERSUS POSITIVE VIEWS ON THE DOLLAR The negative outlook for the dollar has plenty of strong fundamental reasons as support, particularly these five.

1. **U.S. government debt** is massive, leading Standard & Poor's to downgrade U.S. debt.
2. A **downgrade of U.S. credit** from its top-notch AAA rating by Standard & Poor's could trigger massive selling of U.S. dollars by countries worldwide, as well as a huge hit for the United States as it loses its first-class financial-strength status.
3. No end can be seen to U.S. dollar devaluation due to **massive money printing** by the Fed. As long as the Fed continues to print money, the dollar is expected to continue to drop. And since no clear sign has been given regarding the end of money printing, the dollar could drop more.
4. **Rising inflation**, seen in commodity and food prices yet largely ignored by the Fed, will further devalue the dollar.
5. **The end of the dollar as world reserve currency** could take place if the above-mentioned possibilities materialize. The end of the dollar as a "safe-haven" could quickly cause the dollar to plummet as world economies move out of the U.S. dollar to diversify their reserves. One large source of potential trouble: China holds between 65 and 75 percent of

its reserves in U.S. dollars; a lowered rating or simply the decision to diversify could severely hurt the dollar.

The positive outlook for the dollar is largely based on extreme pessimism and overblown fears, as illustrated in these five possibilities.

1. **Bad news and inflation fears already priced in?** With nearly everyone believing the dollar is hopeless, and even running to hard assets such as gold or silver to protect themselves from a dollar collapse, the big drop in the dollar may have already taken place. If much of the bad news is already factored into the price, the dollar may be near a bottom.
2. **The end of QE2 and effective Quantitative Easing** will strengthen the dollar, as the Fed ceases to buy treasuries and dollar devaluation ends.
3. **Tighter monetary policy** in response to soaring energy and commodity prices will ease inflationary concerns and, in turn, strengthen the dollar. The Fed has already shown some signs of future rate hikes, which would bring an end to the easy monetary policy that has severely weakened the dollar.
4. **Increased dollar buying by countries** in an attempt to slow down their own currency appreciation could strengthen the dollar. As a number of currencies have seen tremendous appreciation while the dollar has fallen, some countries are finding their strong currencies to be detrimental to trade and future growth. By buying the U.S. dollar then, some countries could attempt to slow down their own currencies.
5. **Chart technicals are showing a potential upcoming bounce or reversal.**

Looking at Figure 6.30, a long-term chart of the U.S. dollar dating back to 2001, we can see the big drop. Yet even though the dollar has dropped significantly over the past 10 years, it may be heading for an explosive breakout to the upside. The chart above shows that while the dollar has dropped, the MACD has been rising—a positive divergence while the dollar is in a downtrend could signal a reversal. In other words, the drop has occurred on increasingly contradictory momentum and the dollar may start to rise.

Moreover, while gold has soared and while dollar-bears have been calling for the collapse of the dollar, the dollar has not made a new low since 2008! If we just listen to commentary or news, we would think the dollar is the worst it's ever been; but the dollar is still above the 2008 lows and may actually be in the midst of a recovery.

Dollar Comeback Marks Gold's Demise

Not only has the dollar failed to make new lows since 2008 (which should quell some of the "dollar demise" arguments), but it appears that the very

FIGURE 6.30 U.S. Dollar Decline, 2001 to 2011

Source: BigCharts.com, Chart Prophet LLC.

strong recent surge in the dollar signals the beginning of a new uptrend for the currency and a renewed downtrend for stocks and commodities.

According to two Elliott Wave views of the dollar (see Figures 6.31 and 6.32), we may be setting up for a sharp dollar rally very soon. In fact, since we have not made new lows in the dollar index since early 2008, the 2008 low may be the long-term bottom. Unless we see new lows below the 2008 lows, the dollar's gyrations since the early 2009 highs may have just been a correction before the next (and larger) leg up. And the dollar strength will prove to be highly jeopardizing for the gold theme.

Perhaps one of the biggest determinants of the future direction of the stock market, commodities, and emerging markets, the U.S. dollar's comeback points to a deflationary period generally accompanied by falling stock prices and recessions. The majority of the world has been extremely negative on the future of the U.S. dollar, with many even calling for the dollar's collapse. Understandably so, the dollar has been so greatly devalued due to excessive money-printing by the U.S. government that it has been hard to argue *for* the dollar. This, in turn, has fueled the massive rally in stocks, commodities, gold, and foreign currencies, as the falling dollar was seen as a sign

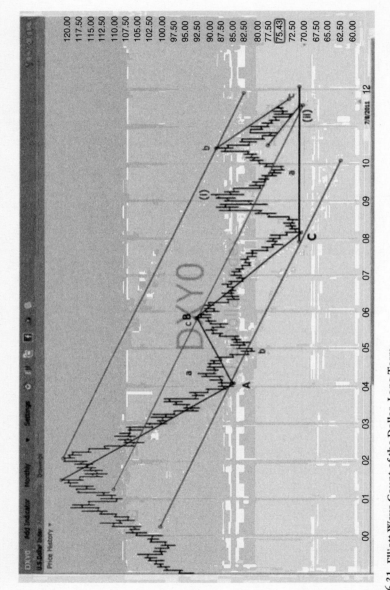

FIGURE 6.31 Elliott Wave Count of the Dollar, Long-Term

Source: studyofcycles.com.

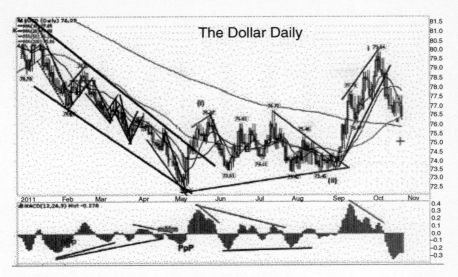

FIGURE 6.32 Elliott Wave Count for the Dollar, Short-Term
Source: chartpattern, YouTube.[14]

of mounting inflationary pressures that would justify rising prices in just about every asset class.

However, as we warned in late April 2011, the dollar's "demise" is over-blown. Instead, the extreme pessimism over the dollar, the slowdown in emerging markets, and the deflationary period that will accompany the upcoming recession all point to a dollar recovery. Rather than a period of soaring inflation and dollar collapse, we continue to expect global economic slowdown and a dollar recovery. The U.S. economy and the dollar are still not healthy in almost all cases, but the *relative* strength of the United States and the dollar over the now-struggling emerging markets and foreign currencies (Euro included) will help the dollar outperform, signaling deflation and falling stock and commodity prices.

Emerging Market Troubles

The collapse of the emerging markets, especially China, India, and Brazil, will have a huge ripple effect on the rest of the world's economies, and will plunge most countries back into a global recession.

One of the major drivers of the markets over the past two years has been the "unstoppable" and highly promising future of the emerging markets— especially China. As millions of inhabitants in emerging countries begin to enter the developed world and middle class, their consumption habits and

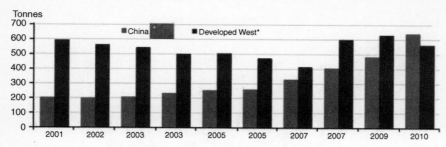

FIGURE 6.33 China's Gold Demand Overtakes Developed World
Note: Demand includes gold jewelry and bar and coin demand only.
*Developed West includes the United States, France, Germany, Italy, Switzerland,
United Kingdom, and other Europe.
Source: GFMS World Gold Council.[15]

their effect on the economies of countries all over the globe increases. And
as millions of people contribute to the growth of China, India, and other
countries, they will require extra food, energy sources such as gasoline and
oil, cotton for their increased consumption and clothing needs, industrial
metals for their new cars and technology, and many other materials that a
growing and evolving population needs.

China's massive growth has also fueled the gold bubble, seen in Figure
6.33. According to the data presented below, Chinese demand for gold has
grown tremendously as the wealth of its citizens has dramatically increased
(Figures 6.34 and 6.35).

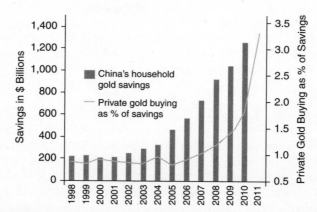

FIGURE 6.34 Chinese Citizens Putting Their Wealth into Gold
Source: BullionVault, BIS, IMF, GFMS.[16]

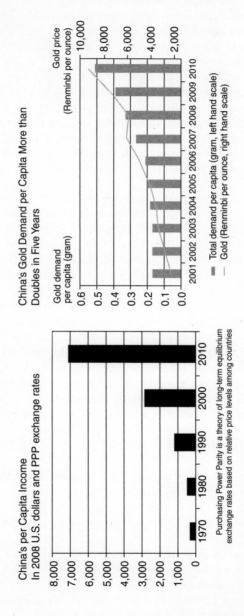

China's per Capita Income
In 2008 U.S. dollars and PPP exchange rates

China's Gold Demand per Capita More than
Doubles in Five Years

Purchasing Power Parity is a theory of long-term equilibrium
exchange rates based on relative price levels among countries

FIGURE 6.35 Growing Chinese Wealth

Source: PIRA, World Gold Council, GFMX, Bloomberg.[17]

The problem that may emerge, however, is that there is no guarantee that China and other emerging countries will actually meet our lofty expectations. Emerging markets have been growing at such a rapid pace (7 to 10 percent or higher compared to 1 to 3 percent for the United States) that their development may have set them up for housing bubbles, high inflation, and uncontrollable growth.

Moreover, with all the enthusiasm over the future growth of emerging markets, investors have piled into stocks and ETFs in hopes of capitalizing on the emerging markets theme. The reasoning behind these moves is that worldwide consumption of food, commodities, and energy will continue as growing and developing populations require more supply. And with more and more people expected to consume at an increasing rate, investors assume food and commodity prices will continue to rise.

Therefore, in order to profit from the expected continued growth in emerging markets, investors have thrown billions of dollars into emerging markets (EEM) such as China (FXI), India (EPI), Brazil (EWZ), and others; grains and agriculture (JJG, DBA, DAG, MOO, AGF); steel (SLX), copper (JJC), silver (SLV, SIL), tin (JJT), and other industrial metals; energy (OIL, USO, OIH, XLE); and just about anything else that could rise if global economies continue to expand.

The problem—and it's a major one—with this emerging markets theme that has dominated for the past two years is that all the expectations and projections investors have had may be way too optimistic. With China and others showing very troubling weakness and attempting to slow their growth in order to prevent economic turmoil, a huge economic dip is not out of the question. Add to that the possibility that all the growth is already factored into the commodity and stock prices (that investors have speculated tremendously in all EEM-related themes and that current prices reflect future expectations), and any stumble or slower growth could send prices plummeting as they attempt to adjust to more realistic growth.

In simple terms, here are the four stages of emerging market growth that many investors have been relying on:

1. Emerging markets are expected to grow at a rapid pace for the next 50 years.
2. Rapid growth will require more supplies and more inputs.
3. As demand grows for food, commodities, and energy, the prices of these inputs will continue to rise.
4. The plan: Buy and invest in emerging markets and commodities in order to take advantage of this continued growth.

And here are the possible four stages that derail economic recovery and hurt emerging markets investors:

1. Emerging markets have been set up with lofty expectations for growth that will not be achieved due to unsustainable commodity and food prices, as well as unsustainable growth rates.
2. The double-digit growth rates that many investors have been relying on do not actually materialize. More reasonable growth rates of 5 to 8 percent do.
3. Since prices have run up at such massive rates and steep angles, they must come back down to reflect the more reasonable growth rates that have surfaced.
4. Prices for emerging markets, commodities, food, and energy drop considerably in order to better reflect current conditions and revised future expectations.

In other words, unless emerging markets continue to grow as expected, economies will suffer and investors will see heavy losses as reality sets in and expectations are missed.

Emerging Market Warning Signs

The slowdown that has been surfacing in China, Brazil, and other emerging markets is visible on many fronts. The warning signs include the following:

- Surging inflation that threatens sustainable growth.
- Soaring money supply that fuels bubbles in stocks and real estate.
- Credit bubbles.
- Massive and understated loan exposure.
- Tightening monetary policy that could put the brakes on the economy.
- Inverted yield curves that usually appear before recessions.
- Real estate bubbles evident in ghost towns and empty malls.
- Overconfident buying at auctions.
- The infamous *skyscraper indicator* (see section further on in this chapter).
- Fraudulent companies that have attracted investment from around the world when they are nothing but "shell" companies with unproven financials.
- Most important: The stock markets of China, Brazil, and others have been deep into bear-market territory in 2011—down between 20 and 30 percent from their peaks.

SURGING INFLATION Many countries around the world are experiencing surging inflation that could threaten steady growth. With consumer prices rising significantly, especially due to the sharp rise in food and commodity prices, countries like China (6.4 percent annual inflation rate, June 2011) could have major problems. The price of pork, China's staple meat, soared 65 percent between July 2010 and July 2011.[18] Though many countries have been attempting to cool the inflationary threats, consumer prices have continued to rise. And even if these countries can slow inflation, they may also be halting growth at the same time.

MONEY SUPPLY

> *Speculative manias gather speed through expansion of money and credit.*[19]
>
> —Charles Kindleberger

While most economists and investors have been arguing for the demise of the dollar and the death of paper currency due to government money-printing, many fail to notice that China's money supply has actually grown at a much more rapid pace than the United States' money supply (see Figure 6.36). With M2, a broad measure of money supply, rising 15.9 percent by June 2011,[20] the rapid growth of money supply and the devaluing of Chinese currency have fueled asset bubbles in real estate, investments, and gold, and may be setting China up for a very sharp financial crisis as money supply shrinks and credit dries up.

CREDIT BUBBLES Foreign banks increased their lending to China by 86 percent in 2010.[21] In addition, off-balance sheet loans have increased by 110

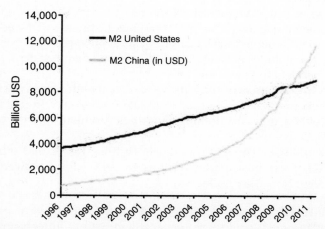

FIGURE 6.36 **M2 Money Supply United States versus M2 China (in U.S. Dollars)**
Sources: Datastream, Erste Group Research.

percent and tremendously raise the risk of bank defaults because these loans are not accounted for in the same way as traditional loans. It has been estimated that the value of off-balance sheet items for 16 Chinese banks is around $3.5 to $4 trillion, making up 25 percent of total assets.[22] This highly increased leverage, much of which has been achieved through hidden activity and therefore results in understated credit exposure, could easily cause major problems for banks in the event of a credit downturn or liquidity crunch.[23]

Such massive credit growth is almost a guarantee of future asset bubbles, especially as China has been attempting to cool the overheating real estate market. And if economic growth slows, China's banks could be left with a toxic portfolio of nonperforming loans.

Economist Hyman Minsky developed a model to explain financial crises as a result of cyclical changes in the supply of credit. Minsky pointed out that the supply of credit increased during economic booms and decreased during economic slowdowns. During expansions, investors were increasingly more optimistic about the future and became more likely to borrow. Lenders were also more likely to lend, since the expansionary phase had increased their risk tolerance and also lowered their assessment of the underlying risk. Furthermore, Minsky argued that the increases in credit supply during booms and decreases during busts made financial crises much more likely.[24]

The emergence of countries like China, India, Brazil, and other modernizing areas has coincided with the sudden and rapid growth of credit. Developed markets have had access to credit for decades—from mortgages to credit cards to low down payments and many other forms of credit extension. Emerging markets and developing countries, however, had been on a cash-only basis until only 20 or 30 years ago. The development and availability of credit has allowed individuals within these emerging markets to increase spending and investment. This increased credit and spending leads to a "domino expansionary effect"[25] in which the economy grows rapidly due to the large sudden increase in available credit. The growth of credit has an almost immediate positive impact as the expansion of business results in double-digit growth in many sectors of the economy.

Growth can only continue at this pace if credit continues to be available. As the credit expansion reaches a saturation point however, the unsustainable cycle of credit growth begins to weaken. Credit begins to dry up as lenders are less willing to lend, and as loans must be repaid. Individuals and businesses can no longer rely on more credit to fuel their existing loans and activities, and economic growth is hit with a sharp slowdown. The unavailability of credit sharply halts further expansion, and the economy may fall into recession as slow or negative growth takes hold. The massive credit and expansionary cycle can only be sustained through continuous credit growth; but credit can't grow forever, and economies inevitably must face contractions as growth comes to a halt.

In the case of China and other emerging countries, credit has grown so rapidly and has fueled such massive expansions, that the economic slow-down resulting from shrinking credit availability could be severe. The large asset bubbles in stocks and real estate that have been appearing in many emerging markets are the results of unsustainable credit expansion that will lead to economic shocks as a saturation point is reached and credit growth is no longer possible.

LOAN EXPOSURE Moody's, the credit ratings agency, recently said that China has underestimated by half a trillion dollars its exposure of state-owned banks' to local government loans.[26] China has also suspended more than 80 percent of its railroad construction projects due to safety concerns and high debt burdens. The Railway Ministry is facing over $300 billion in liabilities, bringing its liability-to-asset ratio up to 59 percent.[27] Banks have stopped lending for railway construction, which stands as a stark warning of a looming liquidity crisis and credit crunch.

TIGHTENING MONETARY POLICY China's central bank has increased interest rates three times and its reserve requirement rate (RRR) for banks six times in 2011 by the end of July. Tighter monetary policy is an attempt to cool the rampant inflation that has been threatening to spiral out of control. While inflation is generally a sign of growth, very high inflation could be damaging to the economy as prices begin to hurt companies and consumers. Tighter monetary policy has therefore been a method of controlling unwanted inflation. However, while stricter policies that limit easy money and easy credit are necessary to prevent rampant inflation, they can also slow growth considerably as they dry up credit and put the brakes on economic expansion. In fact, tighter policy is many times such a shock to the economy that it can send it into recession as rapid growth turns to contraction. Tighter policies are an attempt to slow the economy in a controlled fashion in order to achieve a "soft landing" (instead of a sudden collapse); however, tightening policies also slow down the "liquidity pump" that has been fueling the massive growth leading up to that point. In short, tighter policy is necessary to prevent the unwanted and dangerous inflation that usually leads to asset bubbles, but many times also ends up halting economic growth and severely hurting markets.

China's attempt to cool inflation through tighter monetary policy may dry up the massive credit bubble that has allowed the country to grow at such a rapid pace. The dominos may then begin to fall, as high inflation leads to tighter monetary policy to slower growth to investors fleeing, and to the Chinese economic collapse contagion.

INVERTED YIELD CURVES   Normally seen before recessions, inverted yield curves have surfaced in Brazil and India. The inversion of yield curves takes place when short-term rates rise above longer-term rates, signaling that investors will accept lower rates in the future—because they anticipate an economic downturn. Richard Bernstein, formerly a chief investment strategist at Merrill Lynch, pointed to the inverted yield curve as a sign that a "central bank has tightened too much." Furthermore, "the most inverted yield curves are Greece, Ireland, Portugal, and then comes India and Brazil. There is your warning sign that no one is talking about."[28] With interest rates at over 12 percent in Brazil and India, tightening may really hurt the economy as it could sharply halt economic growth. Slowing the economy down by tightening halts growth, but tightening may be the only effective way of preventing future asset bubbles at this stage. Tightening makes credit harder to get, which severely slows expansion and can even act as a negative shock that sends the economy into recession as it returns to equilibrium.

SLOWING GROWTH   Most economists, analysts, and investors expect China and many emerging markets to grow at a nearly double-digit pace. If China and other countries fail to meet expectations, however, markets could crash hard as investments and stocks adjust to new, and less optimistic, circumstances. In fact, a slowdown that leads to very negative reactions could be growth of even 7 percent![29] Moreover, China's Purchasing Managers' Index (PMI), which measures growth in manufacturing activities, fell below 50 in July 2011[30]—signaling a potential upcoming contraction. With the lowest reading in 28 months, the deceleration in China's industrial activities should be a severe warning of a broader economic slowdown. Additionally, China's customs bureau warned of "severe" challenges as export growth slowed to 17.1 percent in September 2011 from 24.5 percent in August 2011. Moreover, the trade surplus declined for the third straight month, falling from $31.5 billion in July 2011 to $14.5 billion by October 2011.[31] Brazil has been even weaker, with four consecutive months of contraction in manufacturing, as PMI dropped to 45.5 in September 2011. If China and Brazil can't continue to grow at a rapid pace, while simultaneously controlling inflation, things could quickly spiral out of control.

INFLATION RATE OUTPACING SAVINGS RATE   With inflation rates over 6 percent in China and other countries, having money deposited in savings accounts that pay approximately 3.5 percent is detrimental to the account holder. When inflation is higher than the return on savings, the money in the savings account is actually losing relative value over time; inflation makes money worth less, and the same amount deposited a year earlier has less purchasing power as time passes. Since households lose money by keeping it in the bank, individuals in these countries are either losing purchasing power as inflation outstrips their savings rate of return, or they are further adding fuel to the fire by investing their money into other assets that they hope will outperform inflation. And by investing their money into other assets, such as housing or stocks, they are further inflating the asset bubbles that are unlikely to be sustainable over the long term.

SOARING INVESTMENT   Investment as a share of gross domestic product (GDP) reached a record 46.2 percent in 2010.[32] Even though the country may still be developing, having investment comprise nearly 50 percent of GDP is a huge sign of risk and unsustainable euphoria.

REAL ESTATE BUBBLES   As we recently experienced in the United States, many emerging markets will soon undergo massive real estate collapses when investors realize that housing prices cannot go up forever. With heavy investment from inhabitants and foreigners into emerging market real estate, asset bubbles have been almost inevitable. The claim has been that the massive population growth and increasing wealth will spur many to search for new homes and apartments. But with residential housing investment making up 9 percent of economic output (3.4 percent in 2003), a three-month unsold inventory of apartments (which means that supply has outgrown demand), and massive risk exposure to real estate by banks, the upcoming real estate fiasco could truly derail world economies.[33] Even government officials and real estate executives have been warning of housing bubbles, especially in Hong Kong, where home prices have risen more than 70 percent since the start of 2009.[34]

Ghost towns are appearing, with one city equipped with museums, libraries, suburbs, and four-lane highways and built for 1.5 million people, but only housing approximately 20,000 people.[35] It has been estimated that there are currently as many as 64 million empty homes in China.[36] So, too, with the South China Mall in Dongguan (one of 500 malls built in China over the past five years[37]), which was built with the capacity for 1,500 tenants but has filled only 15 to 20 spots (a nearly 99 percent vacancy rate).[38]

Confirmation of a slowing real estate market on the verge of collapse continues to surface: China's big cities reported decreases in apartment sales in September and October 2011, with apartment sales in Beijing dropping 22.8 percent year over year during the week-long National Day holiday.[39] With declining prices and sales during what are supposed to be the "boom months," a real estate bubble is increasingly clear.

OVERCONFIDENCE IN BUYING

One of the most natural ways to find overconfidence in the market is to look for world record prices, or any type of world record set from

> *an asset perspective. That is usually a sign of national hubris and*
> *overconfidence being manifested in the form of buying behavior.*[40]
>
> —Vikram Mansharamani

Chinese overconfidence and extreme speculation is evident in the re-cord-setting bidding at art auctions (a Picasso purchased for $110 million), the growing market in expensive wines, a dog that was sold for over $1 million, the world's most expensive racing pigeon, and "mutton fat jade"—once used to fill bags to hold back flooding rivers—now selling for more than twice the price of gold![41]

SKYSCRAPER INDICATOR   The speculative and arrogant behavior inherent in massive skyscraper construction may be distinct proof that the investment mania and period of rapid growth is nearing its end.

As Vikram Mansharamani, Yale lecturer and author on financial booms and busts, points out, the construction of record-setting skyscrapers is a major indicator of speculative excess and a warning of impending economic slowdown. He points to New York in 1929, where three sites competed for the status of world's tallest building—40 Wall Street, the Chrysler Building, and the Empire State Building—right before the Great Depression; to the early 1970s, with the construction of the World Trade Center and the Sears Tower, followed by a decade of stagflation; to 1997, with the completion of the Petronas Towers in Malaysia right before the currency crisis of Southeast Asia; to 1999, with the beginning of construction on Taipei 101, at the height of the technology bubble; to 2007 to 2008, with the record-setting building of Burj Dubai at the height of the credit bubble; and now to China, where 5 out of 10 of the largest towers in the world are under construction.

> *Why does this indicator work? Because the world's tallest skyscraper un-der construction is usually a sign of, first, speculative excesses—remember they are built by developers not the people who plan to occupy them. Second, there is no economic reason to pursue world's tallest status—that's a simple manifestation of hubris and national overconfidence. And third, easy money—these things are never built with full equity financing—they're usually built relying heavily on other people's money.*[42]

FRAUDULENT COMPANIES

> *One of the characteristics of manias, especially in their final days, is that they are usually riddled with fraud . . . . The uncovering of such dishonesty adds fuel to the downward spiral in prices.*[43]
>
> —Martin Pring

A number of Chinese companies listed on U.S. and Canadian exchanges have been exposed for committing accounting fraud.[44] It has been relatively easy for fraudulent companies to gain access to U.S. investors and list on foreign exchanges, since the massive euphoria regarding the Chinese economy has created the illusion that nearly all Chinese companies could be profitable. Just like the dot-com bubble in the late 1990s to 2000, investors have simply bought almost any company that has any connection to the profitable China theme. In 2000 it was any technology company, now it's any Chinese company. When investors begin to realize that much of their investment has been speculation, especially in fraudulent companies without proven financials or profits, the China theme may come to an end.

UNNOTICED FALLING MARKET   One of the biggest threats to global markets is the "invisible" and largely unnoticed declines in the stock markets of emerging markets in 2011. Most U.S. investors still base much of their investment decisions on the assumption that emerging markets are the future for growth, and they refuse to accept most negative news that may disprove the emerging markets thesis. In the meantime, however, emerging countries have seen their stock markets fall nearly 30 percent! Not only are these drops much greater than the U.S. stock market declines, but the larger failure of emerging markets over U.S. markets could be a very severe warning that the emerging market theme is over. Without emerging markets leading the way for global growth, most investors who based their investment decisions on continued rapid growth will no longer be able to justify their claims. Instead, the economic and financial turmoil that may ensue in countries like China and Brazil could derail the global market.

As seen in Figure 6.37, China's Shanghai Stock Exchange has not made new highs since August 2009! Brazil's Bovespa Index is now in a bear market[45] following a drop of over 30 percent since November 2010 (see Figure 6.38).

The ongoing and largely unnoticed weakness in emerging markets is a huge threat to continued global growth. Emerging markets may have led the way into the 2009 to 2010 recovery, but they may also be leading us back into recession as their growth has spiraled out of control and as excess speculation has created asset bubbles across real estate and stocks. If China, Brazil, and other emerging markets continue to show weakness, global economies will likely enter a renewed recession. A renewed recession will not only result in falling stock prices, but will also take its toll on commodities as emerging market growth no longer supports the massive increases we've seen in commodity prices. And if commodity prices fall, they will likely drag gold down with them.

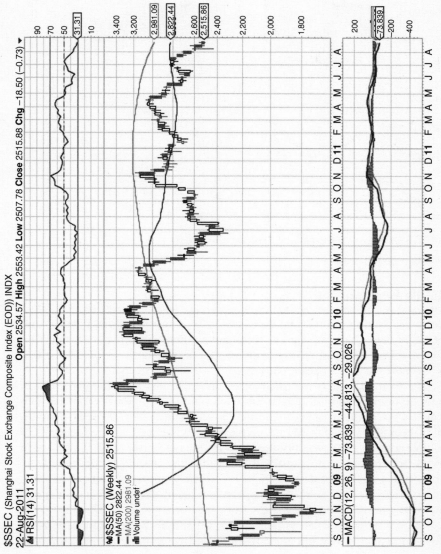

FIGURE 6.37 Shanghai Stock Exchange Fails to Make New Highs

Source: StockCharts.com.

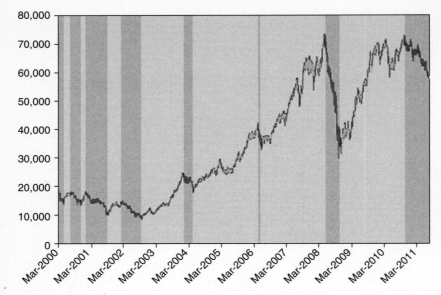

FIGURE 6.38 Brazil's Bovespa Index Enters Bear Market
Source: Bespoke Investment Group.

Middle East Upheaval

Problems continue in the Middle East, following upheavals in Egypt, Tunisia, Libya, Syria, Yemen, Algeria, Iraq, and a number of other countries. Citizens revolted over oppressive regimes, unfair treatment, poor economies, high costs of living, and other injustices.

We warned readers in January and June 2011 that all of the instability in the region was a sign of more trouble to come. A number of countries' citizens have attempted, or succeeded in, ousting leadership. Even if the political upheaval was to subside (which it hasn't), the economic effects would still materialize; the revolutions and protests have undoubtedly put a strain on the region's economy and will likely affect segments of the rest of the globe. The United States' and others' involvement in such matters will affect their own economies, as they attempt to stabilize the region, feel some trade disruption, and may engage in new wars.

Moreover, we warned in January 2011 that a housing bubble may have formed in Israel, and could affect the rest of the region. A housing bubble in Israel is not confined to Israel, and could affect other parts of the world as well. It may be the case that the United States' real estate bubble preceded bubbles in other parts of the world, and that the bursting of these other bubbles (in countries like China) will follow. Regardless of whether or not stability returns to the region, economic damage has been done that may trigger a worldwide crisis—especially with the addition of slowing emerging markets, a European banking crises, and economic contagion.

Egyptian Stock Market Bodes Poorly for Middle East

Originally published June 24, 2011: "Egyptian Stock Market Bodes Poorly for Middle East," *Seeking Alpha.*[46]

Egyptian Revolution of January to February 2011.

As protesters were able to effectively oust President Hosni Mubarak from office following their strong campaign against police brutality, lack of free elections and freedom of speech, corruption, state of emergency laws, high unemployment, inflation and other economic issues—the market (as represented by the Egypt ETF [EGPT]) bounced back after sharply falling in January over the upheaval in the country.

Yet while the market bounced back a considerable amount following the successful overthrow of Mubarak, the market has actually dropped to new lows since then (see Figure 6.39). In other words, even though

FIGURE 6.39 Egypt Stocks Make New Lows

Source: StockCharts.com, Chart Prophet LLC.

it seemed as if the majority of the problems in Egypt were solved, the market may be telling us that they are far from over. A poor economy stands as a very big hurdle for Egypt's future; and Egypt's revolution and economic future may highly affect surrounding countries in the Middle East region.

The Egyptian Revolution sparked protests in other Arab countries as well—Yemen, Jordan, Bahrain, Libya, and Syria. Protests may prove to be socially beneficial in the longer term, but can severely disrupt the economy in the short to medium term.

With Egypt's apparent market and economic weakness as of late—and especially since the market is actually lower today than it was at the height of the revolution—it appears that the Middle East and surrounding areas may see some increased weakness and potential for economic and social upheaval. The weakness in the area bodes poorly for those countries and, potentially, Middle-East-related stocks and markets.

Housing Bubble in Israel?

Originally published January 25, 2011: "Housing Bubble in Israel?," *Seeking Alpha*.[47]

With housing prices soaring nearly 20 percent in 2010, as well as continued fears of an overheated and unsustainable housing market, Israel's central bank has raised interest rates a number of times in order to cool the frothy markets.

After cutting interest rates from 5.25 percent to a record low 0.5 percent over the past few years, Israel's housing market has seen rapid price acceleration that has made it difficult, and even impossible, for many of Israel's inhabitants to purchase homes. And the loose monetary policies that Israel has employed have made easy loans and speculative buying an all-too-common occurrence in recent times.

With three-bedroom homes in Tel Aviv selling for $600,000 while the average salaries of Israelis are nowhere near high enough to properly sustain such high-value mortgages, a bubble is increasingly likely. Just as we have seen in the U.S. housing bubble, easy loans and exorbitant housing prices are the crucial ingredients of a housing bubble; and these factors seem to be exactly what is occurring in the Israeli market.

Three warning signals in particular have already surfaced.

1. Interest rates have increased from 0.5 percent to 3.25 percent in an effort to cool the soaring housing prices and potential inflation troubles.
2. The Bank of Israel's governor, Stanley Fischer, has warned of an impending bubble, saying "Prices have risen over 20 percent in the past

FIGURE 6.40 Israel ETF Plummets
Sources: thinkorswim, Chart Prophet LLC.

year, and if they continue to rise at this pace we will have a bubble." These are not comforting words from the man in charge of controlling these scenarios.

3. The Bank of Israel issued stricter mortgage lending rules in June 2010, lowering the loan-to-value ratio from 70 to 60 percent—in effect requiring homebuyers to put more money down for their purchases than was previously required. This is a sign that loans have been too easy, and another sign of an overheated housing market with loan defaults on the horizon.

The combination of soaring home prices, loose monetary policies, easy loans, and speculative buying have made an Israeli housing bubble very likely.

With prices so far beyond reasonable in comparison to the average Israeli salary, it appears that a similar housing bubble to the one we have just experienced in the United States is underway. With the threat of hostilities in the region constantly on the horizon (which sent home prices down 11.6 percent in 2006 due to the war between Israel and Hezbollah) and the Bank of Israel's recent interest rate hikes to control inflation and cool the housing market, Israel's housing market may be in a bubble that is on the verge of deflating.

In fact, since the writing of "Housing Bubble in Israel?," the Israel ETF (EIS) is down nearly 30 percent as of September 2011 (see Figure 6.40).

European Crisis

Perhaps one of the largest threats to the global economy, Europe's tremendous instability could ensure a global economic catastrophe. Similar to

Lehman Brothers' role in triggering or exacerbating the financial meltdown of 2008, Greece's massive financial troubles may drag all of Europe into a domino-like economic collapse. Since many of the European countries are economically tied to each other through the Euro, the financial collapse of any Eurozone country could severely impact all the other countries. And with the Eurozone countries attempting to stop the contagion by bailing out the failing countries, they could be dragged into the financial mess themselves.

Greece is in no way the only problem. Italy, Spain, Portugal, Ireland, and others are all at huge risk of collapsing and dragging the rest of the world into their mess. Unemployment levels have reached over 20 percent in some countries, with youth unemployment nearly double that. The strongest countries, Germany and France, have been greatly impacted by the massive financial upheavals—having already entered bear markets, as their stock markets are down approximately 30 percent from their peaks. Europe's leaders, together with central banks, have attempted to fix these disastrous conditions; but unless the contagion can be contained and limited to Greece, we can expect financial meltdown in "snowball" fashion to ensue—as collapse and default spreads from country to country, dragging financially responsible countries like Germany into the mess created by Greece, Italy, Spain, and others.

Just take a look at the massive leverage taken on by European banks in Table 6.3—more than twice that of American banks before the 2008 crisis.

TABLE 6.3 European Banking Crisis

Bank	Leverage	Tangible Equity
Landesbank Berli	53.04	1.43%
Dexia SA	52.83	1.49%
Deutsche Bank-RG	37.82	1.83%
Danske Bank A/S	30.68	2.55%
Credit Agricole	30.56	1.97%
ING GROEP-ADR	26.37	3.36%
Commerzbank	26.32	3.39%
UBS AG-REG	25.40	3.19%
Barclays PLC	23.93	3.60%
Nordea Bank AB	23.67	3.67%
BNP Paribas	23.33	3.59%
Credit Suiss-ADR	22.86	3.51%
Soc Generale	22.21	3.71%
Lloyds Banking	21.14	4.17%
Royal BK Scotland	18.91	4.29%
Fortis Banque	17.75	5.61%

Source: http://hussmanfunds.com/wmc/wmc111017.htm.

Conclusion

Gold depends on more factors than most people realize. Not just limited to economic uncertainty or currency devaluation, the factors that affect gold prices include the stock market, the direction of the U.S. dollar, emerging market growth and demand, and global crises stemming out of the Middle East and Europe. Gold's massive rise over the past decade is attributable to growing fears over failing and stagnant stock markets, as well as the loss of faith in paper currencies. Ironically, however, gold's massive rise has also been heavily reliant on continued emerging market demand and rising commodity prices—factors that will not persist if a global recession develops. In other words, gold is expected to provide a "safe haven" in the event of economic catastrophe, but that will likely not be the case, as gold plummets together with other asset classes if a worldwide recession takes hold. Instead of benefiting from a falling dollar, continued emerging market growth, and an inverse correlation to stocks, gold is likely to collapse as the dollar makes a comeback, emerging countries lead the global economy into recession, and stock markets drag gold and other asset classes down. Exacerbated by Middle East upheaval and a European crisis, economic shocks will likely be felt across the globe, hurting stock markets and commodity prices as future growth expectations are not met. Gold is not immune to plunging asset prices. Gold's "safe haven" status is a myth.

Now that we have pointed out the signs of a gold bubble, the probability that gold is an *unsafe* haven, and the factors that are likely to contribute to the end of gold's massive bull market, it is time to look for the reversal signals confirming that a peak is rapidly approaching.

CHAPTER 7

Calling the Top: Signs of Reversal

S potting a bubble is not enough. In order to accurately predict a bubble and successfully profit from its collapse, it is tremendously important to anticipate when the peak will occur and not to risk too much until the coming collapse is confirmed. Betting against a bubble with extreme momentum behind it could wipe you out financially. It is therefore critical that claims of a bubble be confirmed with signs of an imminent top, and that those who wish to profit from the collapse of a bubble limit their risk until a peak is near certain.

A number of signs pointing to an imminent peak and upcoming reversal in gold have surfaced.

Lagging Mining Stocks Signal Reversals in Gold and Silver Prices

Originally published May 10, 2011: "Mining Stocks Signaling Reversals in Gold and Silver Prices," *Seeking Alpha.*[1]

Gold prices have set considerable new highs since late 2010, but the gold miners continue to lag behind.

After dropping from the all-time-high price of $1,435.70 an ounce set in December 2010, gold has since broken out to new all-time-highs above $1,900 an ounce. Over the same time, however, the stocks of many gold miners and especially the broad gold miners ETFs (GDX and GDXJ) have not made new highs in the same fashion—and may be signaling an upcoming drop in gold.

Shares of companies related to the underlying commodity tend to move together with the commodity itself. Rising oil shares tend to accompany rising oil prices, rising gold miner shares tend to accompany rising gold prices, and so forth. Furthermore, the stocks of the related companies usually change direction before the commodity itself does. Therefore, when commodity-related companies start rising while the commodity has been falling, it is a good buying opportunity before the commodity itself turns up. On the flip side of that, as the related company shares start to drop while the commodity continues to rise, it is an early warning of a possible trend change. It can be said, therefore, that energy shares are a leading indicator for oil and that gold mining shares are a leading indicator for gold.

If, in fact, stocks tied to a certain commodity (like oil or gold in our case) do lead the underlying commodity itself, the direction of those stocks can serve as the leading indicator of the upcoming direction of the commodity. In our case, since the gold miners have been lagging behind gold itself, we may be seeing the beginning of the turn down in gold.

As shown in Figure 7.1, gold miners have been significantly lagging behind gold as of late.

The same could be said for silver (SLV) and the silver miners (SIL). The divergence between the miners and silver itself (seen in Figure 7.2) could even have alerted investors to be wary of silver *before* the big drop from May to October 2011, in which silver prices fell nearly 50 percent. Silver (SLV), top line, Silver Miners (SIL), bottom line.

Time will tell if the recent divergences between gold (GLD) and the gold miners (GDX) and between silver (SLV) and the silver miners (SIL) were only warnings for the corrections we saw recently, or if they stand as stark warnings of a much greater upcoming reversal that could see the bursting of the precious metals bubble.

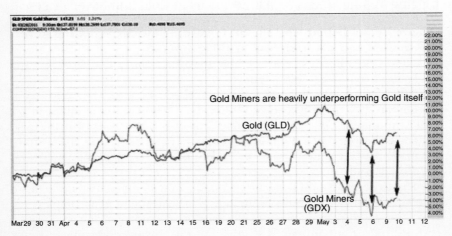

FIGURE 7.1 Gold Miners Lag Gold
Source: thinkorswim, Chart Prophet LLC.

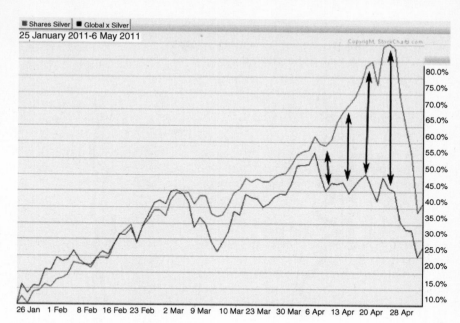

FIGURE 7.2 Silver Miners Lag Silver

Source: StockCharts.com, Chart Prophet LLC.

Gold versus Gold Miners

Compare the new highs in the Gold ETF (GLD) with the failure in the Gold Miners ETF (GDX), shown in Figure 7.3.

Gold has been outperforming the miners for much of the past four or more years (2006 to 2011), as Figure 7.4 shows.

GOLD/GOLD MINERS RATIO According to the ratio of gold to the miners,[2] the miners outperformed from late 2000 until 2004, when gold began to out-perform. With gold's summer 2011 rallies, it has likely broken out of the channel in Figure 7.5 and has continued its outperformance over the miners.

While gold has continued its run to over $1,900 an ounce from late 2010 until September 2011, the gold miners (GDX) have moved sideways over the same time period and have not held new highs since December 2010. The failure of the miners to make and hold considerable new highs is a major warning sign, especially when the lagging of the gold miners has lasted nearly a year. Gold may have continued to run up; but without confirmation by the gold miners, the gold theme may be nearing an end. These diver-gences in the gold miners should be given very close attention as a potential early warning.

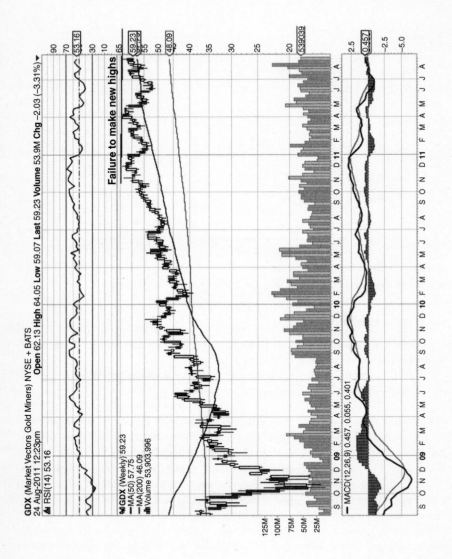

GDX (Market Vectors Gold Miners) NYSE + BATS
24-Aug-2011 12:23pm   Open 62.13 High 64.05 Low 59.07 Last 59.23 Volume 53.9M Chg −2.03 (−3.31%) ▼

RSI(14) 53.16

53.16

Failure to make new highs

GDX (Weekly) 59.23
— MA(50) 57.75
— MA(200) 46.09
Volume 53,903,996

59.23

48.09

539039

MACD(12,26,9) 0.457, 0.055, 0.401

0.457

146

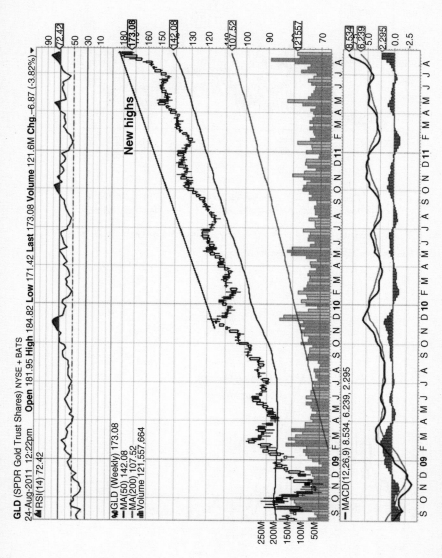

FIGURE 7.3 Miners Fail and Gold Makes Significant Highs

Source: StockCharts.com, Chart Prophet LLC.

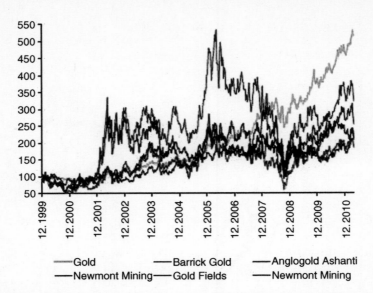

FIGURE 7.4 Performance of Gold versus Performance of Major Gold Producers
Source: Datastream, Erste Group Research.

FIGURE 7.5 Gold/Gold Miners Ratio
Source: Erste Group Research, Datastream.

Bernanke and Buffett "Puzzled by Gold Rally"[3]

The likelihood that investors and speculators would heed the warnings of a government official when asset prices are increasing at annual rates of 20 to 30 percent a year is not especially high.[4]

—Charles Kindleberger

Federal Reserve Chairman Ben Bernanke—the man in charge of the whole country's monetary policy, with the responsibility of maintaining a stable financial system and preventing panics—has admitted that he does not "fully understand movements in the gold price."[5] Generally, huge rallies in gold are interpreted as upcoming inflationary pressures, as investors buy gold as a hedge against inflation. But, as Bernanke pointed out, inflation is not being signaled by other asset classes as it is with gold: yields on Treasury bonds, which usually rise when investors expect inflation, have actually fallen; and prices of other commodities have been falling as well. Yet the gold price continues to reach new highs. When the highest official in charge of financial markets and monetary policy is puzzled by huge increases in the price of gold, a bubble is very possible.

Adding to the confusion, Congressman Ron Paul asked Bernanke in July 2011 if gold is "money." Bernanke responded "No: Gold is an asset." He then continued, saying "the reason that people hold gold is as a protection against what we call tail risks: really, really bad outcomes."[6] It is true that many investors have bought gold as a hedge against worst-case outcomes; however, if gold is not money, but an asset bought in speculation of severe upcoming economic turmoil, it will drop significantly if the expected calamity doesn't materialize. Moreover, even if severe economic collapse does take place, gold may still lose much of its value since recessions decrease the value of nearly all asset classes. Gold may hold strength *relative* to other asset classes, but its *absolute* value will drop. If the most powerful banking and financial government official is confused by the gold rally, investors should be very wary.

Stock market icon Warren Buffett doesn't seem to care for gold either:

"Look," he says, with his usual confident laugh. "You could take all the gold that's ever been mined, and it would fill a cube 67 feet in each direction. For what that's worth at current gold prices, you could buy all—not some—all of the farmland in the United States. Plus, you could buy 10 Exxon Mobils, plus have $1 trillion of walking-around money. Or you could have a big cube of metal. Which would you take? Which is going to produce more value?"[7]

Dollar Strength and Market Weakness

As we've illustrated, the value of gold depends greatly on dollar weakness and emerging market strength. However, I predict the dollar will likely recover and emerging markets will enter a period of disappointing growth or even recession. And so far, it appears the predictions are coming true, as the dollar is showing increasing momentum and has not made new lows since early May 2011 (see Figure 7.6). At the same time, emerging markets have not made new highs since late 2010, and are even down close to 30 percent in Brazil and China (see Figure 7.7).

Although U.S. investors have been extremely optimistic about emerging market growth and the global investment story, many investors may be ignoring the ongoing troubles that continue to surface in many countries from Greece and Italy to China and Brazil. And unless the emerging markets are able to deal with their inflationary concerns, rapid and potentially dangerous growth, and overheating housing and investment speculation, they may lead the rest of the world back into recession.

FIGURE 7.6 Dollar Strength
Source: StockCharts.com.

FIGURE 7.7 Emerging Market Troubles
Source: StockCharts.com, Chart Prophet LLC.

Healthy markets require confirmation from most or all parts of the economy—all or most market caps, all or most sectors, and especially all or most of the economic world powers. If countries like China and India, on which our world economy ultimately depends, are struggling, we may inevitably be affected. If segments of our own economy (such as the transports, small-caps, or financials) fail to confirm the overall market direction, we should at least be paying some attention. This may be a critical juncture that could impact the next few months or even years. Finally, if the dollar gains strength and emerging market weakness persists, the commodity run-up will most likely end as global growth fades. And since much of gold's move has been based on inflation, the commodity price surge, emerging market growth, and the demise of the dollar, the gold bubble could be coming to an end.

Declining Momentum

Though the price of gold has continued to soar, the momentum behind future increases has declined. The most obvious and visible sign of

08/12/2011 c=1740.2 +91.4 o=1697.0 H=1781.3 L=1697.0 Mov Avg 3 lines

FIGURE 7.8 Open Interest Divergence

Source: tradingcharts.com.

momentum is a continued run-up in prices, but if that momentum is not confirmed by other, more discrete indicators, a reversal is possible. In the case of gold, both open interest and ETF holdings are failing to confirm the record-high gold prices. Gold has continued making new highs from late 2010 to August 2011, but both open interest (which indicates future demand via the flow of money into commodity futures) and GLD holdings (which measures the amount of physical gold held in the trust of the most popular gold ETF) have failed to make new highs in 2011 (see Figures 7.8 and 7.9). When indicators that generally trend together with the underlying price fail to make new highs (known as a "divergence"), an early warning is triggered.

Big Guys Selling: "Smart" Money Leads the Way

Gold investors are by no means alone. Their decision to invest in gold is strongly supported by the "experts" and "smart money"—highly recognized individuals and financial gurus such as hedge fund icons John Paulson, Paul Tudor Jones, Ray Dalio, Peter Schiff, and David Einhorn—who have also invested in gold. Billionaire investor George Soros also heavily invested in gold, but disposed of the bulk of his position in 2011, reducing his holdings from 4.721 million shares of the SPDR Gold Trust (GLD) to only 49,400 shares.[8] While he has added stocks of gold miners to his portfolio, Soros's

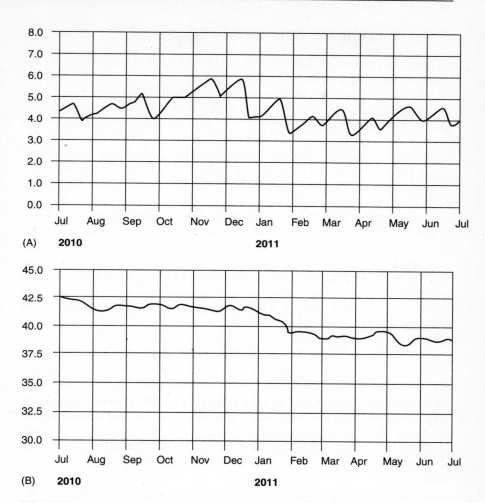

FIGURE 7.9 (A) Declining GLD Option Open Interest (Millions of Contracts) and (B) GLD Holdings (Millions of Troy Ounces)

Source: Richard Bloch, "Gold and Silver Interest: What Options Are Telling Us," *Seeking Alpha,* July 6, 2011.[9]

large exit from the gold trade may signal the beginning stages of the bubble's collapse, as gold bugs begin to realize the risks and as selling pressure mounts. As more gold investors decrease their exposure or divest from gold, the negative feedback loop—which carries the bubble on the way down through fear and panic—can gain traction.

Is the Commodity Run-Up about to Reverse Course?

Originally published February 7, 2011: "Is the Commodity Run-Up about to Reverse Course?," *Seeking Alpha.*[10]

With wheat, cotton (BAL), corn (CORN), sugar (SGG), coffee (JO), and the broader agriculture sector (AGF, DAG, DBA) gaining as much as 250 percent from mid-2010 to early 2011, there is no doubt commodities have led the way and will continue to be the center of much attention in the upcoming months. But after such huge run-ups—which have been spurred on by continuing global growth, surging global demand, and a very high degree of speculative buying—is the commodity play about to reverse course? Is it too late to get in?

Admittedly, I have been avoiding the commodity play even as it has continued to soar. Prices have been rising much too sharply for a cautious investor to simply jump in. And since I have been warning of a gold bubble for a few months, I decided it would be best to avoid joining the overspeculation in the rest of the commodity markets as well. Yet while I have missed the boat thus far, as commodities have soared due to inflationary and demand-driven concerns, I believe we are currently at a saturation level and may be setting up for a sharp correction.

It is true that global demand has grown and that more food and supplies are going to be highly sought-after as the world and emerging markets continue to expand. But at what point can we separate the demand that's driven by real world needs and the demand that's driven by the speculation and expectations of global growth? In other words, much of the spike in commodity prices is due to investors and countries betting on prices continuing higher, rather than actual consumer demand for these products. And since prices may be high due to overspeculation, now may be a good time to at least be cautious, if not avoid the commodity play altogether.

I have already discussed why I think the precious metals space is weakening, and why we should avoid the gold (GLD), silver (SLV), palladium (PALL), and copper (JJC) plays, among others. But with the emergence of a wide variety of agriculture and commodity ETFs over the past few years, and the ease with which the common investor can now invest in these commodities, we are seeing very heightened speculative behavior by many market participants.

Here's why the commodity theme may be in danger of correction or reversal: As we've discussed in the case of gold's fifth and final wave, it appears that other commodities such as sugar and cotton have actually peaked first, ahead of gold. An "ending diagonal" pattern has developed in

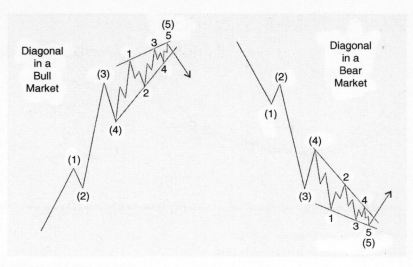

FIGURE 7.10 Ending Diagonals

Source: A. J. Frost, and Robert R. Prechter Jr., *Elliott Wave Principle: Key to Market Behavior*, 10th ed. (Gainesville, GA: New Classics Library, 2005), 37.

sugar and cotton and could be signaling the beginning of the end for the commodity bull market.

As Elliott and later Frost and Prechter pointed out, "an ending diagonal occurs primarily in the fifth wave position at times when the preceding move has gone "too far too fast' . . . . In all cases, they are found at the *termination points of larger patterns*, indicating exhaustion of the larger movement."[11] Figure 7.10 shows what diagonals look like.

Perhaps there is no greater proof of a commodity price surge than in the case of sugar (SGG) and cotton (BAL). Both have been up way over 100 percent in less than a year starting in mid-2010, and have created much strain and potential future burdens on companies who use sugar or cotton in their products. In other words, the higher the cost for the inputs of these companies, the lower the profits these companies can make unless they raise their own prices. And besides for the fact that high commodity prices can severely slow growth, there is some technical weakness in these charts, with Figures 7.11 and 7.12 telegraphing "ending diagonals" in sugar and cotton.

In order to understand the commodity markets, then, we can look at sugar and cotton as our main determinants of the overall commodity sector direction. And as you can see in Figure 7.12, sugar may currently be in an ending diagonal—which will see price break down through the bottom

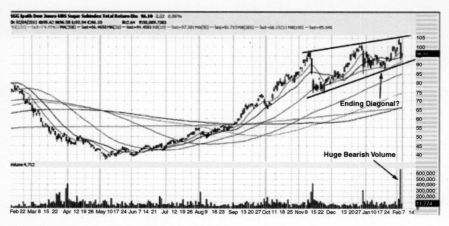

FIGURE 7.11 Ending Diagonal in Sugar

Source: thinkorswim, Chart Prophet LLC.

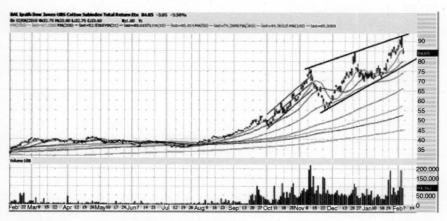

FIGURE 7.12 Ending Diagonal in Cotton

Source: thinkorswim, Chart Prophet LLC.

trendline and enter into a steep correction. Considering we just witnessed a huge down day for sugar, which was backed by huge selling volume, the correction may be upon us. If we do the same analysis for cotton (BAL) in Figure 7.12, we notice the same situation.

Also in an ending diagonal, and on an even sharper price ascent, cotton had two big down days on fairly large volume. Add to that the "outside day" or "bearish engulfing" in terms of candle patterns in early February 2011—which is a very prominent reversal pattern—and we may be right at the top before a severe downturn.

Paying close attention to sugar and cotton, as well as the broader commodity and agriculture sectors, over the next few days or weeks will be vital to predicting future market direction. If we continue seeing weakness, we may be in for some trouble. Our recommendation to investors would therefore be one of caution, profit taking, and even some diligent short-selling. Inflation and continued demand could cause commodity prices to continue higher, but after such huge price run-ups, at such a critical juncture in global economic growth, and with such tremendous speculation currently involved in these commodity plays, we may be nearing a considerable correction. Caution is key.

Commodity Declines in 2011

Commodities have seen massive declines in 2011. Gold may have continued higher, but cotton is down over 50 percent, sugar saw a drop of over 40 percent, wheat dropped 30 percent, crude oil dropped over 30 percent, and copper has been down 30 percent (see Figure 7.13). Not only are these

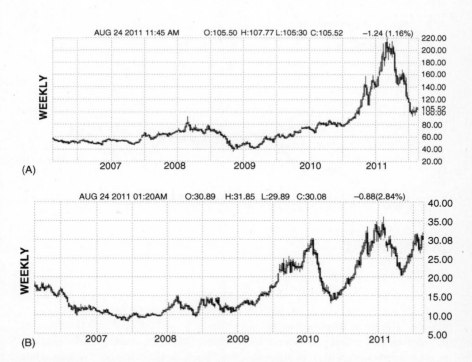

FIGURE 7.13 Commodity Declines in 2011: (A) Cotton, (B) Sugar, (C) Wheat, (D) Crude Oil, and (E) Copper

Source: www.finviz.com.

FIGURE 7.13 (*Continued*)

massive declines forewarning of an economic slowdown and commodity implosion, but when investors start realizing that commodities have actually been plummeting while most people had been optimistic about future price rises, they will likely panic and sell any investments that have commodity exposure. Gold will likely not be safe from the onslaught, and will drop together with the broad commodity space.

Copper and Oil Signal Recession

Originally published October 12, 2011: "Copper and Oil Signal Recession, but Battered Japan May Outperform," *Seeking Alpha.*[12]

Copper and oil have historically been regarded as indicators of economic conditions. When copper and oil prices are rising, industrial growth is expected to follow, which results in economic expansion. The opposite case—when copper and oil prices are falling—indicates an economic slowdown and potential recession.

COPPER As shown in Figure 7.14, copper had broken above the 2008 highs it set before the onset of the Great Recession, but has fallen very sharply since its early 2011 peak—with prices collapsing by over 30 percent from August through September. Copper is looking to rebound from these levels, but will likely not regain recent highs. Instead, the sharp drop in copper may be signaling the onset of a renewed recession. China and emerging markets are slowing down, which lowers demand for copper. Lowered demand and slowing growth may result in recessions.

The best way to invest in copper through stocks had traditionally been Freeport McMoRan (FCX), seen in Figure 7.15. FCX provided investors with exposure to copper, as the company operates gold and copper mines. FCX was one of the only copper-related stocks around for years. FCX is therefore a pretty good indicator for future copper prices, and in turn also the future of the economy.

While actual copper prices broke above their 2008 highs by approximately 20 percent, FCX broke above its 2008 highs by less than 1 percent. It also did not hold above the previous highs, and failed at that level—marking a *double top* formation at $60 per share. This double top

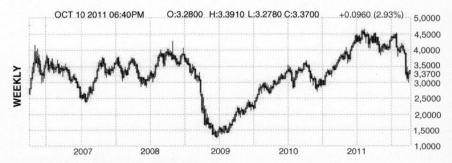

FIGURE 7.14 Copper Signals Recession

Source: www.finviz.com.

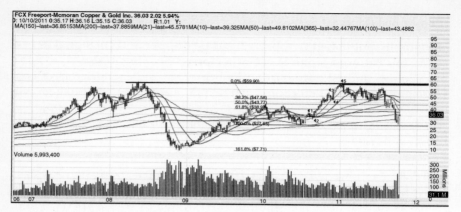

FIGURE 7.15 Freeport McMoRan Fails to Confirm Copper's Rise
Source: thinkorswim, Chart Prophet LLC.

formation should be hard to break above and hold; previous highs should act as very strong resistance if prices approach them. FCX may bounce here after retracing to the 2010 lows, but unless previous highs are exceeded and maintained, recession is much more likely as copper has signaled a downturn.

OIL AND ENERGY   Oil prices soared in 2007 and 2008 only to come crashing down with the onset of the Great Recession. Oil and energy essentially turned into a bubble as investors piled into crude oil and energy-related plays as a way to profit from the soaring prices. However, recessions generally result in lower demand for energy, as economic growth is not there to boost prices. Oil was the best example of a commodity bubble, as its tremendous collapse in 2008 is clearly visible in Figure 7.16.

Oil, as represented by the oil ETF (OIL), has bounced from its 2009 low, but has recently resumed the downtrend as it appears to have broken down from an "ending diagonal" that signaled a sharp drop, seen in Figure 7.17.

The huge drop in Crude, from $115 to nearly $75, is a signal of a slowing global economy. If the economy slows, less oil is demanded. Oil's drop, together with the drop of many other commodities like sugar (SGG), cotton (BAL), platinum (PPLT), and silver (SLV), is signaling an economic slowdown or renewed recession. While commodity prices may bounce from the September or October 2011 lows, they will likely not break above recent highs and have likely peaked. Gold is a commodity as well, and a plunge in the broader commodity space bodes very poorly for the gold bubble.

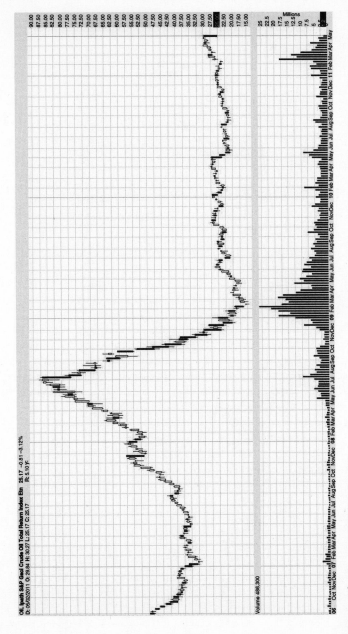

FIGURE 7.16 The Oil Bubble Collapse

Source: thinkorswim.com

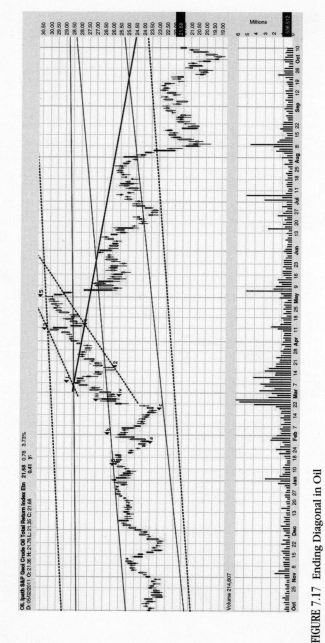

FIGURE 7.17 Ending Diagonal in Oil

Source: thinkorswim, Chart Prophet LLC.

Commodities Still a Bubble, but Prices May Continue to Rise

Originally published May 9, 2011: "Commodities Still a Bubble, but Prices May Continue to Rise *Seeking Alpha*.[13]

After a 900-plus percent and nearly 500 percent skyrocketing run-up in silver and gold prices, respectively, since 2001, the market finally woke up in early May 2011 and corrected the soaring investor enthusiasm that has carried the prices of precious metals, oil, and commodities to extreme and historically unsustainable levels. Moves of such magnitude are *never* sustainable and are almost always inevitably due for a much more severe collapse as institutions, skilled investors, and—most devastatingly—the average investors who got in too late, panic and sell as prices continue to plummet.

Notice the massive gains in gold and silver while stocks have lagged heavily (Figure 7.18).

Gold was the first focus of investor enthusiasm, for the following five reasons.

1. Gold offered a much better alternative to the struggling stock market.
2. It was expected to offer the only real store of value at a time when dollars and paper money seem to be doomed to fail.
3. It would protect investors from both inflation and deflation (though someone has to be wrong).
4. It continues to see demand growth across the globe.
5. It has many fundamental reasons to continue rising.

As gold continued to rise, silver started rising at an even more rapid pace, as enthusiastic investors bought it in a frenzy because it was both more affordable and has industrial uses. Figure 7.19 shows how silver tremendously outperformed gold from August 2010 to May 2011.

Not only has silver utterly destroyed gold in terms of performance, it has also taken a much bigger hit as investors flocked out of it in early May 2011. Silver dropped nearly 30 percent, while gold dropped less than 10. The massive drop in silver shows us what can happen when extreme enthusiasm comes to a screeching halt—something that could easily happen to gold and the entire commodity space almost instantly.

Moreover, the relatively small drop in gold over the same period shows that gold has some more strength behind it. At the same time, however, the massive drop in silver has taken a lot of attention away from gold—and since I expect gold and silver to move up and down together, I think that the largely ignored move in gold will lead us to much more severe downturns in gold in the future. In other words, when people forget about the huge drop in silver and start to remember that gold could be in

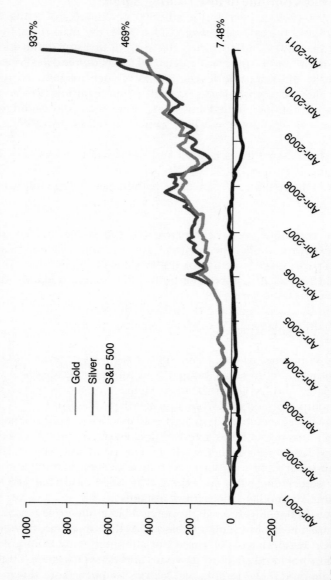

FIGURE 7.18 Ten-Year Percentage Change of Silver, Gold, and the S&P 500

Source: Bespoke Investment Group.

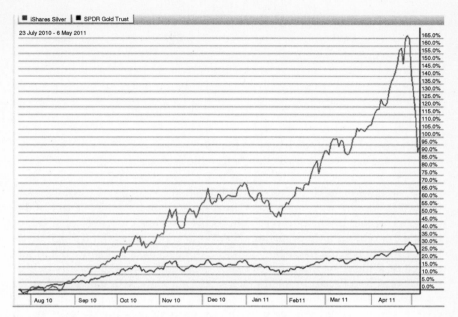

FIGURE 7.19 Silver versus Gold Performance, August 2010—May 2011
Source: StockCharts.com.

danger as well, they will start selling their gold—and prices will drop much more rapidly.

When the bubble bursts—and I am almost completely sure it will, since the evidence is too hard to ignore—you can bet that the drop will not be limited to one or a few commodities. You will certainly see a massive drop in oil, gold, silver, cotton, sugar, platinum, palladium, corn, and just about any ETF or investment that has soared while investors have poured their money into the commodity space.

Has the Bubble Popped?

The question now is whether the commodity bubble has popped or whether it is just a correction before the next leg up. Since I am a full believer that this commodity bubble will pop and will tremendously hurt the average investor, I would caution investors to stay away from the commodity space unless they can monitor it constantly and set very close stops in case prices start to tumble.

On the other hand, such a huge correction is definitely due for at least a short-term bounce as the next wave of investors piles their money into silver, gold, and other commodities. Moreover, I am still unsure if the bubble has truly popped. I am seeing increasing signs of froth and danger in the commodity theme, but I cannot yet rule out a continued run-up that sees even more extreme enthusiasm as investors jump aboard for the final run.

Just as on the way up, prices cannot move straight in one direction without taking breathers or corrections. Therefore, if we have reached the top of the bubble, we will undoubtedly see corrections as some investors buy gold and commodities at what they think to be a bargain price. We are left with two choices:

1. The top of the bubble has been reached.
2. This has just been a correction before the next leg up.

If we have reached the top of the bubble, these temporary bounces and corrections on the way down are a great entry point for selling short. In this case, one would be making very good bets by selling short gold or silver, or buying put options to leverage the drop in prices. On the other hand, if this is just a correction before the next leg up, short sellers must be careful not to stay short if new highs are made. Since I am a believer that this commodity bubble will ultimately collapse, I would rather wait for a more definitive sign that we have reached the bubble top. In my opinion, this has been a very sharp correction and we could still see gold prices reaching new highs—even much higher prices. But whether we have reached the top or will continue to rise to new highs, there is one thing I am sure about: Gold and commodities are in a bubble and will ultimately collapse to the utter shock of millions of people across the globe. We could see a continued run-up to new, and even extreme, highs—but we are entering the final move, if we have not seen it already.

Signs of a reversal have surfaced and have greatly strengthened our argument that gold is in a bubble on the verge of collapse. In addition to the numerous signs pointing to overspeculation, massive publicity, and extreme expectations, we are seeing increasing confirmation that a peak is approaching: stocks of gold mining companies are lagging the move in gold itself; the dollar is recovering to the detriment of gold and commodities; stock markets and economies from the United States to Europe to China are seeing massive declines that could bring gold down with them; momentum is declining; smart money is selling gold; and most of the commodity space has seen major declines in 2011.

The commodity bubble in general, and the gold bubble in particular, has lasted over 10 years. Much of the move has already taken place, and the enthusiasm has had time to build. Now, with much of the fundamental story already factored in, it is time for investor emotions and expectations to take control. Will investors rush to buy as enthusiasm peaks? Or are we just taking a breather before the next, and much steeper, drop? The possibility of a further frenzy and soaring prices is still out there; but even if it is, it will ultimately end in massive drops in prices, huge losses, and a big fat "I told you so!"

CHAPTER 8

Ways to Profit from the Collapse of the Gold Bubble

S potting a bubble and confirming it with evidence of overspeculation and signs of reversal is the first step. But in order to maximize the benefits of correctly predicting a bubble, investors must know how to profit from its collapse. It is one thing to recognize a speculative bubble and avoid investing in the underlying asset; but to be able to profit tremendously while prices fall could be a once-in-a-lifetime opportunity.

This chapter provides a number of ways to profit from the collapse of the gold bubble, from simple and straightforward bets against gold to increasingly complex "pair trades" and options strategies. Readers will have the option to either focus only on gold, or to hedge their bets by targeting the weaker beneficiaries of the gold bubble—such as the gold miners and rare-earth companies. Additionally, since a large part of profitable investing has to do with buying undervalued stocks that offer larger upside potential and relative outperformance, this chapter also presents investment strategies in diamonds and housing—two asset classes that we expect to outperform on a relative basis as the gold bubble collapses.

As with all investing, caution and risk management are key. Investors must limit their risk, cut their losses, and carefully monitor their positions. The following strategies are various ways to profit from the impending collapse of gold, but are not recommended for inexperienced investors. It is strongly advised that investors consult a financial expert before implementing the following strategies.

Short Gold

Perhaps the most direct way to profit from the collapse of the gold bubble is to bet against gold. This can most easily be done by selling short the gold

ETFs, like the GLD, SGOL, and IAU. Short-selling involves potential for unlimited risk, however, so if selling short is not an option, investors can buy an inverse ETF, which goes up if gold goes down—the Gold Double Short (DZZ). The double short ETF has risk limited to what the investor has invested, but should still be closely monitored in order to protect from losses.

Short Gold Miners

Simple short bets on gold may prove to be profitable, but gold's drop won't be as violent as that of most of the gold miners. Just as individual stocks may have a higher risk component (beta) than the broader market, so too the miners generally have a higher risk component than the broader commodity, gold. Add to that the fact that the miners' earnings will plunge significantly when gold prices drop, plus the miners' risky dehedging practices (discussed in Chapter 3) put them in a much more vulnerable position. Miners are therefore set to lose an even larger percentage of their value when the bubble collapses. Investors have taken increased risk by investing downstream from gold to the gold miners. They will, in turn, see greater losses.

In order to profit, then, one could short the gold miners broadly, by shorting GDX or shorting the junior miners (GDXJ). One could also short individual names like Newmont (NEM), Goldcorp (GG), Barrick Gold (ABX), Freeport-McMoRan (FCX), and others in order to take advantage of weakness in specific mining companies. Timing and risk management are key.

Options Strategies

Betting against gold or the gold miners could bring very nice gains as the gold bubble collapses, but gains from simple short bets are nowhere near as profitable as gains from well-executed options strategies. A simple short bet is limited to a 100 percent gain, since the underlying stock cannot lose more than 100 percent of its value. An option, on the other hand, can gain hundreds of percent if the proper strategy is chosen. Options are much more volatile and can lose a larger chunk of their value in a shorter time span; but options also help limit the money at risk, protect investment portfolios or holdings, and offer very profitable leveraged opportunities for those willing to take the risk.

Options strategies can be profitable both for short-term and medium-term moves. Options offer a trader the "option" to buy or sell a stock for a predetermined amount at some point in the future. If an investor thinks the price of a stock will rise, he or she buys "call" options; if the investor thinks the price will drop, he or she buys "put" options. In our case, with gold, investors can buy put options on GLD or GDX to take advantage of the upcoming drop.

To better understand simple options strategies with gold, let's create an example:

We'll assume an investor has $10,000 to bet against gold. If the investor put all $10,000 on a short bet against GLD or GDX, his upside would be limited to a $10,000 gain. Plus, if gold continued higher, the investor could lose a large amount of money as he has to cover his short bet. On the other hand, the investor could use only $1,000 or $2,000 on put options and limit his risk while setting himself up for big potential gains.

In order to profit from an options strategy, one could buy put options on GLD or GDX that don't expire for 200 to 500 days. The long time span gives the investor a considerable amount of time to be right. Moreover, the put options should be bought "out of the money": if GDX, for example, is near $60, the investor can buy put options with a strike price of $50 to $53. An option out of the money is not only cheaper (to make up for the lower strike price), but can offer much bigger gains if the thesis is correct. Instead of paying $10 per share to buy the $60 puts, the investor could pay $5 or less to buy the $50 puts. The same $1,000 or $2,000 the investor was willing to bet can now buy twice the amount of options at the lower strike price. If the price then drops, the cheaper options can gain significantly even if the price doesn't reach the lower strike price. And if the price actually falls to the lower strike price, the profits made on "out of money" options can be massive. Since a collapse of the gold bubble would send gold and gold mining stocks plummeting, "out of the money" put options with a strike price significantly below current prices could still show large returns, as collapsing prices rapidly approach the puts' strike price. Options strategies must be carefully planned and executed with caution.

Short Rare-Earths

Targeting the weakest link could reap the best rewards. By shorting rare-earth related companies like Molycorp (MCP), Rare-Earth Elements (REE), and others, one could target the most speculative of the investments made during the gold bubble.

As investors have continued downstream to derivative plays on gold, like the gold miners, silver, platinum, palladium, and others, they have exponentially increased the speculation and risk now involved in nearly the entire precious metals market.

Rare-earth companies have seen increases of hundreds of percent in less than a year. Their founders and executives have shown some evidence of shady practices, and Molycorp's CEO even called the surge in prices a "bubble" (See Chapter 3). Shorting rare-earth companies may therefore present a leveraged way to profit from the collapse of gold.

Betting on History: A Gold-Platinum Pair Trade

Both a sign that gold is in a bubble and a profitable investment opportunity, platinum prices have dropped below gold prices for the first time in nearly twenty years. Platinum has consistently been worth more than gold as far back as the data goes, with gold being worth more in late 1974 till July 1975, December 1980 to April 1983, July 1984 to October 1985, August 1991 to January 1992, and October 1993 to January 1994.[1] Other than these few instances where gold was more expensive, platinum has continuously regained its title as most expensive precious metal. In fact, every time platinum prices dipped below gold prices, it turned out to be a great buying opportunity for platinum, as platinum prices recovered and even soared in relation to gold. Moreover, other than the brief 1974 to 1975 period during the gold bull market of the 1970s, gold prices have been higher than platinum prices only during bear markets in gold. In other words, when platinum is cheaper it is usually not a good time to buy gold. Figure 8.1 shows how platinum has been approximately equal to or more expensive than gold for most of the past 30 years or longer and has recently become cheaper than gold for the first time since 1994.

Since platinum has historically been more expensive than gold, a great way to profit from the unsustainable gold prices is to short gold and buy platinum. Platinum will fall together with gold when the gold bubble bursts, so it is important to monitor your platinum position and make sure it isn't

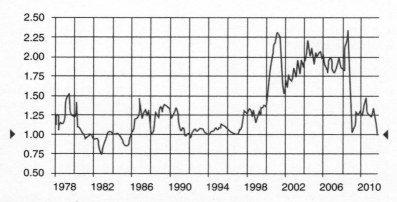

FIGURE 8.1   Ratio of Platinum to Gold, 1978 to Present
Source: Richard Bloch.

falling faster than gold. Buying platinum and shorting gold allows the investor to be *protected* from rising gold prices while still *profiting* from falling gold prices. This platinum-gold "pair trade" works as follows: If gold prices continue to rise, the short positions on gold will lose value but will be offset by rising platinum prices and gains on the long-platinum positions; on the other hand, if gold prices fall, the short position on gold will gain and offset losses in the long-platinum position. Simply put, platinum should be a relative outperformer compared to gold over the next few years, since platinum has historically been more expensive. Therefore, by buying platinum and shorting gold, investors would effectively be betting that the historical relationship between gold and platinum will hold true.

A word of caution, however: platinum still has a chance of falling faster than gold even if the gold bubble collapses. If this is the case, the platinum-gold pair trade would be a loser. Moreover, a pair trade involving such highly correlated metals like platinum and gold provides very little profit potential compared to simple short bets or options strategies. To maximize profits using this pair trade, then, one should closely monitor his or her platinum position and make sure it is not falling faster than gold. Furthermore, if a gold peak is confirmed, one could remove the long-platinum position and keep the short-gold position. Other strategies could include shorting gold and buying call options on platinum, thereby limiting the risk on the long side, or limiting risk by keeping this pair trade through options only (put options on gold, call options on platinum). Regardless, this pair trade offers some insight on how to profit from the gold bubble while still protecting in case gold prices continue to rise.

Forget Gold, Buy Diamonds[2]

As investors, speculators, governments, and funds have piled into gold and other precious metals, they seem to have forgotten about the most valuable asset in the world—the diamond. Symbolizing wealth, quality, and love for centuries, the diamond shares many similarities to gold. Yet, while gold prices have surged nearly 500 percent in 10 years, the prices of diamonds are nearly flat. And though gold offers better use as a store of value and currency hedge, diamonds may begin to catch up as global demand increases and the gold/diamond ratio returns to its historical average.

Seven Reasons Why Diamonds Are a Good Investment

In order to profit as the gold/diamond relationship returns to normal, investors should look to diamonds rather than gold. The following list gives seven reasons in particular why diamonds offer better opportunities than gold.

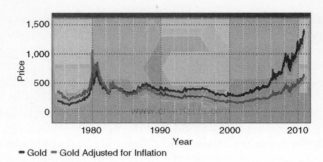

FIGURE 8.2 Gold Prices (Nymex Futures)
Source: Chartfacts.

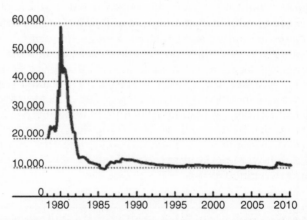

FIGURE 8.3 Diamond Prices: Average Wholesale Price, One-Carat Top-Quality Stone, in 2010 Dollars
Source: Rapaport Diamond Index, U.S. Labor Department.

1. **Diamond/gold price disparity.** While gold is up nearly 500 percent in 10 years, has surpassed its all-time record price of around $800 in 1980, and is nearing its inflation-adjusted record price (also in 1980), diamond prices have almost completely flatlined since the early 1980s, as shown in Figures 8.2 and 8.3.

   As you can see, both gold and diamond prices surged in the late 1970s. But while gold prices have increased tremendously since 2000, diamond prices have lagged heavily.

   If we compare gold and diamond prices from late 2008 until late 2010, it is even more apparent (see Figure 8.4).

PerfChart: GLD

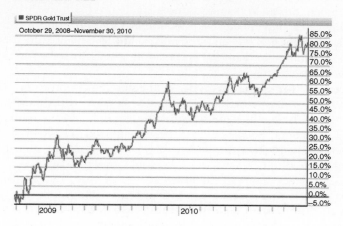

IDEX Online Polished Diamond Price Index

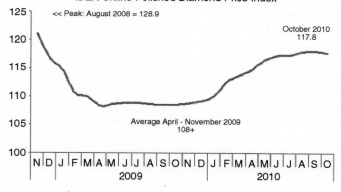

FIGURE 8.4 (A) Gold versus (B) Diamonds
Source: StockCharts.com, IDEX.

While the gold ETF (GLD) was up over 80 percent, diamond prices based on the IDEX Diamond Price Index were actually down about 3 percent over the same time period. With such a wide disparity in price movements between the two precious assets, it may be time to buy the lagging diamond—unless you think gold no longer listens to history and will stay far ahead of diamonds. History usually wins.

2. **Diamonds have industrial use.** Having the highest hardness and heat conductivity of any bulk material, diamonds possess tremendous value for industrial use. Able to polish or cut any material among other uses, diamonds are used in saws, abrasives, construction, computer chip

production, lasers, surgical equipment, and, ironically, mining. In fact, 80 percent of mined diamonds are actually used industrially. With such a staggering percentage used as nonjewelry and noninvestment, the value of diamonds is even more apparent. It is not just valued based on jewelry demand or diamond speculation; it actually serves an important industrial purpose.

3. **Necessary for global growth.** With emerging countries growing rapidly, large infrastructure development is necessary. Roads and highways have to be built, cities must be able to expand, and the required tools must be bought. And since diamonds are utilized in many tools used for stone cutting, highway building, and other technologies, demand for diamonds should increase alongside global growth. Therefore, if emerging economies continue to grow, we can expect diamond usage to grow as well. And if demand grows, prices will likely follow.

4. **Developing nation wealth will increase demand.** Similar to reason number 3, as developing nations and emerging economies grow, demand for diamonds will increase. Yet, while reason number 3 stresses the industrial usage and demand for diamonds due to global growth, this one focuses on the individuals within these countries.

   As emerging countries grow, their populations will become wealthier. And as the individuals become wealthier, they will increase demand for diamonds because they will then be able to afford them. If there are many more people demanding diamonds across the globe, you can expect prices to rise.

5. **Highest value per unit weight.** Diamonds are the most valuable items in the world. A handful of diamonds could make you a multimillionaire. That said, diamonds are the best "portable emergency disaster fund" available. What I mean by that is that diamonds are the lightest and easiest way to store wealth in case of emergency. Stories have been told about people who had to flee their homes and were able to take their precious gems with them as portable wealth. Not that people will have to evacuate their homes and take all of their belongings with them any time soon; but if people are buying gold because it's the best store of value in case of emergency, would you rather carry a diamond or a bunch of gold bricks?

6. **If the consumer is stronger, demand is higher.** If you believe that the economy is recovering, you could expect consumers to recover as well. Consumer confidence has improved since the 2009 lows. If that trend continues, you could expect disposable income and spending to increase as well. And if consumers have more to spend, and actually do spend more, you could expect them to buy more jewelry and more diamonds. Add to that some stronger holiday shopping, and diamond demand increases.

7. **Diamonds have emotional value.** The value of diamond jewelry given as gifts is greatly increased by the emotional component involved. Engagement rings, anniversary gifts, and Valentine's Day presents are just a few examples of how the value of an already-valuable item is exponentially increased. As long as men want to make their women happy, diamonds will continue being valuable assets.

Three Ways to Play This

Considering the wide disparity between gold and diamond price movements since 1999, as well as the multitude of reasons why diamonds should outperform as the gold bubble deflates, an investment in diamonds could reap great benefits—especially when paired with bearish bets on gold or gold miners.

The collapse of the gold bubble and the likely deflationary effect on asset and commodity prices will probably hurt diamond prices as well, but diamonds should be relative outperformers over gold, since they haven't seen as massive run-ups as gold. The following are three ways to pair-trade diamond bullishness with gold bearishness.

1. **Sell gold, buy diamond retailers.** There is currently no diamond ETF or fund, but a good bet on diamonds is either through diamond miners or diamond retailers. If diamond prices start catching up to gold, or if gold prices begin to drop to more sustainable levels, we can expect companies involved in diamond exploration or retailing to outperform gold and gold miners.

    Therefore, a good pair trade would be to sell short gold through the Gold ETF (GLD) or through the Gold Miners ETF (GDX) and to buy diamond retailers such as Zales (ZLC), Blue Nile (NILE), or Tiffany (TIF). As always, monitor your investments, especially since these diamond retailers are individual companies and carry more risk than a broad basket of stocks.

2. **Sell gold miners, buy diamond miners.** If diamonds outperform gold, we can expect diamond miners to generally do better than gold miners. Therefore, you could sell Gold Miners either through the Gold Miners ETF (GDX) or the Junior Gold Miners ETF (GDXJ), or by shorting individual mining companies such as Freeport-McMoRan (FCX), Barrick Gold (ABX), or Eldorado Gold (EGO). To pair that short sale, you could buy companies that mine diamonds exclusively such as Mountain Province Diamonds (MDM) and Harry Winston Diamond Corp. (HWD).

3. **Sell gold miners, buy "multipurpose" miners.** If you want the best of both worlds, you could sell the Gold Miners ETF (GDX) or the individual miners (see earlier mentions) and buy Rio Tinto (RIO), which

mines a wide array of minerals such as aluminum, copper, gold, silver, and diamonds, or BHP (BHP), which has its hand in everything from metals to diamonds to potash to crude oil to coal.

Diamonds have been the most valuable assets for centuries, and have generally moved together with gold. When gold prices surged in the early 1980s, diamonds surged to record prices as well. But since 2000, gold prices have increased tremendously while diamond prices have been flatlining. The price increase in gold is mainly due to increased demand, currency fear, inflation protection, and the need to hold onto a "stable," "tangible" asset at a time when everything else seems to be in danger. Yet, while the underlying reasons for buying gold are definitely understandable, they don't necessarily justify the exorbitantly high prices. Moreover, diamonds offer plenty of reasons as to why they should be rising alongside with, if not catching up to, gold: important industrial usage, highest value per unit of weight, necessary for global growth, and high emotional values. If the saying is really true that "a diamond is forever," the time to buy diamonds may be now.

Buy Stocks Instead

The May 2011 collapse of silver, as well as the poor performance of oil and the broader commodity space from May through September 2011 requires investors to exercise caution as well as rethink their strategies regarding the precious metals and commodities trade. As I've said on multiple occasions, there is tremendous risk involved in gold and commodity investment that many investors are not aware of or simply refuse to acknowledge. In my opinion, gold and commodities will see severe drops that will come as a shock to many who failed to see or accept the warning signs. I will not rehash my arguments here; but suffice it to say that even if gold and commodities continue to go up, there are plenty of investment opportunities out there that will outperform them. In my opinion, there are four possible scenarios that could play out:

1. **Gold, commodities, and markets continue to rise.** In this case, since the markets continue to rise, there will be plenty of stocks that outperform gold and commodities.
2. **Markets fall, gold and commodities rise.** If gold is truly a protection against stock market catastrophe, it will rise while markets fall and could outperform many individual stocks. But since I believe gold and commodities to be a bubble, I believe a drop in the markets will be accompanied by a drop in gold and commodities.
3. **Markets fall, gold and commodities fall.** Since many of the market moves over the past two years have been accompanied by rising

commodity and energy prices, a drop in stocks would likely be accompanied by a drop in gold and commodities as well.

4. **Markets rise, gold and commodities fall.** If gold has been soaring because it stands as a protection against market drops and uncertainty, a sustained increase in stocks could put an end to the gold run. If markets continue to rise, gold interest could fade.

In other words, only a drop in markets and rise in gold and commodities would see gold outperform sound investment choices in stocks. Three out of four scenarios favor good stock picks over gold and silver.

And that's not to say I am bullish on stocks either. I see an extreme amount of cause for concern over the next few years in the stock market; so much so, that I am yet to be convinced that a double-dip recession is not upon us. But, even with the growing fear that the market may be setting up for a fall, I am almost certain that the potential for profits would be much better achieved through selective stock picking and avoidance of the precious metals and commodity trade.

My reasons for choosing stocks over gold and silver are as follows:

- **Avoid the bubble.** Gold and silver are a bubble and pose tremendous risks.
- **Stocks offer higher returns.** Even if gold and silver continue to rise, or even soar, I do not see them gaining more than 50 percent from here. Individual stocks, on the other hand, can see much higher returns if picked correctly.
- **Limit your losses.** With good stock picks near strong support levels, investors can limit their risk by selling out of positions if the trade goes against them. If they're right, they will likely outperform gold; if they're wrong, they'll cut their losses at defined support levels.

Buy Physical Property, or Invest in Housing Stocks?

Originally published April 27, 2011: "Playing a House Recovery: Buy Physical Property or Invest in stocks?" *Seeking Alpha.*[3]

While most people attempting to profit from a housing recovery have done so by buying homes and real estate, betting on housing through stocks requires considerably less time invested, is free of maintenance costs, has the potential for much higher returns, offers enormously greater liquidity, and even greatly reduces risk.

Though a double-dip in housing has been confirmed by the S&P/Shiller Housing Price Index, I'd still rather invest in housing than in gold and silver. Housing has been so beaten up, that I believe the fear and avoidance of the sector by many is offering good investment opportunities for those who do so carefully.

Housing Bubble Revisited

Following the recent devastating recession brought about by massive credit and real estate bubbles, is it time to invest in housing again? With the broader stock market up over 100 percent from the 2009 bottom, while the housing market is still near its lows, down 30+ percent, does real estate present a tremendous buying opportunity if the economy continues to recover? Is the worst of the housing debacle behind us? And if housing does provide a great investment opportunity, which option offers the greatest rewards: physical real estate or housing stocks?

Home prices surged nearly 83 percent from 1997 to 2006 according to the Case-Shiller Index created by Yale economist Robert J. Shiller, seen in Figure 8.5.

With the advantage of the long-term perspective offered by Shiller, it's much easier to see how dramatic the housing bubble actually was—and how sharply and rapidly prices have since collapsed.

Bubbles tend to overextend and overreact to the downside in much the same way that they overreacted on the way up. They even tend to correct to prebubble levels or below. In other words, just as housing prices skyrocketed above long-term averages in the formation of the bubble, they could very well plunge below current levels and even drop an additional 25 or so percent to the lows of the 1970s and 1980s (as depicted in Figure 8.5).

According to Figure 8.6, prices are still above the prebubble trend.

As you can see, prices diverged significantly from the price trend-line from 2000 to 2006, only to come crashing back down.

Recovery or Double-Dip?

Questions remain, however: Have we seen the worst of the housing market collapse? Or is this just a temporary pause before the next leg down? With seven straight months of price declines leading into March 2011 there is a growing concern over a continued drop—what many, including Shiller himself, expect to be a double-dip in housing.

Is the recent decline in home prices on a year-over-year basis (seen in Figure 8.7) just a temporary and minor correction or the beginning of the double-dip?

On the positive side, housing may improve with the recovering job market, low mortgage rates, and highly depreciated prices, which increase affordability and make purchasing a home much more attractive at these levels. The verdict is also still out as to whether the Fed's Quantitative Easing programs

A History of Homan Values

The Yale economist Robert J. Shiller created an index of American housing prices going back to 1890, it is based on sale prices of standard exisiting houses, not new construction, to track the value of housing as an investment over time. It presents housing values in consistent terms over 116 years, factoring cut the effects of inflation.

The 1890 benchmark is 100 on the chart. If a standard house sold in 1890 for $1000,000 (inflation adjusted to today's dollars), an equivalent (standard house would have sold for $66,000 in 1920 (66 on the index scale) and $199,000 in 2006 (199 on the index scale, or 99 percent higher than 1890).

DECLINE AND RUN-UP Prices dropped as mass production techniques appeared early in the 20th century. Prices spiked with post-war housing demand.

DOOM TIMCS Two gains in recent decades were followed by returns to levels consistent since the late 1950's. Since 1997, the index has risen about 83 percent.

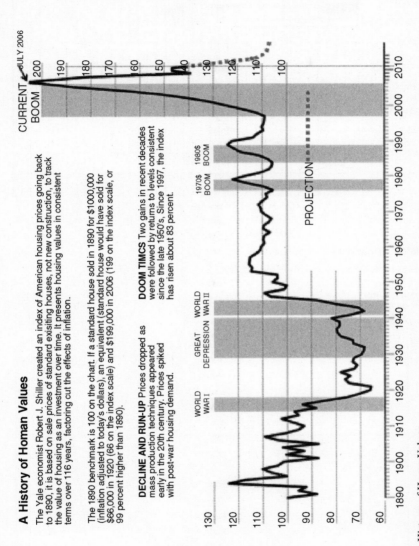

FIGURE 8.5 A History of Home Values
Source: Robert Shiller, Barry Ritholtz.

179

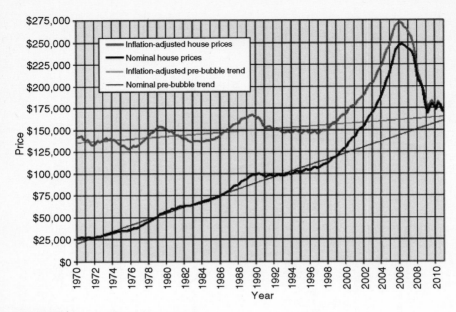

FIGURE 8.6 United States House Prices

Source: www.jparsons.net/housingbubble/.

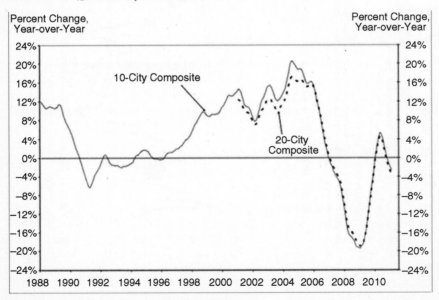

FIGURE 8.7 S&P/Case-Shiller Home Price Indices

Source: Business Insider, Standard & Poor's & FiServ (April 26, 2011).

will be successful in reflating the housing market; inflation is visible in energy, food, and commodity prices (though largely ignored by the Fed), but is still missing in housing. If the Fed's plan works in creating enough inflation to spur housing growth, the housing double-dip may be avoided.

On the negative side, however, a huge inventory of foreclosed homes, massive existing supply, high unemployment, high gas and food prices, difficulties in qualifying for a mortgage, potentially rising interest rates, and the overall lack of confidence in the housing market could all weaken the consumer and severely hamper any near-term growth.

It is therefore very hard, if not impossible, to truly predict the future direction of housing. The double-dip could be underway, which would likely bode poorly for the economy as a whole. And with China and others raising rates in order to combat the dangerous inflation that has been recently surfacing, among many other warning signals—an overheated tech startup sector, housing bubbles in China and other emerging markets, toxic bank balance sheets, the threat of war, and more—the potential for an economic slowdown and a global economic double-dip is growing. On the other hand, with so much widespread pessimism regarding housing, now may be the perfect time to buy—when few dare.

So for those looking to bet on a housing recovery, as there are companies and individuals purchasing real estate in hopes that their investments are made at bargain prices, what is the best way to do so?

Physical Real Estate versus Housing Stocks

While most people attempting to profit from a housing recovery have done so by buying homes and real estate, betting on housing through stocks requires considerably less time invested, is free of maintenance costs, has the potential for much higher returns, offers enormously greater liquidity, and even greatly reduces risk.

BUYING PHYSICAL REAL ESTATE

Pros:

- **It's physical, tangible property.** A house, building, or land is a tangible asset. Unlike many investments around, such as stocks, a house or the land it sits on will always have value. That value can, of course, fluctuate significantly, but at least you can safely bet that the value won't drop to zero. Moreover, owning property or a house offers the buyer a place to live or go on vacation.
- **Potential income from rent.** Buying physical real estate allows the owner to rent it out while he or she waits for the property value to increase in order to sell it. Owning physical property, then, is a good way

of generating supplemental income while awaiting higher real estate prices. Finding people to rent that house or property is not always easy, though.

Cons:

- **Large monetary outlays required.** Buying land or a house generally requires a significant investment. Though there are ways to purchase real estate as part of a group investing together, buying a house easily requires an investment of upwards of $100,000—money which the average investor or speculator does not always have and most times does not want to risk, even if a loan or mortgage is involved.
- **Nonliquid investment.** A house is not easy to sell, especially with current market conditions. Selling a house requires a real estate agent, interested buyers, and time—all factors that make a house fairly illiquid. If the owner needed money immediately, selling his property may pose big problems; many times, desperate selling results in a much lower selling price—if a buyer is even found.
- **Requires considerable input of time.** Buying and owning a house takes time. If you want to make sure you find a good house, in the right location, for the right price, you're going to have to spend a lot of time researching and visiting different properties for sale. Once you find the house you like, you're going to have to spend time involved in the negotiation and buying process, dealing with the bank, and taking care of all the laborious details involved. Then, once you buy the house, you're going to have to spend time and/or money looking for renters, maintaining the property, and checking up periodically. If you don't have much patience for tasks and long processes, buying a house as an investment is not for you.
- **Extra costs for maintenance, property tax, and insurance.** Owning a house will require additional capital for the costs of maintaining the property, fixing what needs to be fixed, paying property taxes, and buying insurance. The costs don't simply end the day you buy the house.
- **Generally requires good credit.** If a buyer purchases a house with the help of a mortgage or loan, he generally needs good credit for mortgage qualification. Since not everyone has acceptable credit, buying a house as an investment is sometimes difficult if not impossible.
- **Selection, location, and house risk.** Not all houses are created equal. If the housing market improves and home prices increase, there is no guarantee that all areas will benefit. Depending on the specific selection and purchase made by the owner, the increase or decrease in price over time could vary significantly. Since there is a risk that the buyer chooses a weak location, poorly or improperly built home, or just a house that is

difficult to sell down the line, investing in physical real estate poses more risks than many assume.

INVESTING IN HOMEBUILDER STOCKS

Pros:

- **Low investment minimum required.** Unlike buying physical property, investing in stocks does not require upwards of $100,000. Individuals or companies looking to profit from a housing recovery through stocks can invest whatever sum they see fit, even as low as a few hundred dollars. Rather than having to take out loans or make a sizeable cash outlay, which many cannot afford or simply do not want to undertake, investing in housing stocks allows the investor to choose the proper investment amount.
- **Highly liquid investment.** Betting on housing through stocks allows the investor to buy and sell whenever he or she wishes, without the risks, costs, or time associated with selling a house. Rather than having to wait a considerable amount of time until the property is sold or having to lower the asking price in order to sell it sooner, investing in housing stocks or ETFs is generally highly liquid and leaves the power in the hands of the investor to buy and sell almost instantly.
- **Requires a lot less time.** Though monitoring one's stock portfolio and the individual companies involved requires some time and is highly recommended, it does not even come close to the time and painstaking labor required in searching for suitable property, negotiating the purchase, maintaining and physically visiting the property, and eventually selling it. A few hours a week, at most, and you could monitor and manage a housing stock portfolio. You could even just buy housing stocks or ETFs and let them sit; just remember to establish some stop-loss points to limit losses if you do so. Regardless, you can invest in housing stocks from the convenience of your own home—without all the hassle involved in purchasing physical property.
- **No maintenance, property tax, or insurance costs.** Unlike physical property or housing, a stock investment incurs no costs other than capital gains taxes if you profit.
- **No credit barriers or approval necessary.** Anyone can invest in stocks, regardless of credit score or financial history. All you need is an online brokerage account.
- **Eliminates selection and location risk.** Since housing and homebuilder companies own many properties across a relatively wide range of locations, investing in their stock eliminates the risks associated with a single property investment. By buying homebuilder stocks, you are

essentially investing in a basket of real estate properties; and, in doing so, you limit or eliminate the risk of picking a poor location, damaged house, or hard-to-sell property.

- **Allows for diversification.** Instead of risking a huge sum of money on one house or property, investing in housing through stocks allows for both diversification and risk protection. By having the ability to spread your total investment among several housing stocks, you will not be at risk of losing it all if one company struggles while others grow. Buying physical property, on the other hand, leaves you heavily invested in one or a few locations and highly increases risk.

- **Allows for protection and risk control.** If you buy a house, your money is essentially trapped until you sell it. And if home prices begin to plunge, you may be stuck with a rapidly depreciating property that becomes difficult or impossible to sell. In other words, you can easily lose a large percentage of your investment value even if you try selling the property before prices really begin to fall; it's just too hard to quickly sell a house as property values decline. On the other hand, if you invest in stocks, you can limit your risk as well as buy protection. By setting stop-loss points, you can quickly sell out of your position if housing or the stocks begin to fall further than you're willing to risk. If, for example, you decide that you're only willing to risk 10 percent, you can simply enter a stop-loss limit order to sell your stock if it drops to a price below a 10 percent loss. Additionally, if you want protection from a steep decline in price, you can buy put options as a hedge against your long stock position. With a cost of only a few percentage points or a few cents or dollars per share, you can protect your entire portfolio from disaster. You can't really do that with physical property or housing.

- **Potential for much greater returns.** If housing does recover, the right stock investment could generate a much greater return than a physical property or house investment. Realistically, home prices will gain 50 to 100 percent *at most* if a recovery takes hold. You could even stretch it and argue that a property's value may double or triple in value if the housing market makes a strong comeback. But bet on the housing market through stocks or options, and you could easily see returns of a few hundred percent if the housing market recovers. Add to that the possibility and ability to lock in profits by selling at highs and buying again near lows, and you could increase those returns even more. Why work so hard, spend so much time and money, and take so much extra risk by buying physical property when it probably won't even increase your return?

Cons:

- **No rental income.** Unlike physical property, housing stocks don't generate rental income while you wait for home prices to increase.

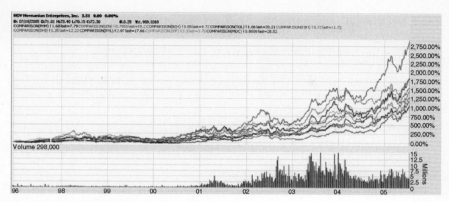

FIGURE 8.8 Homebuilder Gains (1997 to 2006)

Source: thinkorswim, Chart Prophet LLC.

Investing in stocks would therefore limit your supplemental income in the interim. Certain stocks do pay dividends, however, and will supplement you with some income to offset the lack of rental payments.

- **May not mirror actual home price changes.** Though I strongly believe that homebuilder stocks will benefit even more than actual home prices, I am still open to the possibility that housing prices could outperform the homebuilders and that homebuilder stocks may stagnate while home sales pick up. The reason for this is that there is currently a huge supply of homes due to foreclosures and lack of buying. Since homebuilders benefit mainly from *new* housing, an overhang of supply could limit their growth and profits.
- I will point out, however, that while home prices rose 83 percent from 1997 to 2006, homebuilder stocks *tremendously* outpaced them (as seen in Figure 8.8)—with all major homebuilder stocks gaining more than 1,000 percent!

Investing in homebuilders instead of actual property makes way too much sense: limited risk, high liquidity, little or minimal time investment, no extra costs, diversification, and exponentially higher returns. Why do it any other way?

How to Play It

Chart Prophet LLC is currently managing private accounts and structuring a "Housing Recovery Fund" that will create a basket of housing stocks from a select group of homebuilders, retailers, and housing-related companies. We will then actively manage the fund in order to maximize profits from stock price fluctuations and implement risk-protection through hedging and options strategies.

As for the homebuilder stocks, we're currently watching:

- Broad Homebuilder ETFs to bet on the sector: XHB, IYR, ITB.
- DR Horton (DHI)
- Pulte Homes (PHM)
- Lennar Corp (LEN)
- Hovnanian (HOV)
- Beazer Homes (BZH)
- Toll Brothers (TOL)
- KB Homes (KBH)
- Ryland Group (RYL)
- Standard Pacific Corp (SPF)
- MDC Holdings (MDC)

Conclusion

Having established that gold is in a bubble and set for collapse, we presented a number of ways to profit while gold falls. Readers now have an arsenal of strategies at their disposal—from simple and straightforward bets against gold or gold miners, to riskier but more rewarding options strategies, to more complex pair strategies that allow investors to hedge their bets by shorting gold and buying assets that we expect to outperform. While gold falls, assets such as platinum, diamonds, housing, and carefully selected stocks should suffer less and could offer protection for bets against gold. We have presented our claims of a gold bubble and our in-depth analysis of how to profit from its collapse. We favor shorting the gold miners through careful options bets. It is now up to you to implement whichever strategies you see fit. As always, be careful, monitor your investments, and never risk more than you can afford to lose. Good luck!

CHAPTER 9

Other Investment
Land Mines to Avoid

O verspeculative asset bubbles are not limited to gold. Rather, there are usually a number of overly risky and overrated investment themes that should be avoided. Since they may not be as clear-cut as in the case of gold, I cannot call them absolute bubbles, but I do consider them to be tremendously overhyped and overvalued "mini-bubbles" that pose severe risks for investors.

The appearance of these mini-bubbles together with the larger gold bubble is a sign that a broad speculative mania has infected more than just one sector of the investment world. Speculative manias tend to spill over into other parts of the markets. This chapter presents a number of highly risky and overcrowded investment themes that should be avoided or even shorted.

"Cloud Nine" Computing: Sign of a Renewed Technology Bubble?[1]

With the recent housing bubble and its subsequent collapse at the forefront of investors' minds, the technology bubble that preceded it appears to be more far removed from investors' memory than it should be. And that loss of memory could be leading us into a renewed technology bubble.

The technology bubble, or dot-com bubble, saw the NASDAQ climb 584 percent from 1995 to its peak in early 2000. Spurred on by the growing use of the Internet and the speculation that this new technology was the wave of the future, stock prices soared as investors piled into Internet-based companies, sometimes simply based on the fact that they included an "e-" prefix or ".com" ending to their names. And though investors were correct in assuming that the Internet and technology were the future of business, the

187

exorbitant prices they were willing to pay for companies that hadn't even turned in a profit should have stood as a stark warning.

But what could investors have done? The Internet was rapidly gaining in popularity, stock prices were soaring, and the argument that this was a "new age," where old valuation measures no longer applied, was becoming the norm. Things were "different this time," and you'd be crazy not to join the party.

Yet while investors were correct in asserting that the Internet and technology were to be the wave of the future, their expectations led them to get a little ahead of themselves, and their blind faith in almost any company in the technology space was unwarranted. If you joined the party too late, you would have lost almost everything (see Figure 9.1).

It seems like we may be making the same mistake again. As housing collapsed and financial stocks were almost completely wiped out, focus has increasingly shifted towards technology companies with the huge potential to serve the growing needs of the next generation of computer-savvy, social-media-loving consumers. And rightfully so, it seems; Facebook, YouTube (GOOG), Twitter, and others will find a way to make huge profits sometime in the future, right?

Venture capital firms seem to believe so. They've been piling money into startups recently in hopes of striking it big. And there has been a shift among startups, away from IPOs and towards private growth and investment. Some of these companies sell out to bigger powerhouses,

FIGURE 9.1 NASDAQ versus S&P 500: Technology Bubble
Source: thinkorswim, Chart Prophet LLC.

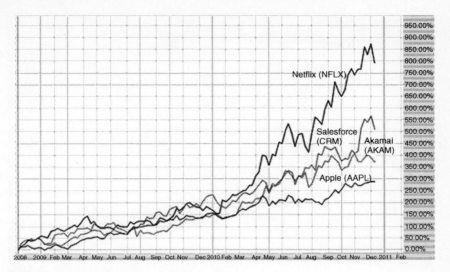

FIGURE 9.2 High-Flying Technology Stocks
Source: thinkorswim, Chart Prophet LLC.

others—like Facebook—await bigger and better opportunities through an eventual IPO somewhere down the road. But with companies such as Groupon, which was recently offered a $6 billion buyout offer by Google (GOOG) and rejected it, gaining such huge momentum, is there much more upside left? What happens if Facebook loses its steam as MySpace (NWS) did a few years ago? Will Mark Zuckerberg regret not selling the company at its peak while he had the chance?

You can even forget about the private companies for now. What about the public technology companies that have recently gained huge popularity and attention as their future potential seems to be almost limitless? Netflix (NFLX), Salesforce.com (CRM), Apple (AAPL), and Akamai (AKAM) are just a few of the stocks that have doubled, tripled, or soared almost nine-fold in less than two years (see Figure 9.2).

As you can see, some of these technology stocks are flying high. They're doing so for good reason—because of good track records and expectations for future growth. But how can we tell if expectations for the future are getting a little too exuberant?.

Five Reasons Why Cloud Computing Could Be Signaling Overenthusiasm

1. **Price run-up.** The most basic of reasons to be wary of stocks, a tremendous price increase should at least send out some warning signs. See Figure 9.3

FIGURE 9.3 Cloud Computing Stocks Price Run-Up
Source: thinkorswim, Chart Prophet LLC.

As you can see over the past two years, while the S&P 500 is up approximately 50 percent, cloud computing companies such as Salesforce (CRM), F5 Networks (FFIV), and VMWare (VMW) are up anywhere from 300 to 550 percent! While such a run-up may be justified, the probability of price increases like this continuing are not favorable; when stock prices inflate this much over such a short span of time, they usually must correct, if not outright plummet. And with cloud computing no longer a secret, with fund managers and the average investor fully aware of the "cloud story," I see more risk than reward in this trade. Have prices reached the "clouds"?

2. **Price-to-earnings (P/E) ratios.** Price to earnings ratios are a measure of how much investors are willing to pay today for the earnings a company will produce in the future. If investors believe a company will continue to grow at a rapid pace, they will generally be more willing to pay higher prices for a company's stock. In other words, if a company is expected to gather momentum or continue its tremendous growth, it will generally have a high P/E ratio as investors clamor to buy the stock.

The question becomes, however—when is the price paid for future growth too high? When are investors expecting too much from a company, regardless of its tremendous potential? Historically, P/E ratios around 30 or slightly above are somewhat acceptable for growth companies. But when the ratios start breaking above 50, it's time to be a little careful.

At the height of the dot-com bubble, investors were ignoring the massive P/E ratios. That mistake ended up costing them, as companies generally can't meet extreme expectations. What do we see now, as the cloud companies have soared? Investors are once again ignoring P/E ratios, assuming these companies have entered a revolutionary market niche and will be able to justify their stock prices as they continue to grow rapidly. Salesforce (CRM) has a trailing P/E of 247 and a forward P/E of 88! Riverbed (RVBD)—231 trailing, 45 forward; VMware (VMW)—124 trailing, 49 forward; Rackspace Hosting (RAX)—100 trailing, 59 forward. These aren't just slightly inflated ratios; they're tremendous! Compare that to Apple (AAPL), with a trailing P/E of 21 and forward P/E of 14, and you can easily see the huge difference. Are these growth estimates sustainable? Or are investors just overly exuberant and setting up for disaster?

3. **"It's different this time."** As in most bubbles and overly euphoric investor behavior, the argument that this time things are different has surfaced once again. In the dot-com bubble, the argument was that the new age of technology and the Internet had arrived. In the housing bubble, land values were going to continue to soar because land was only to continue to become scarcer as the population grew and people needed homes; the extravagant prices were seen as a result of new valuations for homes.

And now, cloud computing is the new paradigm. Technology is shifting from hardware storage and on-site databases, to off-site cloud-based storage, where people can access their programs and information from anywhere. Yes, it is a revolutionary technology; but is it really a "new paradigm" that should cause us to completely disregard valuation methods and rational investing? Technology stocks have highly outperformed the broader S&P 500 (see Figure 9.4), to an even greater extent than at the 2007 peak.

4. **Insider selling.** When high-ranking officers and employees believe in the future growth of their company, they generally hold on to their shares or even buy more. If the people actually working for the company buy the stock, it's a good sign that the ones with the important information expect the stock to continue to perform well.

When the insiders start selling their shares, however, it could be a reason for concern. And if they do it in an extreme fashion, it may be a reason to panic. Why should an investor in the company continue to hold his shares if the high-ranking employees are dumping theirs? Where is their confidence in their own company?

What has happened over the past six months with these cloud companies? They're rapidly dumping their shares onto the unsuspecting

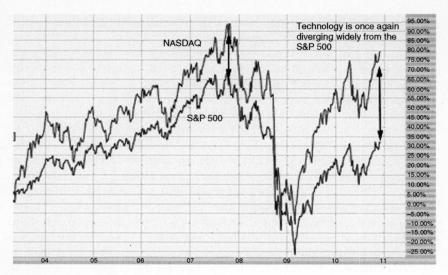

FIGURE 9.4 Technology Outperformance
Source: thinkorswim, Chart Prophet LLC.

public: Salesforce (CRM) CEO Mark Benioff and other insiders have sold over 2 million shares; F5 Networks (FFIV) insiders have sold 45 percent of their holdings; Rackspace (RAX) insiders have sold over 2 million shares; and RedHat (RHT) insiders have sold over 83 percent of their shares! These aren't just numbers to gloss over; they should be sending extreme warning signals.

5. **Cloud Bandwagon.** As the cloud sector gains hype among investors, companies are doing all they can to join the cloud group and see their stock prices appreciate as investors jump in. Companies that have some exposure to cloud computing are highly misrepresenting their cloud participation. In other words, many of the cloud companies that have seen their stock prices soar are simply the benefactors of the cloud craze, when they actually have negligible potential in the cloud space. They've simply jumped onto the cloud bandwagon, and when investors realize that, these companies' stock could plunge.

Silicon Valley has seen a revival since the dot-com bubble collapsed in 2000. But with venture capital flowing into start-up companies in an almost exuberant fashion, offering massive sums of money for companies with barely any track record, the threat of a renewed technology bubble is looming. Groupon rejected a $6 billion offer only four years after the much bigger YouTube accepted a $1.65 billion offer. Facebook remains a private company, but is allowing investors to trade derivatives on its shares.

Cloud computing may have a more tangible business model than did many of the dot-com era companies; but after multi-hundred-percent price moves, massive insider selling, extreme P/E ratios, and the arguments that "it's different this time"—can we really trust the cloud computing story? Or is it starting to look a bit more like "foggy" computing?

Betting against Facebook[2]

Facebook has transformed the way we live and interact, has flooded the world with opportunities in a rapidly developing social-media era, and may have even become the "second Internet."

But with dot-com bubble valuations, growth limitations, and potential legal hurdles standing in the way—are we nearing "social network overload"? And if the social-media craze is overdone, are there ways to make money in the event of a social-media crash?

There is no doubt that Facebook is one of the most dominant and exciting companies around, with seemingly nothing holding it back from becoming the first website, or Internet-based company, to have control over every country in the world. Just take a look at Figure 9.5 showing Facebook's global dominance.

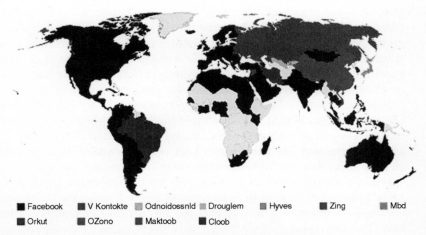

FIGURE 9.5 World Map of Social Networks, December 2010
Source: Courtesy of Vincenzo Cosenza Vincos.it.

With an ever-growing worldwide recognition as *the* social network, and continuous penetration into competitive markets of emerging countries which offer a nearly untouched consumer base with multiple avenues for giant profits, Facebook's hype is absolutely warranted. It is a platform for connecting with people, a source of news and updates, and an ever-evolving landscape for gaming, business, media, and technology.

Yet with all the massive potential it offers, how can we be assured that Facebook's dominance will actually translate into profits? And how can we determine if expectations are getting ahead of themselves? After a period of tremendous growth that has seen Facebook's user base grow from 150 to 600 million and its perceived value rise from less than $10 billion to over $50 billion (in less than one year!), is it time to jump in before it really takes off? Or is the Facebook hype and mass-awareness a sign of irrational exuberance for a business model founded on free-usage and mirage-like profit potential?

Four Reasons Facebook Could Succeed

Facebook is undoubtedly one of the most revolutionary companies in the world, and therefore has a number of reasons it could succeed:

1. **It is becoming the "second Internet."** Already the largest networking, photo, and gaming site, with very impressive upcoming opportunities in apps, television, its own e-mail service, and just about every aspect of the Internet, Facebook is not too far from being a one-stop source for people to manage their social lives, stay informed about current events, and find great deals on everything from travel to clothing. In fact, with over 30 billion pieces of content (links, news, blogs, photos, etc.) shared each month, developers from over 190 countries building with the Facebook platform, an average of 10,000 new websites being integrated with Facebook every day, and the recognition that Facebook is likely the number-one means for interconnectedness and mass exposure, it is not a *complete* shock that Facebook took over Google's (GOOG) title of "most-visited site" in the United States for 2010 (see Table 9.1). If a monopoly on the Internet is ever possible, Facebook may have the best chance.
2. **Much room left for new ideas and opportunities.** It may have already revolutionized the ways in which we communicate, behave, and spend, but there is still much growth left in this rapidly developing social cyber-world. Far from exhausting its innovative talents, Facebook continues to impress us with new apps, new ways of engaging its user base, and big dreams for the future. And many believe that the money will soon flow into Facebook once it firmly takes hold. If Facebook does figure out a way to improve its advertising capabilities and

TABLE 9.1 Top 10 Most-Visited Websites

2009	2010
www.google.com	www.facebook.com
mail.yahoo.com	www.google.com
www.facebook.com	mail.yahoo.com
www.yahoo.com	www.yahoo.com
www.myspace.com	www.youtube.com
mail.live.com	www.msn.com
www.youtube.com	www.myspace.com
search.yahoo.com	mail.live.com
www.msn.com	search.yahoo.com
www.ebay.com	www.bing.com

Note: Data is based on U.S. visits for January to November 2009 and 2010.
Source: Experian Hitwise.

monetize its grasp on such a massive audience, it could very well be just in its beginning stages.

3. **Many more people still left to join.** Surpassing the 500-million user mark in July 2010 (see Figure 9.6), and currently having an estimated user-base of more than 600 million users, there may still be plenty more people left to join. The world population is nearing 7 billion! And though many will not be able to join due to age, lack of the necessary

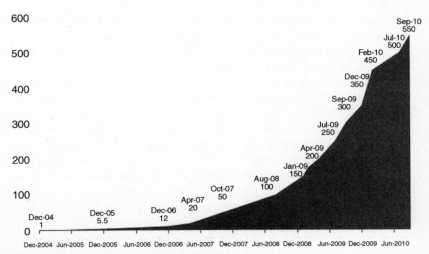

FIGURE 9.6 Facebook User Growth in Millions
Source: Ben Foster (@benphoster).

technology, or simply lack of interest, Facebook founder Mark Zucker-berg has said that "it is almost a guarantee" that Facebook will hit the one billion mark.

As you can see, Facebook's exponential growth since late 2004 is indicative of the tremendous momentum it has gained. If momentum continues as it has thus far, the one billion mark isn't a far stretch, though we do have to keep in mind that previous performance is no guarantee for future results and that it may be much harder to convince another 500 million people to join the site than it was to convince the existing users.

4. **Still no mass investor participation.** After five years of enormous success and public attention, Facebook is still a private company! Com-panies generally go public in order to raise money for expansion and to allow insiders to sell their share of the company. But Facebook has been avoiding the usual need to go public by raising $1 billion in funding (compared to only $25 million raised by Google before going public in 2004), and by allowing its private shares to be traded in secondary mar-kets created by companies such as SecondMarket and SharePost, which allow for insiders and shareowners to sell their privately held shares to institutions and wealthy investors who are willing to pay big bucks for a stake in what could be a highly valuable IPO in the future. In other words, private Facebook stock is currently being bought and sold in a secondary market even though the company isn't public. And though Zuckerberg recently said "Don't hold your breath" when it comes to a Facebook IPO any time soon, an investment in the company now could be very profitable if Facebook does end up going public.

And with Goldman Sachs (GS) announcing that it will invest $500 million in Facebook, creating a "special purpose vehicle" to allow its wealthy investors to buy a stake in the company, the mass-investing phase in Facebook may be only beginning.

On the one hand, more investment funds may soon offer Facebook shares to individuals, which will further inflate Facebook's share value; companies like Felix Investments, EB Exchange Funds, and GreenCrest Capital have already opened Facebook funds in the past year. On the other hand, all this increased investor appetite for Facebook may force Facebook to go IPO earlier than it has been planning to, which could launch the mass-investment phase as the average investor jumps into Facebook stock with hopes it will become the next Google.

Or, in a third scenario, Facebook investing could turn out to be a terrible decision if the inflated private-share prices turn out to be the result of greedy speculation, or if the company and its IPO fail to be as successful as most people believe they will be.

Where are we in the course of a bubble (Figure 9.7) if Facebook turns out to be one?

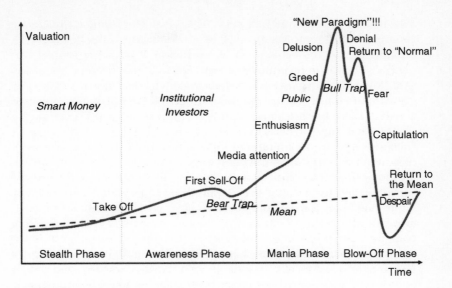

FIGURE 9.7 **Main Stages in a Bubble**

Source: Jean-Paul Rodriguez (http://canadianfinanceblog.com/is-the-current-market-a-return-to-normal/).

Seven Reasons Facebook Could Fail

Since Facebook's tremendous valuation, and the investor enthusiasm that surrounds it, is based on extreme expectations of *future* growth, there are a multitude of reasons why Facebook could fail:

1. **Extreme valuations.** Facebook shares being traded on the secondary market are valuing the company at over $50 billion. That makes it bigger in valuation than Boeing (BA), which is both America's largest exporter and one of the 30 companies in the Dow Jones Industrial Average (DJIA). The $50 billion valuation also makes Facebook worth over 60 percent as much as Amazon (AMZN), one of the worldwide leaders in online retail—ranging from books to consumer electronics (including its Kindle) to shoes (it owns Zappos).

   The $50 billion valuation wouldn't be so much of an issue if Facebook was producing proportional revenues to justify its market cap. And surely much of the money that has been invested in Facebook is being invested because of the potential *future* profits that Facebook *may* produce.

   But Facebook has yet to truly prove its money-making abilities. While it did more than double its revenues of approximately

$800 million in 2009 to $2 billion in 2010, it is still far from producing the revenues necessary to justify a $50 billion valuation. Take Boeing (BA), for example: with a market cap of $49 billion, it far outperforms Facebook's $2 billion in revenues with over $65 billion in revenues. Amazon (AMZN), which is valued at less than twice what Facebook is valued at, still earns 15 times more in revenues. And Dell (DELL), which is valued at half of Facebook's valuation, earns 30 times as much as Facebook.

Another sign of massive speculation and unproven valuation is Facebook's price-to-earnings ratio (P/E ratio). The P/E ratio is a measure of how much investors are willing to pay *today* for a company's earnings *tomorrow*. If a company is expected to grow rapidly, and therefore "prove itself" by earning the required revenues, investors will pay higher multiples for the company's stock; a company with a bright future would therefore be proportionally more expensive than a failing company. But while investors generally benefit from paying more for growth companies, there are big risks involved in overpaying. A 20 or 30 P/E ratio is historically reasonable for a growth company, and a 50 or 60 P/E ratio may sometimes prove profitable; but massive and dangerous investment bubbles have formed and collapsed when P/E ratios reached extremely lofty levels, such as the dot-com bubble that saw the P/E ratios of many overly hyped companies reach over 100, only to send those companies' stock prices crashing down once reality set in.

So why is Facebook's P/E ratio pointing to extreme valuations and potential overspeculation? Because based on its $50 billion valuation and $2 billion in revenues, it currently has a P/E ratio of over 100, with some estimates as high as 400! Compare that to P/E ratios of 22 for Apple (AAPL), 24 for Google (GOOG), and 68 for Netflix (NFLX), and it is very obvious that Facebook has yet to prove itself, if that is at all possible at these valuations.

Figure 9.8 shows what happened to some of the most promising companies in the dot-com bubble, who carried P/E ratios as high as Facebook currently does.

These companies did maintain their leading positions, and remained some of the biggest companies in the world even after the bubble collapsed. But that didn't stop their stock price from dropping as much as 90 percent. Sure, Facebook has the potential to earn the huge amounts expected; but are expectations way ahead of profits?

2. **Unproven ability to monetize.** As mentioned above, Facebook has yet to prove its ability to turn big profits. As a free social-media platform, Facebook's main service provides it with zero payment. Instead, Facebook must generate revenues by offering advertising and other fee-related services. The problem, however, is that Facebook is struggling with monetizing its business. First, Google still dominates the Internet advertisement space; it had a head start, currently has a much more

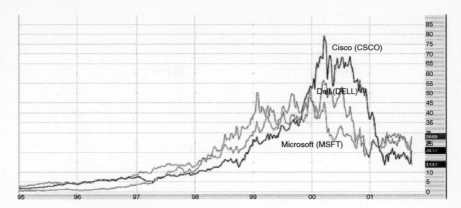

FIGURE 9.8 Tech Stocks Collapse
Source: thinkorswim, Chart Prophet LLC.

efficient system for targeting ads at the right audience, and is better able to mesh its advertising segment with its search business. Second, Facebook hasn't proved that it can truly become ad-friendly; unlike Google, which places well-targeted ads to individuals who are actually searching for something, Facebook is attempting to advertise to individuals who may be using the site strictly for its *social* aspect and could very well be annoyed by such intrusive ads.

Social media is hard to monetize, and Facebook hasn't yet figured out how to make the big profits expected of it; but that hasn't stopped venture capitalists from funneling millions of dollars into Facebook and anything related to social media or the accompanying apps. Yet it may be important to take note that Facebook is not only valued at extreme levels, but is also severely lagging in revenues when compared to the first six years of Google (Figure 9.9). If it can't match Google's initial growth, why should we assume it could be the "next Google," let alone value it at $50 billion or more?

3. **Growth limits and waning interest.** Facebook is taking over the world, but how much growth is left until it does so? And if it does establish itself all over the world, what growth will then follow?

Facebook has already captivated 600-plus million people, and has convinced them to join. It has also spread around the world like an infectious social-media disease, transmitted from friend to friend and further developing the global Facebook obsession. Yet while countries such as Indonesia, Russia, and India (among many others) continue to show strength in adopting Facebook, there is no guarantee that the current rate of Facebook adoption rate will continue. Instead, as opposed to the mainly American audience Facebook was geared towards until recently, Facebook now faces different cultures with different needs,

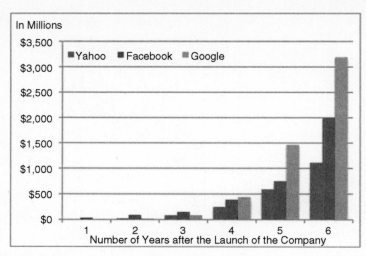

FIGURE 9.9 Annual Revenue for Tech Companies for the First Six Years after Launch
Source: Business Insider; Capital IQ (December 2010).

expectations, and potential political ramifications. China and Japan remain two of Facebook's biggest challenges. If Facebook is able to firmly
take hold of these competitive arenas, it will prove itself as the sole
worldwide king of social media; if it fails to take control, it may set itself
up for very dangerous failed expectations. Either way, however, worldwide domination may already be factored into most people's investment
models or expectations. Facebook's growth may therefore be broken
down into three outcomes—world domination, failed penetration into
China and other important markets, or waning interest which sees Facebook losing even its current user base. I'd bet on something closer to
world domination, but the threats of slowing growth, waning interest,
and expectations that may have already factored in Facebook's global
dominance may make Facebook a very dangerous investment.

In fact, Facebook growth in the United States may be peaking. After
a record 133.5 million unique visitors in October, Facebook saw a slight
drop to 132.7 million unique visitors in November (Figure 9.10). Worldwide, Facebook saw an added 14 million unique visitors; but stagnant
U.S. growth and a decline in interest could be a warning of what's to
come. Moreover, Facebook may actually begin to *lose* users. If months
like June 2010 are any indication (see Figure 9.11), Facebook is not immune to negative growth.

As you can see, Facebook's U.S. growth may be slipping. Not only
was growth negative for the 18 to 44 age range, but Facebook may be

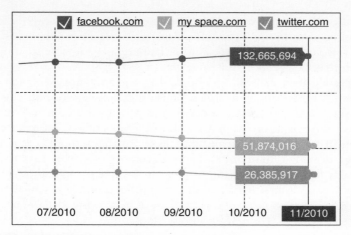

FIGURE 9.10 Facebook Loses Visitors
Source: InsideFacebook.com

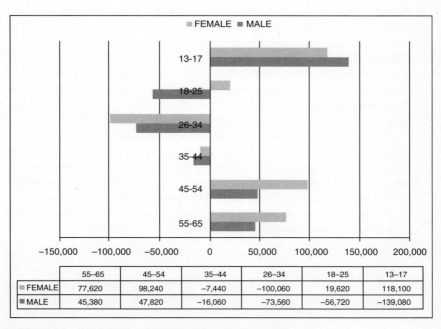

FIGURE 9.11 U.S. Facebook Audience Growth, June 2010
Source: InsideFacebook.com, July 1, 2010.

losing what many consider to be its most lucrative and vital demo-
graphic—the 18 to 35 year olds. Facebook may have simply lost its lus-
ter once everyone's parents and grandparents were able to join; it may
no longer be as "cool" as it once was.

4. **MySpace Part 2?** Until Facebook stole the spotlight, MySpace was by
far the most dominant and promising social-networking site in the
world. It is true that MySpace wasn't as widespread then as Facebook is
now; and it is also true that Facebook offers critical features that were
unavailable on MySpace and that make Facebook more connected and
more dominant than any of its predecessors. But what says that Facebook's fate won't ultimately follow in MySpace's footsteps? MySpace
was the supreme site for years, only to have its title taken away by Facebook's superior competition and by the growing disinterest among
MySpace users. Though Facebook does seem to be better geared for
competition and continued dominance, there is no guarantee that it will
remain on top forever; a revolutionary competing site could theoreti-
cally usurp Facebook of its power. And if a better competitor doesn't
show up, growing disinterest and "Facebook fatigue," as some have
called it, pose the added threat. People are very fickle; Facebook is not
immune to fads and constantly changing interests.

5. **Privacy issues.** As a social network founded on openness and shared
personal information, such as pictures and daily activities, Facebook
has had to deal with many privacy issues. With much private, and potentially dangerous, information open to the public, the threats of iden-
tity theft, stalking, and defamation are much bigger than many realize.
Facebook has had to revise its privacy policies and attempt to appear
more transparent on numerous occasions due to constant public criti-
cism and potential legal issues.

Privacy issues remain one of Facebook's biggest challenges. People
generally prefer that their information be kept private, or at least that its
sharing will be limited to people they know and trust. Facebook's policy, however, is less transparent than it would have us believe. While
Facebook does appear to be strongly supportive of its users' privacy, it
faces very difficult challenges in ensuring that privacy. Their privacy
policy states the following:

> *In order to provide you with useful social experiences off of Face-
> book, we occasionally need to provide General Information about
> you to pre-approved third party websites and applications that use
> Platform at the time you visit them (if you are still logged in to Face-
> book). Similarly, when one of your friends visits a pre-approved
> website or application, it will receive General Information about
> you so you and your friend can be connected on that website as*

well (if you also have an account with that website). In these cases we require these websites and applications to go through an approval process, and to enter into separate agreements designed to protect your privacy . . . . You can disable instant personalization on all pre-approved websites and applications using your Applications and Websites privacy setting. You can also block a particular pre-approved website or application by clicking "No Thanks" in the blue bar when you visit that application or website. In addition, if you log out of Facebook before visiting a pre-approved application or website, it will not be able to access your information."[3]

As you can see, Facebook generally maintains its right to provide users' information to "pre-approved" third-party websites and applications. Not only is Facebook tracking your activity, but "when one of your friends visits a pre-approved website or application, it will receive General Information about you." And while Facebook does allow users to change their privacy settings, it is really hard to determine how much of each user's personal information is actually protected. Even if Facebook makes sure to protect your information, who says the third-party vendors who somehow get their hands on your information aren't abusing it?

Facebook is vulnerable to many threats that could jeopardize its user safety and, in turn, its success. Facebook reserves the right to share or store much of its users' information, which allows it to harvest information and collect data about users. This data mining is generally done for behavioral targeting in Facebook advertisements, but it is not a stretch to say that Facebook is both sharing our personal information and developing a system of surveillance to monitor our activities. Forget Big Brother, Facebook is watching.

And if data mining and information sharing aren't enough of a scare, the increasing threats of spam, spyware, and fake accounts are making the trade-off between networking and privacy much less attractive. In fact, a researcher recently compiled a list of over 170 million Facebook users and uploaded it on Pirate Bay for anyone to download. The ease with which an ill-intentioned person could access such vital information makes Facebook a haven for hackers, criminals, and data miners looking to wreak havoc or earn ethically questionable profits. If Facebook doesn't tackle the privacy issue before it gets out of hand, it could face growing resentment, a loss of its users, and substantial legal issues.

6. **Mass awareness signals peak.** The best investments are made before the whole world knows about them. The most fashionable clothing is coolest before everyone is wearing it. The most talked-about news story is most interesting before everyone has already "discussed it to death."

The same may be said regarding Facebook—the best time to join Facebook or invest in it is before everyone knows about it and uses it. And based on a few signs, Facebook's popularity may have peaked.

2010 was Facebook's biggest year in many ways. It saw an added 250 million users, the most for a year since it was founded; it neared $2 billion in revenue; it was able to penetrate very important markets in its quest for global growth; it completely revamped much of its online design and introduced tremendously innovative and promising features; and it even took over Google's spot as number one most visited website in the world. But nothing has grabbed the media's attention more than the release of the Facebook movie, *The Social Network*, and the tremendous honor of having Facebook founder and CEO, Mark Zuckerberg, named TIME Person of the Year. Not only did *The Social Network* receive exceptionally positive reviews from critics, but it also opened at number one in theaters and has grossed nearly $200 million since its release in October 2010.

But the tremendous attention Facebook has received may be signaling a peak in popularity. While it is true that Facebook still has plenty of growth left and many exciting opportunities remaining for the future, is there that much room left for the "Facebook obsession" to grow? After a movie based on it came out, its CEO being named TIME Person of the Year, and a special on CNBC entitled *The Facebook Obsession,* how much better can things really get? If anything, most people's attention and love for Facebook is near its maximum levels; and with everyone from grandparents to 10-year-olds now on Facebook, it could be just a short while before many users lose interest.

7. **Risky derivatives and SEC investigation.** Goldman Sachs (GS) along with a Russian investment firm announced that they will be investing $500 million into Facebook, ultimately allowing its wealthy investors to invest up to a total of $1.5 billion into the company. Goldman Sachs will be providing the investment opportunity by creating a "special-purpose vehicle" that will sidestep one of the most critical laws regulating initial public offerings. The law states that companies with more than 499 investors must disclose important financial information in order to limit investor risk and maintain financial integrity—something Facebook has been avoiding since its founding. Zuckerberg wants to keep Facebook a private company, and continues to do so by limiting the number of investors to below 500. The problem now faced, however, is that Facebook is using a tricky loophole to maintain that number under the 499 limit.

Goldman Sachs is a prime example of how such a loophole is used. Even though Goldman will have multiple investors buying stock in Facebook, Goldman will technically only be considered one investor on Facebook's books. In other words, even though Facebook says it currently has less than 500 investors, there are probably many more that are either unaccounted for or simply lumped together as pooled money and counted as one. Adding to this law-avoidance, it appears that the investment risk involved in Facebook is much greater than many believe. Not only are the investments in Facebook being made in a private company with highly inflated and hard-to-value shares, but the secondary markets in which Facebook shares are being traded are completely unregulated and unsecured. The risks involved with investing in a private company such as Facebook are tremendous, and investment in Facebook is by no means recommended for the average investor. Goldman Sachs' creation of a "special-purpose vehicle"—another term for "derivatives"—is not too much different from the "special-purpose vehicle" it created to pump its mortgage-backed securities to its uninformed investors who eventually saw their investments collapse while Goldman walked away mostly unaffected. Facebook may sound like a better bet, but it could be just as risky and ill-advised as any other asset-backed security or derivative.

This hasn't escaped the attention of regulatory authorities either. The SEC is currently investigating Facebook and Goldman Sachs to figure out exactly what is happening with the investments. The SEC knows both companies are avoiding the 500 shareholder laws, and it may begin to clamp down on these shady practices. The SEC could end up forcing Facebook to go IPO in order to avoid these issues, or it could prevent some of these shady investment practices. Though a push for an IPO may make a current investment in Facebook fairly lucrative, the potential risks involved with private-company derivatives are tremendous. Add to that the sensationalism involved in these private shares and the unheard-of $50 billion valuation for a private company with inadequate and unproven revenues, and Facebook could very well be a social-media bubble.

As we've mentioned again and again, Facebook is one of the most interesting and dynamic companies in history. It has revolutionized technology, social networking, and the future of how we live and interact. There is no doubt Facebook has a lot of potential and many opportunities to become one of the biggest companies in the world, already having control over the bulk of the globe and now being the number one most-visited website. There are many more people for Facebook to "convert," many more ideas for it to develop and introduce, and many more investors for it to convince on its way to becoming the "second Internet."

But while investors are clamoring to snap up shares in the private company, and the media continues to be infatuated with anything related to social media, there are many issues lurking that could set Facebook up for serious problems. For one, its valuations are currently at extreme levels not seen since the dot-com bubble; its revenues are by no means enough to justify its $50 billion market cap. Second, it hasn't truly proven itself as a profit-generating business; since its business model was essentially founded on a free service, it has been facing difficulties in monetizing its business. Third, though it has grown extremely rapidly thus far, we should not expect Facebook to continue seeing such astronomical growth; at some point it will have saturated the market. Moreover, while it aims at global growth, it could start losing some of its current users due to disinterest, new competitors, or harmful privacy policies. It could also face some legal troubles both on the privacy front and in its shady and avoidant investment practices. There are so many potential issues involved that could hamper Facebook's growth, jeopardize it legally, or simply see it fail to meet expectations, that an investment in Facebook carries a tremendously higher risk than reward. Money could potentially be made, but the dot-com bubble valuations and the housing-meltdown-like derivatives make investing in Facebook extremely dangerous.

Is IPO Mania Warning of a Tech Bubble 2.0?[4]

IPO mania is setting in with the likes of LinkedIn (LNKD), Groupon (GRPN), Renren (RENN), Pandora (P), and potentially Facebook and Twitter. However, the soaring valuations, risky secondary-market trading, and infectious overenthusiasm in the technology startup space could be warning of an overheated and potentially dangerous market.

There is no doubt that companies like Facebook, LinkedIn, Groupon, and Twitter have revolutionized the way we interact with others and how businesses interact with us. These companies show tremendous user and subscriber growth, promising future opportunities, and huge profit potential. It even seems as if the world would no longer function properly without them. But with unproven money-generating capabilities to justify such exorbitant valuations, and what appears to be an overreliance on the belief that these companies will one day validate investors' expectations, investing in many of these companies may be highly unwise and risky. Moreover, such extreme euphoria regarding the future of these companies could be pointing to a renewed technology bubble that will be met with failed expectations and big financial losses.

I am not saying that a Tech Bubble 2.0 is necessarily here, but the rapid growth in enthusiasm over these up-and-coming technology companies and the willingness to pay high premiums to own shares in their stock should at least be a concern. Particularly when many of these companies have yet to prove their profitability and while expectations are sky-high and possibly unrealistic (See section titled Betting against Facebook).

Soaring Valuations

With valuations of these highly popular companies reaching $10, $20, or even $100 billion in the case of Facebook, investors need to be aware of the pricing basis that determines the amount they must pay to own shares in these companies. It would be one thing if these companies were earning enough money to justify their valuations. But when LinkedIn is being valued at $10 billion, Groupon at near $30 billion, and Facebook at $100 billion— and their revenues don't even come close to established companies with similar market caps—such frothy valuations are not so appealing.

For example, at its current valuation, LinkedIn is bigger than Sirius (SIRI): $10 billion versus $7.5 billion; Groupon is bigger than one of the top cloud-computing companies, Salesforce (CRM): $30 billion versus $18 billion; and Facebook is even bigger than Amazon (AMZN)! That's $100 billion–plus versus $85 billion. It would be fair to say that the new companies could possibly one day earn these lofty valuations, but to be valued at such extreme levels when their revenues don't even compare is risky, to say the least.

So how extreme are the valuations? We can compare them based on two fundamental valuation metrics—Revenues and Price-to-Earnings (P/E) Ratios. In terms of revenues, LinkedIn earned a measly $243 million in 2010 compared to $2.88 billion for Sirius, Groupon saw $600 million in 2010 compared to Salesforce's near $2 billion, and Facebook earned a tiny $2 billion compared to $37 billion for Amazon. These are not just small differences— these are massive discrepancies that the new companies must justify.

Furthermore, these companies aren't even profitable yet! LinkedIn had profits of only $15 million last year while its valuation is at $10 billion; Groupon even saw a *loss* of $413 million (see Figure 9.12). Or take Pandora (P), in Figure 9.13, with an IPO in June 2011. As the hottest company in years, Facebook is still not matching Google's (GOOG) early success, seen in Figure 9.14.

These lofty valuation wouldn't be so much of an issue if the companies were producing proportional revenues to justify their market caps. And surely much of the money that has been invested in Facebook, Groupon, LinkedIn, and others is being invested because of the potential *future* profits that these companies *may* produce. Time will tell, but the probabilities are low.

P/E Ratios

P/E ratios are the second concern. The P/E ratio, or price-to-earnings ratio, is a measure of how much investors are willing to pay *today* for a company's

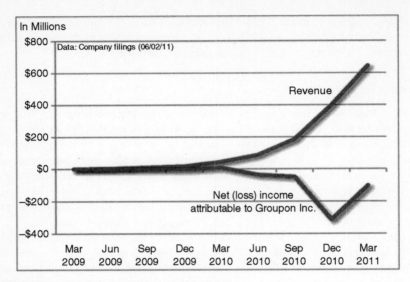

FIGURE 9.12 Groupon: Revenue versus Net Loss
Source: Business Insider; company filings (June 2, 2011).

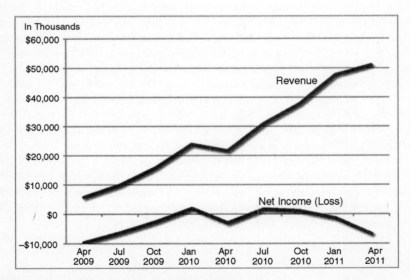

FIGURE 9.13 Pandora's Quarterly Results of Operations
Source: Business Insider; company filings (May 26, 2011).

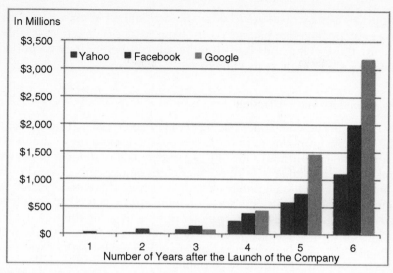

FIGURE 9.14 Annual Revenue for Tech Companies for the First Six Years after Launch
Source: Business Insider; Capital IQ (December 2010).

earnings *tomorrow*. If a company is expected to grow rapidly, and therefore "prove itself" by earning the required revenues, investors will pay higher multiples for the company's stock; a company with a bright future would therefore be proportionally more expensive than a failing company. But while investors generally benefit from paying more for growth companies, there are big risks involved in overpaying. A 20 or 30 P/E ratio is historically reasonable for a growth company, and a 50 or 60 P/E ratio may sometimes prove profitable. However, massive and dangerous investment bubbles have formed and collapsed when P/E ratios reached extremely lofty levels. For example, the dot-com bubble days saw the P/E ratios of many overly hyped companies reach over 100, only to send those companies' stock prices crashing down once reality set in.

So if P/E ratios of over 50 are even dangerous, and ratios near 100 were seen at the height of the dot-com bubble, how high are the P/E ratios for these companies? Facebook's P/E is over 100, Groupon's can't even be determined because it's still losing money, and LinkedIn's P/E is over 1,000! These aren't just concerns, these are warning signs of overspeculation and hype. Keep in mind, even Netflix (NFLX), which many consider to be overvalued, is still only a 75 P/E, and Apple (AAPL) has a P/E of under 16!

Investors are once again ignoring P/E ratios, assuming these companies have entered a revolutionary market niche and will be able to justify their stock prices as they continue to grow rapidly. And a big reason why investors are paying huge premiums to own shares in these companies is because valuating these companies is even more difficult before they go public or before they show a few years of financials.

Risky Secondary-Market Trading

With many private companies having avoided going public through an IPO in the past few years due to poor market conditions and the desire to avoid disclosing their financials to the SEC, secondary market trading of company shares has been gaining a lot of popularity. In other words, instead of buying and selling stock on a public exchange, private shareholders have been selling their stake to outsiders such as Goldman Sachs (GS), T. Rowe Price (TROW), Morgan Stanley (MS), and others without going through the traditional methods of exchange. Secondary markets for private shares, such as SecondMarket, have been growing, and have offered investors a way to buy shares in companies before they go public.

Secondary markets have tremendously inflated prices and risk, however. With little clarity as to how much these companies are really worth, along with the extra excitement and overpricing that the "hard to acquire" status of those private shares have produced, the valuations of these companies have been able to reach what appear to be highly unreasonable levels.

Most of the Price Appreciation Already Over

After investors bought and sold shares on the private secondary markets and brought about massive price increases in these companies, there is probably little upside left. In a traditional market, a stock that is released through an IPO could gain momentum as institutions and investors pile in; but since secondary trading has been taking place for years now, many of the big players are already invested, and the late-comers (average investors) may be the suckers who lose money as the big players pull out.

Just take LinkedIn (LNKD), in Figure 9.15, as the example:

LinkedIn's valuation soared on its way to IPO, and reached a price of over $120/share on its first day. But since much of the trading was done on the private markets, the IPO was an opportunity for those already invested to bail and sell it to the latecomers. The price dropped from over $120 to near $70 in less than 20 days. The same has happened to Renren (RENN), which was down from a high of $23 to just above $8 in less than a month. And the same could happen to the other companies that eventually go public—Pandora (P), Zynga, Living Social, Twitter, and even Facebook.

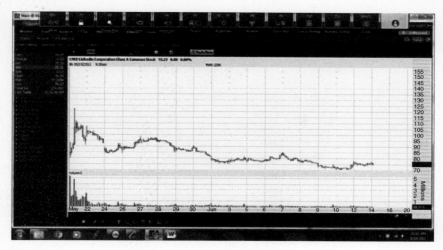

FIGURE 9.15 LinkedIn (LNKD) Dumped by Institutions
Source: thinkorswim, Chart Prophet LLC.

Overstated User Growth?

Facebook supposedly has nearly 700 million users, Twitter has over 100 million, and Groupon has over 80 million. But how many of these users are actually active? And do these users really stand as any value to the companies other than just another person to add to the list?

A large user base is a tremendous advantage to these companies since they can reach a much wider audience and attract advertisers, businesses, and investors. But if the user base is made of inactive or nonprofitable users, their value is limited.

Groupon boasts an 80 million–plus user base, but the actual number of users who have added value is much smaller, as seen in Figure 9.16.

Twitter is also showing an overstated user base (Figure 9.17). This company is my favorite within this space, since it is the least overvalued. However, it still shows a tremendously inflated user number, with only half of its users following two or more people:

Peaking Popularity?

After growing tremendously for years, Facebook is beginning to show weakness. It has lost over 7 million users[5] in the United States and Canada in May 2011. Though growth in Mexico, Brazil, and India has made up for the losses, the threats of peaking popularity and stagnant growth are huge potential problems for Facebook and others. If the growth that most investors

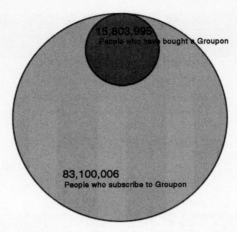

FIGURE 9.16 How Many People Have Purchased Groupons?
Source: Business Insider, Company filing.

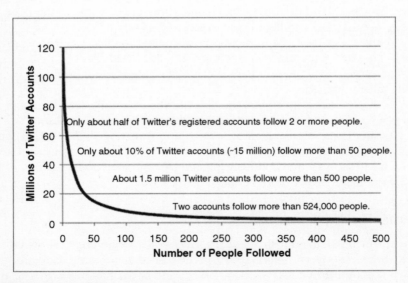

FIGURE 9.17 How Big Is Twitter, Really?
Source: Business Insider, Twitter API.

have expected cannot be sustained, these companies are setting themselves up for a huge disappointment.

Conclusion

After a few years of massive excitement regarding the future of social media, group buying, and the bright future for Internet startups, signs of a bubble are continuously emerging. We've got it all:

- Rapid increases in valuations.
- Extreme P/E ratios that are reminiscent of the dot-com bubble.
- Revenues that do not even come close to justifying company valuations.
- Risky and ambiguous secondary-market trading.
- Overstated user bases.
- Peaking popularity.
- Extreme expectations that may never be met.

These are all signs of mass speculation, euphoria, and huge potential risks that have emerged. They should stand as a warning to investors looking to get in at a time that may be too late.

Netflix: Setting Up for Disaster[6]

Netflix (NFLX) dropped 19.8 percent in 13 trading days after I wrote my last article.[7] It has since bounced back, slightly exceeded the previous February highs, and fallen below again. At the same time, competition has been massively increasing, insider selling continues to reveal dwindling faith in the future of the company, the company's content costs have been soaring, and accounting manipulation trouble may even be on the horizon. If Netflix was a good short candidate in February, it is by far an even better short candidate now.

In a previous article, I noted seven main reasons why Netflix was showing increasing weakness.

1. **Valuation.** Netflix is priced for perfection.
2. **Transitioning business model and competition.** As it shifts from DVD rentals to streaming content, Netflix is entering a market that it no longer monopolizes and which has much bigger competition.
3. **Streaming library is weak.** With much higher costs involved in streaming content, Netflix's video library is very weak compared to what it offers in DVDs. Its content is limited, it takes longer for the company to offer new releases, and it is behind many competitors in terms of content offered.

4. **CFO resigns unexpectedly.** Such a vital company figure resigning suddenly, amidst extreme upward momentum tells me something may be brewing behind the scenes or under the surface.

5. **Heavy insider selling.** Large selling made by CEO Reed Hastings and others is a huge warning signal. If the leaders and executives of the company are pulling their money out of the company, why should the average investor (who has much less clarity into the company's operations) leave his money in? Heavy insider selling is many times a warning of an impending downturn or potential "shady" behavior.

6. **Whitney Tilson gives up.** The capitulation by one of the largest Netflix bears signaled the end of the era dominated by Netflix shorts. Many times, a downturn takes place only after the shorts give up.

7. **Technicals.** Bearish reversal candles marked the $247.55 high as significant overhead resistance—a level to short against.

While the above seven reasons were made three months ago (in our previous Netflix article), they all still hold strongly as very significant reasons to short Netflix. However, while the above reasons were enough then, we can add numerous more with the additional information that has surfaced over recent months.

Reasons to Short Netflix

1. **Valuation.** While the P/E ratio is down to just under 70 from the nearly 80 level it reached in February, it is still tremendously above historically reasonable P/E levels of 20 to 30 for growth companies. Even if we allowed 40 or 50 to be reasonable considering the massive growth Netflix has shown, 70 is way too high for any prudent or rational investor. Add to that the fact that Netflix stock is up over 1,000 percent since late 2008, and it is easy to see why the company may be extremely overbought at these levels.

2. **Transitioning business model.** The streaming business model simply is not as dominant as DVD rentals. Netflix is attempting to dominate the video streaming business, but it faces huge hurdles in the space since streaming is much different than the DVD-rental business model it used to launch itself to the top of the chain. Streaming will cost more, limit the selection, and increase competition.

3. **Competition.** Unlike with DVD rentals, where it had a significant advantage and near-monopoly on the industry—after essentially beating Blockbuster—Netflix now faces increasing competition for streaming content. Many other companies are now attempting to enter the space, duplicate or improve on the success of Netflix, and gain market share.

And these are not just some new, small start-up companies. The companies entering the space include Amazon (AMZN), Apple (AAPL), Hulu, Google (GOOG), Disney (DIS), Dish Network (DISH), Wal-Mart (WMT), Best Buy (BBY), Time Warner (TWX), and Coinstar (CSTR). These companies not only offer services and technologies that may become superior to Netflix, but they also have tremendous financial resources to back them up—something Netflix is quickly running out of. To present the recent growing competition surrounding Netflix, let's document the competitors:

Coinstar (CSTR): Offers Redbox video rentals and announced on February 17 that it is "gearing up to launch[8] a Redbox subscription-based online streaming movie service that will take on Netflix's dominance." (*SeekingAlpha* Market Currents)

Amazon (AMZN): Launching its own rival streaming video service on Februrary 23, Amazon became a huge competitor for Netflix. Not only does Amazon have the potential to offer a much greater selection with a much greater financial backing, but "turns out that Netflix outsources a 'huge' portion[9] of its operations to a division of Amazon," Andrew Wallenstein writes. "Talk about the fox guarding the henhouse: Netflix basically entrusts the brains behind its vast operations to a company poised to be its biggest competitor." (*SeekingAlpha* Market Currents).

Time Warner (TWX) and Facebook: Announcing on March 8 that it will release the Batman film *The Dark Knight* on Facebook, Time Warner's plan[10] to offer $3 film rentals on Facebook may not pose severe challenges in the short term, but has even Goldman Sachs warning that "Facebook could become a credible threat."[11]

Google (GOOG): With its "big overhaul"[12] of YouTube and the addition of about 3,000 movies[13] to its rental service, Google is a significantly growing threat[14] to Netflix. According to Wedge Partners: "Unlike other streaming video competitors, YouTube is on nearly every device platform on which NFLX is running today. We believe that it is this platform distribution in particular that gives GOOG a significant leg up on the competition versus NFLX. Time will tell how aggressive GOOG will be in competing with NFLX, but we think the threat is substantial."

Dish Network (DISH) and Blockbuster: Taking up several paragraphs in its annual letter to shareholders, Netflix mentioned the looming threat of competition. While it hopes that fast growth and more content will help it stay on top, it also mentioned that "Dish Networks is likely to launch a substantial subscription streaming effort under the Blockbuster brand." (Netflix: Yes, Blockbuster Is Coming After Us[15])

Wal-Mart (WMT) and Best Buy (BBY): Attempting to also capitalize on the video streaming space, Wal-Mart and Best Buy are planning[16] on offering "Internet-like" video services as well.

Hulu: Already a big player in online streaming video content, Hulu recently launched its subscription-based "Hulu Plus," which will also compete with Netflix.

Apple (AAPL): Even Apple may be in the midst of plans to compete with Netflix, as Jefferies analyst Peter Misek claims "Apple to Launch Assault on the Living Room" by building two massive data centers[17] in North Carolina and may launch a "video-focused cloud-based service" that will rival Netflix. Don't forget, Apple also rents and sells videos on iTunes.

As we can clearly see, Netflix's competition is growing tremendously. It is not only going against companies with considerably greater access to content, superior partnerships, and significantly stronger financial backing; it is also struggling to maintain control over a video-streaming market which it is attempting to transition to and in which it is only relatively new to.

As Whitney Tilson wrote in his article "Why We're Short Netflix":[18]

> *In short, Netflix is moving from a business in which it was competing against smaller, dying, heavily indebted companies with inferior business models to some of the largest, most powerful, aggressive and deep-pocketed companies in the world, which have big competitive advantages over Netflix.*

4. **Streaming library has weak/poor selection.** Because it offers such low-cost subcriptions of under $10 a month, Netflix doesn't necessarily have the resources to pay high fees for streaming content. Increasing costs and the unfeasibility of providing customers with the newest or most popular releases results in Netflix having a weak streaming library and largely incomplete selection. Not only does it frequently take a month longer for Netflix subscribers to gain access to new releases, but the number of available movies in the streaming library is well below much of the competition.

Quoting Whitney Tilson again:

> *To come up with a representative list of popular movies, we took the top 50 grossing movies of all time, Internet Movie Database's 20 top-ranked movies of all time, Rotten Tomatoes's 20 top-ranked movies of all time, and the 10 top-selling, top-renting and top-video-on-demand DVDs for the week ending 11/28/10.*

> *Here's the summary: of these 120 movies (including dupli-cates), Netflix has a mere 17 (14.2 percent, and 0 percent of the current most popular movies) versus 77 for iTunes (64.2 percent), 63 for Vudu, 62 for Amazon, and 41 for cable.*

Figure 9.18 depicts the results graphically.

Netflix may be regarded by many as the top video provider, but if we look at the data in this case it does not appear so.

5. **Streaming costs.** After releasing earnings numbers and offering a dis-appointing Q2 EPS guidance[19] of $0.93 to $1.15 (versus $1.19 consen-sus) on April 25, Netflix finally acknowledged their dramatically growing streaming content costs. If the company was fairly valued and the stock reflected slowing growth, I wouldn't necessarily have much of an issue. But with the company expected to grow tremendously over the next few years, as reflected in its exorbitant 70 PE ratio, a growing issue of rising costs and slow growth is big-time trouble.

How big are the streaming costs? New movie and TV deals resulted in cash outlays on content of $530 million in 2010, more than double the previous year. Such rising costs are going to cut into Netflix's profits—and that's even before this year and coming years, where content costs will be even higher as competition increases.

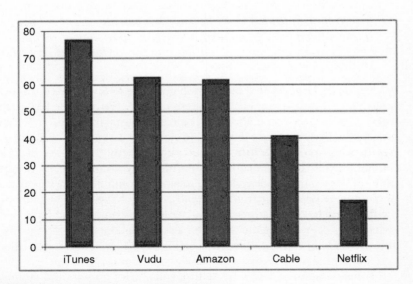

FIGURE 9.18 Available Streaming Movie Titles

Source: Whitney Tilson (T2 Partners), *Seeking Alpha*.

TABLE 9.2 Cost of Subscription Detail ($ Millions)

Year	DVD Amortization	Streaming Content Costs	Total Content	Postage and Packaging	Streaming Delivery	Total Content Delivery	Other
2010	160	252	412	542	55	598	144
2009	175	72	246	494	25	519	144
2008	168	32	200	407	10	417	144
2007	167	20	187	327	5	332	146
2006	134	0	134	257	0	257	141
2005	91	0	91	174	0	174	129
2004	74	0	74	114	0	114	85
2003	40	0	40	59	0	59	49
2002	15	0	15	29	0	29	33
2001	20	0	20	15	0	15	15

Source: Jim Pyke, "Digging Into Netflix's Cost of Subscription Part 1." *Seeking Alpha*, May 16, 2011.[20]

Table 9.2 shows how rapidly costs have been rising.

And content costs are only rising from here. According to Goldman Sachs,[21] Netflix is facing an uphill battle for content:

> *We fully expect content owners to increasingly "flex their muscles" and make it incrementally harder for Netflix to acquire more content. However, until a worthy competitor emerges to either bid away or bid up the price of content, we believe that content owners will still gain and grow the overall revenue pie for themselves by selling their catalog content to Netflix.*

Goldman believes that Netflix will continue to lay claim to the content "until a worthy competitor emerges to either bid away or bid up the price." But as we've seen above, those competitors may already be here and Netflix may soon lose the bidding war.

6. **Accounting manipulation?** Pointed out by Lenny Brecken of Brecken Capital,[22] Netflix is overstating its earnings by amortizing its content costs in a way that makes it appear more profitable than it really is. According to Brecken, earnings would actually have been negative for the third and fourth quarters, and 2010 pretax income would have been reduced by over 80 percent! Brecken also points out that accounts payable are up well over 100 percent (see Figure 9.19)—a figure that bodes very poorly for Netflix's financial stability and future.

It makes sense, then, why Netflix still shows growth and strength while content cost and competition is rising—the full impact of rising costs are not showing up on the company's bottom line because it is amortizing these costs over long periods. In essence, it is attempting to

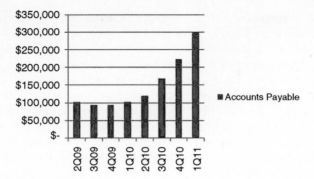

FIGURE 9.19 Netflix Accounts Payable

Source: **Larry Brecken, Reuters Knowledge.**

prolong the time it takes to recognize its costs, and overstates its actual profits, while it hopes to grow fast enough to outpace those costs. However, if it can't continue to grow exponentially, these rapidly rising costs will eventually catch up and destroy its bottom line.

It is my opinion, then, based on these newly revealed facts, that the sudden resignation in December 2010 by CFO Barry McCarthy may be due to a growing concern over accounting fraud or manipulation. With shady accounting practices and overstated earnings (not to mention tremendous insider selling by McCarthy, totaling over $20 million), McCarthy's resignation could have been his attempt at fleeing huge potential legal issues before they surfaced. Again, this is just an opinion based on the available facts, but it seems to fit in very well with what I had written (on *Seeking Alpha*) in February.

> *Barry McCarthy, who had been with the company since 1999 and led it through the IPO, resigned in December 2010. To the shock of many, and with the supposed claim that such a decision was made in order to "pursue broader executive opportunities outside the company," McCarthy's designation immediately set off a warning alarm in my head. Such a vital company figure resigning amidst extreme upward momentum tells me something may be brewing behind the scenes or under the surface. And especially when such a figure was the CFO, who is largely in charge of monitoring the books and maintaining strong finances, such a resignation may be a sign of upcoming trouble. ("Why It May Finally Be Time to Short Netflix"[23])*

7. ***Huge* insider selling.** In my previous article on Netflix I mentioned the heavy insider selling by CEO Reed Hastings and then-CFO McCarthy. As I mentioned then, heavy selling by insiders is many times a sign of a lack

of faith in the company. If those insiders, or people working for the company—who actually have the best direct contact to the company and the most clarity and insight into the company's operations—don't believe the stock price will continue to rise, why should the rest of the investors? And if we factor in the potential underlying fraud that is going on in the accounting practices, it could become understandable why many insiders—mainly CEO Reed Hastings—are selling their shares at a frantic pace.

In fact, after selling millions of dollars worth of shares in 2010, CEO Hastings has picked up his selling pace tremendously in 2011. He has been selling at least 5,000 shares every single week since January 20 (a total of more than $1 million every week).

Readers could easily take a look at his selling by visiting Yahoo! Finance.[24] With over $20 million just from selling his stock, who needs a salary?

And Hastings is not the only one selling. In the past six months alone, over 18 percent of insider shares have been sold, compared to less than 7 percent of institutional shares (see Table 9.3).

Director Jay C. Hoag is also a huge seller of Netflix stock. He has sold approximately $30 million in stock over the past year.

It appears that insiders have lost faith in the company and the stock, and are selling fast. And if accounting fraud or manipulation is one day revealed, or if Netflix begins to suffer, it would be very hard to understand why Hastings, McCarthy, Hoag, and others do not find themselves in big legal trouble.

TABLE 9.3 Insider Transactions

Net Share Purchase Activity

Insider Purchases—Past 6 months

	Shares	Trans
Purchases	n/a	0
Sales	695,219	41
Net Shares Purchased (Sold)	(695,219)	41
Total Insider Shares Held	3.04M	n/a
% Net Shares Purchased (Sold)	(18.6%)	n/a

Net Institutional Purchases—Prior Quarter to Latest Quarter

Net Shares Purchased (Sold)	(2,858,070)
% Change in Institutional Shares Held	(6.83%)

Source: Data provided by Thomson Financial, Yahoo! Finance.

8. **Short interest.** After the most well-known Netflix bear, Whitney Tilson, capitulated on his bearish bet on Netflix and threw in the towel due to a consistent rise in the stock price that hurt his performance, I noted that it was now time to short. The extremely high short interest (people betting against the stock) of nearly 25 percent at the time Tilson covered his position was simply too high to sustain a big drop in the stock. Though I agreed with almost everything Tilson said about Netflix (and he is one of the best fundamental analysts around), I knew that Netflix couldn't fall hard unless some shorts gave up—since stocks usually only collapse when no one expects them to.

When Tilson covered his position, however, I saw that a good opportunity to short was approaching. In fact, as seen in Figure 9.20, short interest has dropped to nearly 20 percent recently.

Counterintuitive to what we would assume, short interest has actually declined as Netflix stock continued to rise. If anything, as the stock price rises, short interest should increase as well—since a higher price has an even higher chance of falling. But that has not been the case; instead, as the stock has reached new all-time highs, the short interest has been falling. Since it is clear that many Netflix bears have removed their positions, now is actually a much better time to short—as the focus on the company has faded, and as the overcrowding by shorts has cleared.

9. **Technicals.** Following a meteoric rise from 2008 until February 2011, Netflix stock is beginning to show considerable technical weakness (see Figure 9.21).

On the one-year chart (Figure 9.21) we can see a clearly defined uptrend from the August 2010 low until now. In terms of the one-year

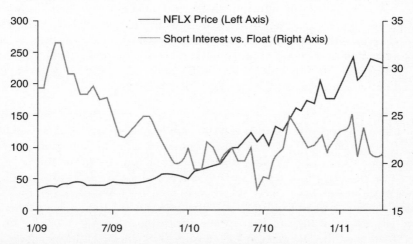

FIGURE 9.20 Netflix Price versus Short Interest (2009 to 2011)
Source: Bespoke Investment Group.

FIGURE 9.21 One-Year Chart

Source: thinkorswim, Chart Prophet LLC.

trend, then, we are still holding up. However, while the stock has moved sideways and even made a new high since February, the momentum (as measured by the MACD) and the relative strength (as measured by the RSI) are in a clear downtrend over that period. The divergences relative to price action, as shown by the two indicators, are revealing decreasing momentum and an upcoming reversal of trend. Price continues to stay above the 50- and 200-Day Moving Averages, but this chart is warning of a major bearish reversal.

The six-month chart, in Figure 9.22, reveals extremely bearish patterns. First, starting with the Bearish Harami candle pattern in February, Netflix stock price failed at the $250 level four times. The failure at a specific level on numerous occasions makes that level very important in the future. The fact that price approached or slightly exceeded the $250 level and failed four times makes $250 a very strong resistance level. We can expect resistance at that level to continue into the future. And unless price breaks strongly above $250, that level may actually be the top.

Moreover, the fact that the $250 level was touched four times highly increases the strength of the resistance. Additionally, the fact that those four

FIGURE 9.22 Six-Month Chart

Source: thinkorswim, Chart Prophet LLC.

touches of the $250 level involve extremely bearish candle patterns (Bearish Harami, Dojis, Bearish Engulfing) and a breakaway gap to the downside on huge volume in late April, makes the $250 resistance level one of the strongest resistance levels I have ever witnessed. Add to that the fact that $250 is a round number and is easily recognized and remembered by the average investor, and it is easily understood why the stock may have tremendous issues breaking above it.

And if all the candle patterns, huge volume downward breakout, momentum and relative strength divergences, and tremendous resistance levels weren't enough—the potential head-and-shoulders pattern that has formed from late March to now should be enough to convince you. The head-and-shoulders pattern is one of the most-recognized and deadliest reversal patterns in technical analysis. Signaling the end of huge run-ups in price led by investor greed or overenthusiasm, the head-and-shoulders pattern is warning of a big potential top. If price breaks below $225, expect a severe correction.

As we have seen, Netflix has been a revolutionary company that has changed the way we watch movies and videos, and has continuously shocked investors as it rose time and time again in the face of high valuations and numerous doubters. But with big competition emerging and

gaining momentum, soaring streaming costs that will cut into its future profits, a transitioning and struggling business model, a weak video streaming
library, huge insider selling, weak and possibly deadly price behavior, and
potential accounting manipulation and fraud, Netflix appears to no longer
justify a sky-high PE ratio of 70 and may be setting up for a huge disaster.

How I Predicted Netflix's Fall, and Why Its Prospects Are Getting Worse[25]

In February and again in May I predicted that Netflix (NFLX) was setting up
for disaster. I had been following the Netflix story for quite a while and saw
way too many reasons Netflix looked like an extremely dangerous
investment:

- Valuations were extreme, signaling Netflix was priced for perfection.
- It no longer had a dominating business model as it transitioned from
  DVDs to streaming content.
- It faced tremendous competition from large, successful companies with
  greater financial backing, including Amazon (AMZN), Apple (AAPL),
  Hulu, Google (GOOG), Disney (DIS), Dish Network (DISH), Wal-Mart
  (WMT), Best Buy (BBY), Time Warner (TWX), and Coinstar (CSTR).
- It struggled with rapidly rising streaming costs, which were cutting into
  its profits.
- Its streaming library was weak, far behind iTunes, Vudu, Amazon, and
  cable.
- Subscriber growth was beginning to stall, signaling expectations were
  too high.
- It was overstating earnings by amortizing content costs over long peri-
  ods, in an attempt to push off its costs until the future, when it hopes to
  grow fast enough to outpace these costs (which is unlikely and may
  constitute accounting manipulation).
- The CFO mysteriously resigned.
- Huge insider selling was warning of a lack of faith by management and
  employees.
- Momentum was beginning to decline.

Netflix may have been a great service and a great business, but that did
not justify an outrageous stock price or valuation. Though the stock had tremendous momentum as it rose over 1,000 percent since late 2008 and continued to defy expectations and hurt short-sellers, it was setting up for a
massive fall as problems began to surface.

MY TRADING STRATEGY   I decided it was time to short Netflix, with $250 be-
ing a strong level to trade against. The $250 level showed great resistance
and distribution, with failures to break above $250 (a round psychological

number) and sideways price movement for nearly four months. This meant that many investors bought and sold around $250 a share, and shares were exchanging hands—from people who had been invested selling to new-comers who wanted to buy. I mentioned that if a last wave of buyers could come and push the stock above the range of $250 to $255, then maybe in the short term it could go up. Regardless though, the fundamental story was bearish, the technicals showed decelerating momentum and increasing weakness, and I expected the stock price to follow—by falling.

I decided to bet against Netflix with the use of options strategies. Instead of betting against the stock in a simple short-sale, and risking a lot more money in case the price continued to run up, I decided to buy put options on NFLX. Put options not only limited the risk, but would also allow me to bet that the stock would fall over the next year. Instead of a $25,000 bet, if I were to sell short 100 shares of Netflix at $250, I could buy one contract of put options (1 contract = 100 shares) on NFLX for as little as $1,000. If I bet that NFLX would fall below $200, $180, $150, or lower, I could make very small bets that Netflix would collapse in the upcoming few months or a year and make tremendous profits if I was right. If I simply sold NFLX short, I would be taking a lot more risk as well as limiting my maximum gains to 100 percent (assuming NFLX collapsed to zero). If, however, I bet against NFLX through put options, I could limit my risk and set myself up for gains of *hundreds* of percent if NFLX fell. I bought out-of-the-money put options because I expected Netflix to collapse if it began to fall. It wasn't simply going to lose a few percentages; it was going to fall hard, closer to 60 per-cent, down to $100 or below.

But stocks do not move straight in one direction; they swing up and down as optimism and pessimism take hold at different times and various magnitudes. If NFLX were to fall, then it wouldn't fall to $100 in one shot; it would take months or longer for it to eventually hit bottom. If it were to fall, it would switch between smaller up and down price movements on its way to $100 per share. The most important point to remember, however, is that the trend is down—all that matters is that price will continue to decline.

I appeared on CNN and BNN TV to discuss my claims. The story gained a lot of publicity, and the video was featured on front page of Canada's lead-ing newspaper, *The Globe and Mail*'s website.[26]

GROWING PROBLEMS   I also mentioned Netflix just couldn't compete with other companies if it charged less than $10 per month for subscriptions. Net-flix recently proved this claim to be correct, as it nearly doubled the sub-scription fees from $8 to 10 per month for DVDs and streaming combined, to $8 for DVDs and $8 for streaming ($16 combined). The stock price has plummeted largely due to this announcement, down nearly 50 percent from its July $304.79 peak. Subscribers have threatened to end their subscriptions due to the price hike, and many have—causing management to announce on September 15 that Netflix had lost 600,000 subscribers in the past quarter—only the second time the company has ever had a quarterly loss in the number of customers.

The very weak growth and loss of subscribers now makes it even harder for Netflix to pay for content. If streaming costs are rising because large competitors are bidding for content, and the number of subscribers is not rising fast enough—or even declining—Netflix will not be able to afford the streaming costs. If it can't afford the streaming costs, it won't be able to buy many movies or shows. If it can't buy movies or shows, its library of videos will be very weak. And if its library is weak, customers won't see as much value in subscribing to Netflix. Other companies with a wider selection will be available.

Even if Netflix can buy content, the lack of subscriber growth will hurt its profits and fail to meet expectations. Investors have expected so much continued growth from Netflix, that any stumble or failure to exceed expectations will result in huge drops in the stock. The stock has run up to such a large extent because investors expected Netflix to dominate and continue to grow rapidly, but that is unlikely to be the case, as many are just beginning to realize.

Adding fuel to the fire, Starz recently announced that it will no longer provide Netflix with its content—Sony and Disney movies. Making up at least 8 percent of Netflix's viewing, the Starz exit is a huge hit to its library, and signals similar upcoming announcements from other large content providers leaving Netflix. If Netflix can't afford content and can't maintain its library, it is doomed to fail.

WHAT TO EXPECT   Netflix is in free-fall territory. Reality is only starting to set in that the company is in trouble. Investors still haven't fully realized that the stock price was not justified, and that they had expected too much from Netflix. Instead of the $300-plus stock that investors were hoping for, the stock is really worth $150, $100, or even lower. And just as the stock and the company had tremendous momentum on the way up, they now have tremendous momentum on the way down, as investors flee to the exits. The massive uptrend was broken at $250, and the stock is plummeting as the bad news piles on.

The competition has Netflix figured out. The companies competing with Netflix or attempting to enter the space now know that Netflix's weaknesses are subscriber growth and nonaffordable streaming costs. Since many of the competitors have greater financial resources, they can better afford the content than Netflix. They can therefore bid up the prices and gain control of the content, leaving Netflix even weaker.

The content owners also have Netflix figured out. With so many competitors now in the space, fighting for content rights, the companies who own the rights to the content know they can charge more. Because the competition makes it almost a bidding war, content owners will be able to sell the rights for much more as the companies fight to buy them. Netflix is bound to lose in this battle, since it was not expecting as much competition and cannot come close to affording it if huge companies like Apple, Amazon, and Google are involved.

ACCOUNTING MANIPULATION AND FRAUD? Bad news is yet to come. The momentum is strongly down, reality is starting to set in, and the competition and costs are rising. Even more troubling to me, however, are the very shady practices by management, massive insider selling, and potential accounting manipulation. There is no doubt management had done an outstanding job in getting Netflix to where it was, as it became the dominant player in DVD rentals and almost the dominant player in streaming. But a few signs over the past year have been pointing to potentially fraudulent activities.

- **Overstated earnings and accounting manipulation.** By amortizing its growing content costs over a longer period into the future, Netflix has been able to make itself appear more profitable that it really is. Its account payables were up over 100 percent, and earnings may have actually been negative for the third and fourth quarters of 2010. Netflix based these numbers on an expectation that it will grow fast enough to outpace those costs, but if Netflix can't continue to grow rapidly, these rising costs will catch up and severely hurt its bottom line. Netflix management has essentially "kicked the can down the road" and avoided dealing with these major issues now, before they escalate into huge problems.
- **CFO resignation.** Still only my opinion and speculation, the sudden resignation of CFO Barry McCarthy in December 2010 may fit very well with my claims of Netflix accounting manipulation: McCarthy's resignation could have been his attempt at fleeing huge potential legal issues before they surfaced. McCarthy was with the company since 1999 and even led it through the IPO; resigning suddenly at the height of Netflix's success did not make sense. McCarthy's claim was that his resignation was in order to "pursue broader executive opportunities outside the company," but as I wrote in February: "Such a vital company figure resigning amidst extreme upward momentum tells me something may be brewing behind the scenes or under the surface." McCarthy was the CFO, the number-one person in charge of the company's finances; if he left suddenly, red flags should have appeared for investors and analysts to better analyze the company's finances, balance sheets, income statements, and numbers. The occurrence of overstated earnings and potential accounting manipulation make McCarthy's resignation even more troubling—was he fleeing the company before the real trouble began?

■ **Massive insider selling; CEO not guiltless.** Don't be so quick to blame it all on ex-CFO McCarthy. CEO Reed Hastings has also shown big signs of knowing what was coming—he has been selling millions of dollars of shares (5,000 or more shares every week since January 20) as Netflix reached all-time highs. Heavy selling by management and insiders is many times a lack of faith in the company's future, or future stock price. If those insiders and management, who have the best view of the company's operations and most clarity into future growth, don't believe in the stock, why should the rest of investors?

Hastings has sold over $40 million in Netflix stock this year alone! The trades have been automatic sales, because Hastings has established an automatic sale of 5,000 shares every week. It is legal for insiders to sell their shares automatically; but to see CEO Hastings sell massive amounts of shares when potential accounting manipulation may have been committed and when investors have been wrongly informed about future growth, makes me wonder if Hastings has committed fraud. Time will tell.

CONCLUSION With the uptrend now broken and momentum strongly negative, Netflix is not safe at all. The stock may bounce up, since nothing rises or falls in a straight line. But with the worst probably still yet to come, NFLX should be sold, avoided, or even sold short if done carefully. A fall to $80 or $100 is likely still in the works.

Will Netflix Disappear?[27]

Once again, I get to showcase my extremely bearish and accurate call on Netflix (NFLX). I warned investors in February and again in May that Netflix was setting up for disaster. I even followed up on September 19th and explained how I predicted Netflix's fall and why things were only getting worse from there. If you listened, you could have made some big profits by shorting or at least saved yourself from huge financial losses by getting out or avoiding getting in.

Netflix's troubles just keep getting worse and worse. To recap the huge red flags that should have warned investors and will continue to plague the company in the future:

■ Netflix's valuations were extreme, signaling that any slip-up would severely damage the stock.
■ The shift from its dominant DVD business to a streaming-content business brought it face-to-face with a business model it could no longer dominate. Huge and growing competition like Amazon (AMZN), Apple (AAPL), Hulu, Google (GOOG), Dish Network (DISH), and many other

companies with deep pockets and tremendous resources meant Netflix would not be able to hold the top rank for much longer.

- Streaming content costs have become unsustainable, and Netflix simply can't afford its own collection of movies and shows. This has cut into Netflix's profits and is a leading cause for Netflix's tremendously weak content library. Netflix has attempted to hide this big weakness by pushing off costs into the future, but it can't run away from its problems forever. Eventually, costs catch up and profitability disappears; and at that point, so does the stock price, which has been based on massive expectations by investors.

- Netflix has lost content right and left, either by failing to renew contracts (with the likes of Starz) or by not being able to afford new content. Since its entire business is based on content, its dwindling video library is almost a sure sign of a dying business.

- By overstating its earnings and hiding much of its liabilities off the balance sheet, Netflix may have been involved in accounting manipulation and fraud, which could bankrupt the company if surfaced.

- Management has been increasingly shady and potentially fraudulent, with a mysterious resignation by the CFO at the end of last year as well as massive insider selling of shares by CEO Reed Hastings and other officers. The CEO has essentially been selling millions of dollars' worth of shares to the late-coming small investors who trusted in Netflix.

To make matters even worse, Netflix recently announced that it would spin off its DVD business and call it Qwikster. Not only did management fail to realize that the Qwikster name was already taken on Twitter by a drug-involved individual (huge PR mess), but it also really angered a lot of its subscribers who would now have to pay as much as double the price for both DVDs and streaming. And since Netflix's success relies largely on subscriber growth, the disgruntled customers' exodus may have sealed Netflix's fate for failure.

WILL NETFLIX DISAPPEAR? As noted recently: "If Netflix can't afford content and can't maintain its library, it is doomed to fail." I still hold that to be completely true. Moreover, with the downtrend firmly intact, I knew a Netflix comeback would be nearly impossible since "Netflix is in free-fall territory." The stock price had plummeted, but many investors still refused to accept the reality that Netflix is in a downward spiral and could be on its way to bankruptcy, or at least on its way to becoming irrelevant. The momentum is very strong on the way down, just as it was on the way up. With competition continuously rising, strengthening, and eating away at Netflix's once-dominant business, I expect Netflix's troubles to continue from here. Competition has finally broken Netflix.

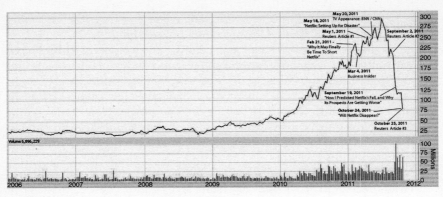

FIGURE 9.23 How I Called Netflix's Collapse
Source: Chart Prophet LLC.

The huge mistakes made by Netflix's management, the increasing and unsustainable costs, the dwindling content library, the failed expectations by investors, the mass subscriber losses, the potential for surfacing accounting manipulation, and the tremendous downward momentum that has taken Netflix from over $300 a share to under $90 a share in less than four months are all reasons Netflix could quickly fade from here. The stock may have fallen back to earth, but the company may still get buried deep under ground.

Figure 9.23 is a chart of Netflix's rise and fall, annotating my articles, interviews, and predictions.

Conclusion

I can calculate the motions of the heavenly bodies, but not the madness of people.

—Isaac Newton

The herdlike behavior and highly speculative participation in gold is pointing to a huge bubble that poses severe risks and may soon collapse.

By analyzing the reasons behind gold's surge; presenting the relevant fundamental stories, projections, and catalysts; studying the price action, supply and demand factors, and technical levels; and pointing out the extreme and very unsettling psychological forces currently involved in the gold theme, we have explained why gold and related stocks and commodities are showing patterns of a bubble and should be avoided.

With global crises, currency devaluations, stagnant recoveries, and a looming threat of war, many funds and investors have flocked to gold as a diversification tool, protection from inflation, and even investment. And with prices up over 600 percent in less than 10 years, many still see more upside for this historic store of value. But with the most prominent banks, research firms, gold mining companies' CEOs, and investment legends predicting gold prices to reach anywhere from $1,000 to $15,000, who do we listen to? And can we really be sure these aren't extremely optimistic forecasts that will never be realized?

It is true that many of the most well-known individuals strongly believe in the continuation of the enormous gold bull market. It is also true that gold has been of tremendous interest to investors and speculators worldwide due to its importance as a fear hedge, as a store of value, as protection against currency devaluation, and as tangible wealth. But after an historically steep 11-year rise and domination of news and media headlines and investor attention for *at least* a few years, are most of the fundamental reasons to invest in gold already factored into the price?

Frankly, this gold bubble, which will eventually pop (if it hasn't already), has been dragging on for longer than I expected. It is completely possible that we will see an additional steep rise if global fears escalate. It is

231

also possible that gold prices will soar for a short period, marking a *blowoff top*—which would also signal the beginning of gold's collapse. But the major issue regarding gold is the risk to average investors who have bought gold recently in hopes of riding along with the rest of the crowd. Not only will many latecomers suffer major losses, but if they have invested in gold in the form of coins or physical gold, they will be stuck with an asset plunging in value and hard to dispose of for a reasonable loss.

I am not arguing with the underlying reasons that make gold attractive. Gold's inherent value is understandable. As we saw in Chapters 1 and 2, the rapid price increase in gold over the past few years is due to mounting fears over currency, poor investment alternatives, and the lack of stability in just about anything else—among other things.

I completely understand the bullish case for gold: It's a "tangible store of value, it can act as a hedge for currency risk, demand is expected to continue to grow, and so forth. What I don't agree with, however, is that the current price of gold is justified. Sure, demand has increased, uncertainty continues, and the threat of financial collapse still lingers over our heads. But at what point have we sacrificed our rational thinking by skyrocketing gold prices just to own a so-called tangible asset? Believing that gold will always retain its value is a complete misconception: Yes, gold will always be valuable; but its actual value relies on how much people are willing to pay for it. Gold would still be valuable at $800 an ounce. But if you buy it at $1,800 and the price drops to $800 because people start to realize they have become a little too exuberant, you still lose a lot of money. Gold may never be worthless but it may become *worth less*, and it could become worth *much* less. Gold is therefore not a screaming buy as many believe. Instead, I think that overspeculation, extreme expectations, faulty arguments, and massive publicity make investing in gold much riskier than many are willing to accept.

We currently stand at a major crossroads between the largest recession since the Great Depression and the uncertain future of the global economy. World markets are more connected to each other than ever before; what happens in one sector on one side of the world can affect companies on the opposite side of the world. Technology, innovation, and the search for profits have turned this entire world into an up-to-the-minute newsroom and stock exchange. Almost anything that takes place across the globe is virtually instantaneously uploaded onto the Internet. We just can't fight it—the world is highly intertwined, and failing to pay attention to any of the never-ending data coming from all corners of the globe could cost us.

We must first understand our current position in history in order to fully understand where we may be heading. Following a period of rapid growth in the 1980s and 1990s, we entered a 10-year period of ups and downs, from the dot-com bubble of the late 1990s through 2002 that brought the Dow Jones Industrial Average above the 10,000 mark for the first time in history and then collapsed on investors who were largely euphoric about the future of technology, investing in nearly any company that put a ".com" after its name; to the housing and credit bubbles that took the Dow to even higher highs from 2003 to 2007, where housing seemed to be the new road to lasting wealth and the introduction of extremely complex derivatives, such as mortgage-backed securities, ultimately caused one of the steepest plunges in stock market history and the failure of financial powerhouses such as Lehman Brothers and Bear Stearns.

But the story is not over. Since that devastating plunge from over 14,000 to below 7,000, the markets have rebounded and recouped almost all of their losses. The economy is nowhere near as healthy or as promising as it was before the stock market collapse, yet the markets are up over 100 percent from their early 2009 bottom. The questions now become: Is the worst behind us? Is the market really recovering? Is it time to invest again? What will be the next big investment opportunity? Are things really better? Are we setting up for a depression?

I am of the camp that thinks the market looks extremely dangerous at these levels. We have not yet fixed the main issues that brought about this recent recession, unemployment is still extremely high, the risk seems to have increased, emerging markets look frothy, and a multitude of other reasons exist for businesses and investors to remain wary.

It seems as if investors have moved from one hot investment to the next for the past 10 years or longer, constantly losing as the hot investment loses steam and collapses. We've gone from technology, to housing, to oil, and now on to what appears to be the new hot investments in technology and commodities. The world depends on emerging market growth, which has fueled investments in all of the emerging market essentials: food, commodities, and construction. But with many signs pointing to an overheated and weakening emerging markets theme, together with the possibility of a third massive bubble in just over 10 years, we may be finding ourselves at the juncture of a major market turning point.

Many clues pointing to a bubble have been hard to notice or accept because gold supporters have had so many counterarguments as to why gold is a good investment. The failing dollar, economic upheaval, volatile and falling stock markets, and unstable political leadership have convinced many investors and institutions to trust in gold as the only "safe" investment. However, the need to find a "stable" asset or investment has made gold a highly speculative and now unstable commodity. Gold has historically been a store of value and a very important tangible asset, but the rush to invest in gold has pushed prices way beyond reasonable levels and have turned it into an emotional trade based on fear and greed. The reasons to buy gold seem to make sense, and have justified the buying of gold for a few years. But the fundamental reasons don't work anymore because gold has turned into an object of mass speculation; the reasons to buy gold have already been priced in. The continued run-up now relies on more investors buying gold, rather than fundamental catalysts that justify higher prices.

Bubbles have a great way of appearing to be safe and profitable, but ultimately collapse on investors unexpectedly. They are supported by strong arguments and the illusion of safety. But safety, profitability, and appeals to emotion are classic factors in nearly all bubbles, and help reinforce investor enthusiasm and convince many to join the herd.

For all the reasons stated here and throughout this book, we think the risks involved in gold are too great to warrant investing in it. Not only have we seen soaring prices, media frenzy, overly enthusiastic investors, extreme speculation, and what appears to be an overly saturated investment theme, we are now seeing weakness, as emerging markets are falling, commodity prices are dropping significantly, and gold has even lost some of its strength as a "safe-haven" play during the Middle East crisis, Japan nuclear turmoil, and large volatile price swings. Furthermore, we think there are other investment opportunities that provide better value and further upside for much less risk.

I continue to hold the opinion that gold looks extremely dangerous at these levels, against what seems to be the entire investing world. With so many clues pointing to the near-definite gold bubble, accompanied by extremely optimistic investor sentiment generally seen in previous bubbles, we are short gold mining companies and awaiting further confirmation to pile on the short-gold trade.

When everyone thinks alike, everyone is likely to be wrong.[1]
—Humphrey B. Neill
The Art of Contrary Thinking (1954)

Sometimes it pays to go against the crowd.

Notes

Preface

1. Charles Kindleberger, *Manias, Panics, and Crashes: A History of Financial Crises*, 5th ed. (Hoboken, NJ: John Wiley & Sons, 2005), 18.

Chapter 1

1. Martin Pring, *Investment Psychology Explained* (New York: John Wiley & Sons, 1993), 19.

Chapter 2

1. Robert J. Shiller, *Irrational Exuberance,* 2nd ed. (New York: Broadway, 2005), 31.
2. Holly Watt and Robert Winnett, "Goldfinger Brown's £2 Billion Blunder in the Bullion Market." *Times Online*, April 15, 2007, www.timesonline.co.uk/tol/news/politics/article1655001.ece.
3. Clive Maund, "The Gold Bull Market Remembers How Gordon Brown Sold Half of Britains Reserves at the Lowest Price." *Marketoracle.co.uk*, April 1, 2007, www.marketoracle.co.uk/Article670.html.
4. Watt and Winnett, "Goldfinger Brown's £2 Billion Blunder."
5. Doug Short, "The Dollar and Gold: A 20-Year Perspective," *Seeking Alpha,* April 25, 2011, seekingalpha.com/article/265165-the-dollar-and-gold-a-20-year-perspective.
6. Watt and Winnett, "Goldfinger Brown's £2 Billion Blunder."
7. Ibid.

Chapter 3

1. Charles Kindelberger, *Manias, Panics, and Crashes: A History of Financial Crises,* 5th ed. (Hoboken, NJ: John Wiley & Sons, 2005), 29.
2. Carl Futia, *The Art of Contrarian Trading* (Hoboken, NJ: John Wiley & Sons, 2009), 41.
3. Robert J. Shiller, *Irrational Exuberance*, 2nd ed. (New York: Broadway, 2005), 2.
4. Futia, *The Art of Contrarian Trading*, 24.
5. Ibid., xii–xiii.
6. Ibid., 41.
7. Ibid., 75.
8. Ibid., 92.
9. Charles Kindleberger, *Manias, Panics, and Crashes.*
10. Erste Group Research, "Special Report Gold" (July 2011), 57.
11. Tom Lydon, "ETF Spotlight: SPDR Gold Shares Becomes the Largest ETF," *Seeking Alpha* 23, August 2011.
12. Michael Johnston, "GDX vs. GDXJ: A Better Way to Play Gold?," *ETFdb* 3, March 2010.
13. Shiller, *Irrational Exuberance*, 50.
14. "SPDR Gold Trust Prospectus." SPDR Gold Trust, May 27, 2010, www .spdrgoldshares.com/media/GLD/file/SPDRGoldTrustProspectus.pdf.
15. Catherine Austin Fitts and Carolyn Betts, "GLD and SLV: Disclosure in the Precious Metals Puzzle Palace," *Solari Special Report* (2010), http:// solari.com/archive/Precious_Metals_Puzzle_Palace/.
16. Erste Group Research, "Special Report Gold," 70.
17. Yuriy Humber and Tara Lachapelle, "Hong Kong Canary Singing Commodities Boom Peaking in Aussie Mine: Real M&A," *Bloomberg*, April 18, 2011, www.bloomberg.com/news/2011-04-17/hong-kong-canary -singing-commodities-boom-peaking-in-aussie-mine-real-m-a.html.
18. "Is Barrick's Bid for Equinox a Warning Sign for Gold Bugs?" *CNBC Fast Money*, April 26, 2011, www.cnbc.com/id/42759747.
19. Ibid.
20. http://chovanec.wordpress.com/2011/10/03/economy-on-the-edge-of -a-nervous-breakdown/
20. Kate Connolly, "Gold Bullion—Coming Soon to a Vending Machine Near You," *Guardian.co.uk*, October 21, 2010, www.guardian.co .uk/business/2010/oct/21/gold-bullion-vending-machines?INTCMP =ILCNETTXT3487.
21. Originally published September 12, 2011.
22. Lee Brodie, "'There May Be a Bubble Occurring,' Says Rare Resource Chief," *CNBC Fast Money*, October 21, 2010, www.cnbc.com/id/ 39786632/.

23. Drew Sandholm, "Molycorp CEO: No Rare Earth Bubble," *CNBC Fast Money*, December 21, 2010, www.cnbc.com/id/40767602/Molycorp_CEO_No_Rare_Earth_Bubble.
24. Ibid.
25. Nigam Arora, "Rare Earth Stocks Poised for a Fall," *Seeking Alpha*, February 22, 2011, http://seekingalpha.com/article/254176-rare-earth-stocks-poised-for-a-fall.
26. Luke Belz, "Why Rare Element Resources Is Unlikely to Ever Mine REEs," *Seeking Alpha*, February 16, 2011, http://seekingalpha.com/article/253132-why-rare-element-resources-is-unlikely-to-ever-mine-rees.
27. Futia, *The Art of Contrarian Trading*, 48.
28. Ibid., page 56.
29. A. J. Frost and Robert R. Prechter Jr., *Elliott Wave Principle: Key to Market Behavior*, 10th ed. (Gainesville, GA: New Classics Library, 2005), 173.
30. Charles P. Kindleberger, *Manias, Panics, and Crashes*, 4.
31. http://seekingalpha.com/article/238208-why-inflation-isn-t-affecting-gold-prices.
32. Charles P. Kindleberger, *Manias, Panics, and Crashes*, 4.
33. http://seekingalpha.com/article/260900-the-impending-collapse-of-the-gold-bubble.
34. Data from Goldinmind.com.

Chapter 4

1. Robert R. Prechter Jr., *Robert Prechter on Gold & Silver* (Elliott Wave International, 2009), 15.
2. Ibid., 23.
3. Ibid., 28.

Chapter 5

1. Yoni Jacobs, *Unsafe Haven: The Impending Collpase of the Gold Bubble* (New York: CP Publishing, 2011).
2. http://canadianfinanceblog.com/is-the-current-marketa-return-to-normal.
3. Quoted in A. J. Frost and Robert R. Prechter Jr., *Elliott Wave Principle,* 10th ed. (Gainesville, GA: New Classics Library, 2005), 207.
4. A. J. Frost and Robert R. Prechter Jr., *Elliott Wave Principle: Key to Market Behavior*, 10th ed. (Gainesville, GA: New Classics Library, 2005), 21.
5. Ibid., 129.
6. Ibid., 129.

7. Ibid., 86.
8. Ibid., 51.
9. Ibid., 52.
10. Ibid., 34.
11. Ibid., 173.
12. Ibid., 40.
13. Ibid., 173.
14. Ibid., 78.
15. Ibid., 86.
16. Ibid., 68.
17. Frank Holmes, "Ready, Set, Gold: The Best Months Are Just Ahead," *Seeking Alpha*, August 9, 2010, http://seekingalpha.com/article/219614 -ready-set-gold-the-best-months-are-just-ahead.

Chapter 6

1. Bespoke Investment Group, "Short Interest Declines to Lowest Levels since 2007," *Seeking Alpha*, December 28, 2010, http:// seekingalpha.com/article/243887-short-interest-declines-to-lowest- levels-since-2007.
2. http://seekingalpha.com/article/257685-what-can-the-great-depression -teach-us-about-our-great-recession.
3. http://seekingalpha.com/article/285061-has-the-500-point-drop -confirmed-a-great-depression-2-0.
4. http://seekingalpha.com/article/231981-stocks-approaching-major -long-term-resistance-is-a-reversal-imminent.
5. http://seekingalpha.com/article/264049-sector-rotation-how-energyand -consumer-staples-may-reveal-a-contraction.
6. http://seekingalpha.com/article/300500-are-etfs-toblame-for-over -speculation-record-correlations-and-a-potential-crash.
7. www.calculatedriskblog.com.
8. Global ETF Research and Implementation Strategy Team, Blackrock.
9. Robert J. Shiller, *Irrational Exuberance*, 2nd ed. (New York: Broadway, 2005), 50.
10. Ibid.
11. http://seekingalpha.com/article/278502-skyy-what-s-in-the-cloud -smaller-stocks-that-pack-a-lot-of-punch.
12. Schiller, 30.
13. http://seekingalpha.com/article/265369-dollardemise-looks-overblown -betting-on-a-short-term-bounce-or-mediumterm-recovery.
14. www.youtube.com/watch?v¼ZVfl39ascQ.
15. http://politicalmetals.com/2011/05/27/chinese-gold/.

16. Ibid.
17. Ibid., 30.
18. Kevin Yao, "Analysis: China May Lean on Rate Rises to Fight Inflation," *Fox Business*, July 12, 2011, www.foxbusiness.com/markets/2011/07/12/analysis-china-may-lean-on-rate-rises-to-fight-inflation/.
19. *Manias, Panics, and Crashes: A History of Financial Crises,* 5th ed. (Hoboken, NJ: John Wiley & Sons, 2005), p. 64.
20. "China New Loans, Money Supply Growth Rebound Even after Cooling Measures," *Bloomberg*, July 12, 2011, www.bloomberg.com/news/2011 -07-12/china-new-loans-money-supply-growth-rebound-even-after -cooling-measures.html.
21. Mark Whitehouse, "Number of the Week: Foreign Banks Bet on China," *Real Time Economics*, May 14, 2011, http://blogs.wsj.com/economics/2011/05/14/number-of-the-week-foreign-banks-bet-on-china/.
22. "Off-Balance-Sheet Loans Double, Boosting Bank Default Risk: China Credit." *Bloomberg*, June 23, 2011, www.bloomberg.com/news/2011 -06-23/off-balance-sheet-loans-double-boosting-bank-default-risk-china -credit.html.
23. "Off-Balance-Sheet Loans Double, Boosting Bank Default Risk."
24. Charles P. Kindleberger, *Manias, Panics, and Crashes: A History of Financial Crises,* 5th ed. (Hoboken, NJ: John Wiley & Sons, 2005), 25.
25. Steven J. Kaplan, "Why Investors Need to Reexamine These Emerging Market Myths.," *Seeking Alpha*, March 7, 2011, http://seekingalpha .com/article/256695-why-investors-need-to-reexamine-these-emerging -market-myths.
26. Dexter Roberts, "Preparing for the (Possible) China Crash," *BusinessWeek*, July 14, 2011, www.businessweek.com/magazine/ preparing-for-the-possible-china-crash-07142011.html.
27. www.cnbc.com/id/44744422.
28. Manuela Badawy and Jennifer Ablan, "Monstrous Risks Seen in Emerging Markets," *Reuters*, June 9, 2011, http://business.financialpost.com/2011/06/09/monstrous-risks-seen-in-emerging-markets/.
29. Roberts, "Preparing for the (Possible) China Crash."
30. Cullen Roche, "China's July PMI: Definite Economic Contraction Underway," *Seeking Alpha*, July 21, 2011, http://seekingalpha.com/ article/280698-china-s-july-pmi-definite-economic-contraction -underway.
31. www.bloomberg.com/news/2011-10-13/china-trade-surplus-drops-to -lowest-in-four-months-as-export-growth-slows.html.
32. Tom Orlik, "Prepare for an Attack of the China Bears," *Wall Street Journal*, May 25, 2011, http://online.wsj.com/article/SB10001424052702304520804576344542708300046.html?mod=WSJ_newsreel_markets.

33. Roberts, "Preparing for the (Possible) China Crash."

34. Frederik Balfour, "Walter Kwok Says Hong Kong Home Prices Have Peaked, May Drop 15% This Year," *Bloomberg*, June 20, 2011, www.bloomberg.com/news/2011-06-20/walter-kwok-says-hong-kong -home-prices-have-peaked-may-drop-15-this-year.html.

35. Andrew Barber, "Is the Chinese Bubble Ready to Burst?," *Institutional Investor*, June 29, 2011, www.institutionalinvestor.com/Article/2856797/ Is-The-Chinese-Bubble-Ready-To-Burst.html?ArticleId=2856797.

36. "The Ghost Towns of China: Amazing Satellite Images Show Cities Meant to Be Home to Millions Lying Deserted," *Daily Mail Reporter*, December 18, 2010, httpwww.dailymail.co.uk/news/article-1339536/Ghost-towns -China-Satellite-images-cities-lying-completely-deserted.html.

37. Barber, "Is the Chinese Bubble Ready to Burst?"

38. Ibid.

39. www.chinadaily.com.cn/bizchina/2011-10/08/content_13851248.htm.

40. Author of *Boombustology,* quoted in Andrew Barber, "Is the Chinese Bubble Ready to Burst?" *Institutional Investor*, June 29, 2011.

41. Barber, "Is the Chinese Bubble Ready to Burst?"

42. Ibid.

43. Martin Pring, *Investment Psychology Explained* (New York: John Wiley & Sons, 1993), 116.

44. Stephen Gandel, "China's Latest Export: Stock Fraud," *The Curious Capitalist,* June 14, 2011, http://curiouscapitalist.blogs.time.com/2011/ 06/14/chinas-latest-export-stock-fraud/.

45. Bespoke Investment Group, "Brazil's Bovespa Enters Bear Market Territory," *Seeking Alpha*, August 2, 2011, http://seekingalpha.com/article/ 284073-brazil-s-bovespa-enters-bear-market-territory.

46. http://seekingalpha.com/article/276516-egyptian-stock-market-bodes -poorly-for-middle-east.

47. http://seekingalpha.com/article/248356-housingbubble-in-israel.

Chapter 7

1. http://seekingalpha.com/article/268995-mining-stocks-signaling-reversals -in-gold-andsilver-prices.

2. Erste Group Research, "Special Report Gold" (July 2011), 83.

3. Jon Hilsenrath. "Bernanke Puzzled by Gold Rally," Real Time Economics, *Wall Street Journal*, June 9, 2010, http://blogs.wsj.com/economics/ 2010/06/09/bernanke-puzzled-by-gold-rally/

4. Charles Kindleberger, *Manias, Panics, and Crashes: A History of Financial Crises,* 5th ed. (Hoboken, NJ: John Wiley & Sons, 2005), 92.

5. Ibid.

6. Charles Kadlec, "The Dollar, Gold, and the Quality of Money," *Forbes*, July 18, 2011, http://blogs.forbes.com/charleskadlec/2011/07/18/the-dollar-gold-and-the-quality-of-money/.

7. Ben Stein, "Warren Buffett: Forget Gold, Buy Stocks." *Fortune*, October 19, 2010, http://money.cnn.com/2010/10/18/pf/investing/buffett_ben_stein.fortune/index.htm.

8. Nicholas Larkin and Pham-Duy Nguyen, "Soros Sells Most of Gold ETP Holdings during First Quarter," *Bloomberg*, May 16, 2011, www.bloomberg.com/news/2011-05-16/soros-sold-most-of-his-gold-etp-holding-during-first-quarter-filing-shows.html.

9. http://seekingalpha.com/article/278169-gold-and-silver-interest-what-options-are-telling-us.

10. http://seekingalpha.com/article/251156-is-the-commodity-run-up-about-to-reverse-course.

11. A. J. Frost and Robert R. Prechter Jr., *Elliott Wave Principle: Key to Market Behavior*, 10th ed. (Gainesville, GA: New Classics Library, 2005), 37.

12. http://seekingalpha.com/article/299097-copper-and-oil-signal-recessionbut-battered-japan-may-outperform.

13. http://seekingalpha.com/article/268866-commodities-still-a-bubble-but-prices-maycontinue-to-rise.

Chapter 8

1. "Platinum to Gold Ratio and Detecting Bubbles," June 21, 2011, http://profitimes.com/free-articles/platinum-to-gold-ratio-and-detecting-bubbles/.

2. Originally published as "Forget Gold, Buy Diamonds," *Seeking Alpha*, December 1, 2010, http://seekingalpha.com/article/239445-forget-gold-buy-diamonds.

3. http://seekingalpha.com/article/265715-playing-a-housing-recovery-buy-physical-property-or-invest-in-stocks.

Chapter 9

1. Originally published as "Cloud 9 Computing: Sign of a Renewed Technology Bubble?, *Seeking Alpha*, December 15, 2010, http://seekingalpha.com/article/241963-cloud-9-computing-sign-of-a-renewed-technology-bubble.

2. Originally published as "Betting against Facebook," *Seeking Alpha*, January 6, 2011, http://seekingalpha.com/article/245157-betting-against-facebook.

3. "Privacy Policy," *Facebook*, December 22, 2010, www.facebook.com/policy.php.

4. Originally published as "Is IPO Mania Warning of a Tech Bubble 2.0?," *Seeking Alpha*, June 15, 2011, http://seekingalpha.com/article/274967-is-ipo-mania-warning-of-a-tech-bubble-2-0.

5. Matt Rosoff, "Facebook Is Losing Users in the Countries Where It Took Off First," *Business Insider* (June 13, 2011), www.businessinsider.com/facebook-is-losing-users-in-the-countries-where-it-took-off-first-2011-6.

6. Originally published as "Netflix: Setting Up for Disaster," *Seeking Alpha*, May 18, 2011, http://seekingalpha.com/article/270618-netflix-setting-up-for-disaster.

7. Yoni Jacobs, "Why It May Finally Be Time to Short Netflix," *Seeking Alpha*, February 21, 2011, http://seekingalpha.com/article/254066-why-it-may-finally-be-time-to-short-netflix.

8. Ben Fritz, "Redbox Digital Service Will Go Toe-to-Toe with Netflix," *Los Angeles Times*, February 16, 2011, http://latimesblogs.latimes.com/entertainmentnewsbuzz/2011/02/redbox-digital-service-will-compete-directly-with-netflix.html.

9. Andrew Wallenstein, "What Worries Netflix about Amazon Isn't Just Competition," *Paid Content*, February 21, 2011, http://paidcontent.org/article/419-what-worries-netflix-about-amazon-isnt-just-competition/.

10. "Market Currents," *Seeking Alpha* March 8, 2011, http://seekingalpha.com/currents/post/70431.

11. Tyler Durden, "Goldman Issues Netflix Update: Sees Facebook as a 'Credible Threat,'" *Zero Hedge*, March 8, 2011, www.zerohedge.com/article/goldman-issues-netflix-pt-200-update-sees-facebook-credible-threat.

12. "Market Currents," *Seeking Alpha*, April 6, 2011, http://seekingalpha.com/currents/post/72797.

13. Salar Kamangar, "Welcome to the Future of Video. Please Stay a While," *YouTube-Global*, May 9, 2011, http://youtube-global.blogspot.com/2011/05/welcome-to-future-of-video-please-stay.html.

14. Matt Phillips, "Google YouTube Overhaul: 'Significant Threat' to Netflix," *MarketBeat, Wall Street Journal*, April 8, 2011, http://blogs.wsj.com/marketbeat/2011/04/08/google-youtube-overhaul-significant-threat-to-netflix.

15. Shira Ovide, "Netflix: Yes, Blockbuster Is Coming After Us," *Deal Journal, Wall Street Journal*, April 25, 2011, http://blogs.wsj.com/deals/2011/04/25/netflix-yes-blockbuster-is-coming-after-us/.

16. Ben Fritz, "Netflix's Days without Competition May Be Numbered," *Los Angeles Times*, April 23, 2011, www.latimes.com/business/la-fi-ct-netflix-20110423,0,3960771.story.

17. Matt Phillips, "Netflix Lookout!: Apple to Launch 'Assault on Living Room,' Analyst Says." *MarketBeat, Wall Street Journal*, April 12, 2011,

  http://blogs.wsj.com/marketbeat/2011/04/12/netflix-lookout-apple-to
  -launch-assault-on-living-room-analyst-says/.
18. Whitney Tilson, "Why We're Short Netflix," *Seeking Alpha*, December
    16, 2010, http://seekingalpha.com/article/242320-whitney-tilson-why
    -we-re-short-netflix>.
19. "Netflix Releases First Quarter 2011 Financial Results," *Seeking Alpha,*
    http://seekingalpha.com/news-article/971831-netflix-releases-first
    -quarter-2011-financial-results.
20. http://seekingalpha.com/article/270103-digging-into-netflix-s-cost-of
    -subscription-part-1.
21. Matt Phillips, "Goldman on Netflix: Content Producers to 'Flex Their
    Muscles,'" *MarketBeat, Wall Street Journal,* March 25, 2011, http://
    blogs.wsj.com/marketbeat/2011/03/25/goldman-on-netflix-content
    -producers-to-flex-their-muscles/.
22. Herb Greenberg, "The Last Short Standing in Netflix," *CNBC Stock Blog,*
    February 11, 2011, www.cnbc.com/id/41535093.
23. Jacobs, "Why It May Finally Be Time to Short Netflix," *Seeking Alpha*,
    February 21, 2011.
24. "Insider Filings—Reed Hastings," *Yahoo! Finance,* http://biz.yahoo
    .com/t/22/382.html, May 17, 2011.
25. Originally published as "How I Predicted Netflix's Fall, and Why Its
    Prospects Are Getting Worse," *Seeking Alpha*, September 19, 2011,
    http://seekingalpha.com/article/294587-how-i-predicted-netflix-s-fall
    -and-why-its-prospects-are-getting-worse.
26. "Is It Time to Short Netflix?" www.theglobeandmail.com/report-on
    -business/video/video-is-it-time-to-short-netflix/article2032415/, May 24,
    2011.
27. Originally published as "Will Netflix Disappear?" *Seeking Alpha*,
    October 24, 2011, http://seekingalpha.com/article/301709-will-netflix
    -disappear.

Conclusion

 1. Humphrey B. Neill, *The Art of Contrary Thinking* (Caldwell, ID: Caxton
    Printers, 1954).

About the Author

Yoni Jacobs, CMT, is Executive Director and Chief Investment Strategist for Chart Prophet LLC, an investment management company that utilizes its proprietary Triple-Perspective Outlook to make investment decisions based on a comprehensive mix of technical, fundamental, and behavioral analysis.

Yoni has developed a programmed formula and backtested timing strategy that has avoided the 2000 dot-com bubble and the 2007 to 2008 housing and financial meltdown, and has shown backtested returns of 915 percent in a 10-year span from 2001 to 2011. He is also a contributing author and Opinion Leader for *Seeking Alpha*, with over 500,000 views, numerous Editor's Picks, most-popular pages, and front-page articles. He has appeared on the Business News Network (BNN), affiliates of CNN and ABC News, and has been featured or quoted in *Reuters,* the *Globe and Mail,* the *Financial Post, CBS MoneyWatch, International Business Times,* and other top sources.

Yoni graduated with top honors from the Macaulay Honors College at Queens College with a BBA in Finance and a BA in History. He has supplemented his education with the Chartered Market Technician (CMT) designation, an MBTI Certification for Behavioral Analysis and Personality Evaluation, and a Chartered Financial Analyst (CFA) candidacy. He also holds the Series 7 (Securities Representative) and Series 66 (Quantitative Methods) licenses.

Index